DISCIPLINE
IN THE
SECONDARY CLASSROOM

A Problem-by-Problem Survival Guide

Randall S. Sprick, Ph.D.

90-1129

The Center for Applied Research in Education, Inc.
West Nyack, New York 10995

10   9

DEDICATION

This book would never have been possible if it were not for the excellent ideas of hundreds of secondary-level teachers. During in-service sessions throughout the country, teachers have openly shared their successful techniques with me. These ideas and methods have helped to formulate the procedures included in this book. So, it is to these competent and caring professionals that this book is dedicated.

Library of Congress Cataloging in Publication Data

Sprick, Randall S.
   Discipline in the secondary classroom.

   Includes index.
   1. Classroom management.   2. High school students—
Discipline.   3. Problem children—Discipline.
I. Title.
LB3013.S64   1985   373.11′024   85-12794

ISBN 0-87628-248-6

Printed in the United States of America

ABOUT THE AUTHOR

Randall S. Sprick, Ph.D. (University of Oregon), is director of Instructional Resources, a company providing staff development expertise to school districts throughout the country. Each year, Dr. Sprick conducts in-service workshops and classes for more than 4,000 teachers and administrators.

Dr. Sprick's classroom experience includes teaching students with emotional and behavioral problems. He has also worked with students of all grade levels in the regular classroom as a supervisor and educational consultant.

Dr. Sprick has been a project manager for Follow Through, a federally funded program for disadvantaged students. He is currently president of the Association for Direct Instruction.

ABOUT THIS BOOK

Discipline in the Secondary Classroom addresses your special needs as a teacher of grades 7 to 12 in order to improve your ability to solve behavior problems and to teach students to be self-disciplined and motivated. Working with large groups of secondary students for only 50 minutes at a time, working with up to 180 students in one day, and dealing with long-practiced behavior problems create special difficulties for you.

This is a "how-to" book. It is designed to be a practical resource, translating theory into specific procedures. The techniques are designed to be immediately useful in the classroom so that you can motivate and manage large numbers of students within the existing structure of most secondary schools. For example:

- If you are concerned about students who do not care about grades, Section I (Chapter 2) offers information on designing an effective grading system.
- If you are tired of nagging students, Section II (Chapter 3) has suggestions for improving student–teacher interactions.
- If you have a defiant student or an unmotivated student in the classroom, Section III (Chapter 8) provides step-by-step instructions for teaching the particular student to interact and work more productively.

Read Section I before the school year begins and skim Sections II and III. Then, throughout the year, reread one or more of the chapters each month. Implement a few of the procedures that appear to have the most relevance to your situation. Do not try to implement too many things at once. Effective discipline is a process to be continually revised, adjusted, and improved. Use this book as a resource to gradually improve your discipline policies and procedures.

Section IV, *Troubleshooting Specific Problems,* can be used as a guide for implementing procedures for solving specific misbehaviors. Use this section as a quick and easy reference tool by looking up a specific problem on the Contents page and reading the suggested plan of action in Section IV. Each of the problems and plans suggests specific procedures. If you are unfamiliar with the suggested procedure, a reference is given to one of the previous chapters where that procedure is discussed in more detail.

Remember that problem solving is always a short-term solution. After the problem is alleviated by using Section IV, you should then use Sections I through III to work on improving the process of discipline.

Every procedure in this book is based on two premises:

- You can make a difference in the lives of students. A teacher is not a babysitter, but a professional who is dedicated to teaching skills and concepts that students would probably not acquire on their own.

- You must be committed to teaching all students and must try to find ways to motivate even those without the interest or maturity to understand the benefits of education and the joy of learning.

It is assumed that you will always treat each student with dignity and respect when implementing any suggested procedure. No management tool should serve as an excuse for humiliating or degrading another human being. Effective classroom management will help students learn to function to their fullest potential, which takes place only in an atmosphere of professionalism and positive regard. Students will learn to respect those who respect them.

Randall S. Sprick

ACKNOWLEDGMENTS

I would like to express my gratitude and appreciation to Marilyn Maeda Sprick for her tireless efforts in editing and rewriting the original manuscript. Without her assistance and ideas, this book would not be complete.

I would also like to acknowledge the helpful feedback and encouragement from Debbie Holmes, Kathy Robinson, and Francie Steinzeig.

CONTENTS

Section I
PREPARATION
AND ORGANIZATION

Many problems with student behavior can be prevented. The major goal of this section is to help you prepare and implement a classroom management plan that will teach students the behaviors needed to be successful in *your* classroom. You can plan for the beginning of a new semester and design a grading system that will actually serve as a motivational tool. By following the guidelines in this section, you can significantly reduce the amount of misbehavior from students. Always try to think in terms of problem prevention before thinking about problem solving.

Chapter 1
BEGINNING A NEW SEMESTER

> At the beginning of a new school year with high school sophomores, Mr. Fraley is work-
> ing at his desk as first-period students enter the classroom. While waiting for the bell
> to ring, most students stand in clusters, talking quietly, but a few students are rather
> loud and boisterous, cruising around the room, causing a commotion with every group
> they pass. Not wanting to be overly negative on the first day of school, Mr. Fraley says
> nothing.
>
> By the time the bell rings, most of the class has become loud and boisterous. Realizing
> that this is going to be an immature class that will need to learn self-discipline, Mr.
> Fraley remembers the classroom management suggestion he learned in college, "Don't
> smile until Christmas and be tough on the first day." Therefore, he commands, "You
> people sit down and be quiet. We need to get this class started."
>
> From the time of role call to the time Mr. Fraley is passing out textbooks and then
> throughout the introductory lesson, several students are loud and sometimes obnox-
> ious. Mr. Fraley continually tells the students to be more quiet, but they don't listen.
> By the end of the first period, Mr. Fraley wonders whether his going into teaching might
> have been a mistake. He wanted to teach to help young people learn, but these students
> just don't seem to care. The joy of teaching is certainly lost, he thinks, when you spend
> your whole day disciplining students instead of teaching them.

A lack of student motivation is extremely frustrating to professionals who are dedicated
to teaching their subject. Though it is certainly easier to work with students who are self-
disciplined and mature, teachers can encourage these qualities in every student from the
first day in the classroom. If the teacher starts the year off right, even the most immature
students can learn self-discipline.

At the beginning of a new semester there are two major factors that will have a
lasting impact on the motivation and behavior of students. First, the teacher must carefully plan and organize course content and motivational procedures before students begin
school. Second, the class must be conducted in a manner that teaches students self-discipline and cooperation.

If the first week goes well, students will discover that the teacher maintains high
expectations for student behavior and academic performance. They will recognize that
there are effective procedures for monitoring their behavior and work and that there are
consistent consequences for misbehavior. Most students will strive to meet high expectations set in an academically productive environment.

If the first week goes badly students will discover that expectations for behavioral
and academic performance are unclear and inconsistent. Students will experiment with
various types of misbehavior to determine how much "goofing around" they can get
away with and how little work the teacher will accept.

This chapter provides strategies for increasing the likelihood that the semester will
begin well. The first part of the chapter focuses on preplanning steps, preparing handouts,
making up lesson plans, and setting up behavioral procedures for the first day of class.
The second part of the chapter presents suggestions for how to conduct the first day and
the remainder of the first week. Finally, there is a list of questions for teachers who are
new to a building. This list will help ensure that they have all the information needed to
begin the first day of school.

ADVANCE PLANNING–BEFORE SCHOOL BEGINS

A major difference between effective and less effective teachers is the degree to which they have defined and communicated their expectations of students. An effective teacher knows exactly *how* he wants students to behave and *what* he hopes to accomplish during every activity. The following section will take you through a seven-step planning process to help clarify your expectations and develop a clear, consistent discipline procedure. The remainder of the chapter will focus on how to conduct the introductory activities on the first day and teach students how to conduct themselves during class activities.

PLANNING YOUR DISCIPLINE POLICIES

Step 1: List all types of classroom activities.

Identify every type of activity that might be included in your course. Rules and expectations will be designed on the basis of this list. Some of the activities that might be included are:

Listening to lectures

Participating in discussions

Watching films

Working on computers

Participating in lab activities

Working independently

Taking tests

Working on group projects

Step 2: For each activity, imagine how you would like students to behave.

For each activity listed, imagine how your class would look if it were composed of only mature and cooperative students. This class would be composed of the full range of academic abilities, but within that range, all students would be motivated and responsible.

In imagining how an ideal class would function, you will be identifying your precise expectations for student behavior. For example, are students talking during independent work times? If so, how loudly? How many people are involved in a conversation? For how long? How much off-task behavior is occurring? How much laughing and joking is going on? If you know your expectations, you can define them for the students. Clarity will reduce the need for students to test you and will help you respond more consistently to the testing that does take place. Examples of the types of questions you should answer when imagining your expectations for a given activity follow.

- Listening to lectures:
  Are students talking?
  Are students raising their hands to ask questions?
  Are students working on other tasks while you are lecturing?
  Are students taking notes?
- Doing independent work:
  Are students talking? How loudly? To students how far away?
  How are students getting help?

Are students out of their seats? For what reasons?

What are students doing when they have completed tasks?

Continue imagining how you would like each activity to look if you had only mature and responsible students. Once you know how you would like students to participate in class activities, you are on your way to teaching students to meet your positive expectations.

Step 3: Design classroom rules.

If you have completed Steps 1 and 2, you have a firm idea of how students should conduct themselves for each type of activity. Write four or five positively stated rules that reflect these expectations. A positively stated rule implies to students that you expect them to function in a mature and responsible way. Below is an example of a set of positively stated rules.

1. Always give every task your best effort.
2. Cooperate with other people in the class.
3. During independent work, work quietly at your desk until your work is completed.
4. Raise your hand if you have something to say or need help.

Avoid stating rules as negative expectations using the word "don't." A rule that specifically addresses a negative behavior tends to communicate a negative expectation. "Don't talk while someone else is talking," tends to imply, "I expect you to be rude and to interrupt people; don't do it."

Because the potential list of misbehaviors is endless, negatively stated rules also tend to be unmanageable. Massive "don't" lists make it difficult to respond consistently to misbehavior. If rules are negatively stated, students may feel a need to challenge every "don't."

Positively stated rules will be relatively broad and general. They will serve as an overall expectation, not a specific code for students to follow. It will be your responsibility to teach students what "cooperation" and "give every task your best effort" mean. Specific procedures for teaching students to translate general rules into actual behavior will be discussed later in this chapter. For now, it is important to write four or five positively stated rules that inform students they are with a teacher who will demand their best—who will not tolerate anything less.

Write your rules neatly in large, bold letters and post them permanently in the front of the classroom. Posted rules let students know they must work to meet your expectations throughout the semester. This is also a visible demonstration to students that there may be different rules in different classrooms, but that in your room the rules will be consistent and enforced.

If you wish to have students design their own rules, wait until the third or fourth day of classes. In the meantime, post temporary rules so students know what is expected for the first several days. Throughout the term, it is perfectly acceptable to modify the rules, using student input if you wish. The major goal of classroom rules is to be fair to students by clarifying and encouraging acceptable and productive behavior.

Step 4: Design consequences for severe misbehavior.

Identify three to four misbehaviors that you feel very strongly about, and their specific consequences. On the first day of class you will need to discuss these behaviors and their consequences with students. For ideas on designing consequences, see Chapter 8, *Classroom Consequences.* Your list might look like the following:

Hitting or fighting—Referral to the office

Direct defiance of the teacher—Referral to the office

Talking during lectures or study time—Three minutes owed at lunch

While you do want to avoid addressing a long list of "don'ts," it is important to include a few. If students have no idea how you will respond to misbehavior, they will test you to find out what will happen. If this occurs, you must either provide a consequence that has not been discussed or let the misbehavior go by. If you implement a consequence for the misbehavior, students may feel, justifiably, that they have not been treated fairly. If you fail to implement a consequence, students will feel that misbehavior is acceptable. It is obviously better to discuss the consequences for intolerable behavior beforehand. Students need to be informed.

If some of the behaviors you identify are already covered in the school's discipline policy, you may choose to omit them from your list. In class, it will be important to let students know they are accountable for every behavior discussed in the school discipline policy as well as the additional behaviors you have identified.

Note: This list of misbehaviors should not be posted. Post your positive expectations, but not the negative behaviors and consequences. Posting the negative behaviors can serve as a reminder to some students to engage in the misbehavior. Simply inform the class about consequences for misbehavior. If students misbehave, implement the consequences for misbehavior quickly and firmly and then focus on teaching students to behave appropriately.

Step 5: Design a grading system that encourages motivation and participation.

Students must learn that their behavior in class and their effort and cooperation will affect grades in a positive or negative manner. It is important for students to know that their actions and performance will be monitored and evaluated. Students must see that the teacher is keeping systematic and ongoing records of their performance in class. For information on setting up such a grading system, see Chapter 2, *Effective Grading Systems.*

Step 6: Design routines for assigning and collecting in-class assignments and homework.

Late papers and incomplete assignments are a problem in most secondary schools. Teachers frequently find themselves nagging students with little or no result. Routines for assigning and collecting work can increase the probability that students will turn completed work in on time. An example of a regular routine: The teacher can lecture the first half of class and then provide class time for assignments due at the end of each period. Homework might be assigned every Monday and be due every Thursday, assigned every Thursday and be due every Monday. Routines encourage students to become self-disciplined by following a set schedule. Early in the term, students will learn to organize their homework routine, as your expectations will be very clear.

Without a set routine, students may have heavy homework assignments one week and no assignments the next week. This lack of consistency makes it difficult for students to plan their time. Only the brightest and most mature students can adjust to a continually shifting pattern of work. The majority of students need the security of daily and weekly routines.

Students also perform better when they are given short assignments due on a relatively frequent basis, rather than long assignments due at the end of each week or at the end of the term. The more immature your students, the more important it will be to break homework assignments into small increments.

If your students have difficulty getting homework assignments in on time, it may be necessary to ask parents to help monitor work that should be completed at home. A regular routine will make it possible for parents to determine whether their children have completed assignments.

Routines do not take the spontaneity out of teaching, nor do they restrict teachers from adjusting lessons to the needs of students. When a break in routine is needed, you will find that it is refreshing for everyone. To have a break in routine, however, you must have a routine in the first place. Establish a daily routine. Get students adjusted and then provide periodic breaks as needed.

Your routine should include procedures for assigning work. Students can learn to check a section of the board each day for homework and daily class assignments. Another effective method for giving assignments is to provide a worksheet at the beginning of each week listing all assignments for the week. In some cases, you could even require that students have the sheet signed by their parents. This ensures that parents are aware of course requirements throughout the term and can intervene if students are having difficulty completing assignments.

You must also have a regular routine for collecting assignments. Students must see that any work assigned will be collected on the day it is due. There is nothing more discouraging to students than to work hard to meet a deadline, only to find their work isn't collected until two days later. Work must be collected at the beginning of the period. This will help students plan to have work completed prior to the time they enter the classroom. This alleviates the problem of students trying hurriedly to complete work during your other class activities.

Finally, it is important to record completed work as it is handed in. One method for collecting and recording work is to have students hand in assignments as they enter the classroom. You can record their work as you are greeting the students at the door. Another efficient method for collecting papers is to have students hand in assignments as you call their names for roll. You can record completed assignments and attendance simultaneously.

Step 7: Prepare activities for the first day of classes.

The way you conduct the first day of class leaves students with a lasting impression and usually sets the tone for the remainder of the semester. It is important to communicate encouragement, warmth, and firmness. Students must recognize that you have high expectations, tempered by an understanding of their making mistakes and having limitations. By showing concern and efficiency, you will demonstrate that class time will be used as effectively as possible. Students must understand that you take learning very seriously and expect them to take it seriously as well. This step will help you design activities for the first day to ensure that the semester gets off to a good start.

• Prepare an easy task for students to work on when they first enter the classroom. Tell students to work quietly on the assignment until you have completed roll. If students have to get to work as soon as they enter the classroom, they will learn that every minute of class will be used as effectively as possible. This task can be something as simple as the Student Information Form shown in Figure 1–1. You should suggest that the last part

Figure 1–1   Student Information Form

STUDENT INFORMATION FORM

Name: _____

Address: _____

_____   _____

City   State   Zip

Phone: _____

Name of parent(s): _____

Can your parents be reached at home during the day? _____

If not, provide a number where they can be reached: _____

List any special interests or hobbies: _____

_____

_____

_____

List any activities you enjoy doing in class when your work has been completed or during free time:

_____

_____

_____

_____

_____

_____

_____

_____

_____

_____

_____

_____

_____

of the form include something for students to work on quietly when they have completed the assigned task. It could include crossword puzzles or brain teasers, or you may tell the students you wish them to complete tasks that will give you diagnostic information. For example, if you are a math teacher, you may wish to have students work a series of problems that assess basic skills. If you are a social studies teacher, you may wish to have students practice summarizing paragraphs from your text.

• Prepare handouts on your rules and class expectations, on homework and daily class assignments (as described in the previous steps), and on your grading system (see Chapter 2).

• Prepare activities for the remainder of your first class. These activities should be representative of the types of activities you will have on a normal day. If most of your class time will involve lectures and independent study time, plan to give a short lecture followed by time to get started on a homework assignment. Plan to show students what your class will be like. If you wish to spend time getting to know students, take time later in the week after you have established a constructive academic atmosphere in your classroom.

TIPS ON CONDUCTING THE FIRST TEN MINUTES OF CLASS

Step 1: Stand at the door to greet students.

Greeting students at the door will demonstrate your interest in interacting with students from the moment they enter the classroom. Your presence will also reduce the likelihood of misbehavior. Finally, if any students try to enter your room rambunctiously or disruptively, you can take care of the inappropriate behavior outside your classroom.

As students enter, introduce yourself and give them any directions needed to complete the introductory task. If students are entering the classroom in a loud or boisterous manner, stop them before they actually enter your room. Tell students that they must enter quietly and begin working on their assignment. If students do not quiet down, tell them to remain in the hall until they are ready to enter quietly. Then, if any students remain in the hall as class is about to begin, indicate privately that they must enter quietly and take a seat. If a student does not enter the room, explain that you will have to count her absent unless she chooses to join the class. If you greet students at the door, these last steps are rarely needed.

Step 2: When you are ready to begin class, get everyone's full attention before you start.

Always wait to get everyone's attention before you begin the class. If you start class while some students are still talking or are out of their seats, students will assume that it is all right to engage in those behaviors while class is in session. Make this waiting a habit and give directions or start class activities only when you have the attention of the entire class.

If the students do not quiet down when you tell them you are ready to begin class, wait quietly. If the students get quiet within ten or fifteen seconds, begin the first activity and say nothing about the time it took them to get ready to listen. If they take up to thirty seconds, inform them—when they have gotten quiet—that from now on you will expect them to be quiet and ready to listen within a few seconds of the time you call for their attention. If they are not quiet after thirty seconds, tell them in a firm (not shouting—*firm*) voice that you need their attention. Repeat this instruction until you have the attention of the class.

Step 3: Present class rules and consequences for misbehavior.

When you have everyone's attention, introduce yourself. Let students know you are glad to have each of them in class and hope they will find your class enjoyable and profitable. Present your class rules as procedures for ensuring that class time is beneficial to everyone and then discuss consequences for inappropriate classroom behavior. Give them the handout on rules and expectations and make sure everyone understands how your class will be conducted. This is an important first activity because it allows you to clarify your expectations prior to any opportunity for student misbehavior.

Step 4: Take attendance.

Once you have presented your classroom rules, take attendance. Have students work on completing the introductory task while you call roll. In some schools, it may be necessary to take attendance right after the bell rings. If so, you may wish to take attendance while you are greeting students at the door. During a roll call, students know that they will be involved in the activity for only one thirtieth of the time. If the roll is taken before you present the rules and expectations, students may tune you out even before you have begun.

Step 5: Explain your procedures for assigning and collecting work.

Introduce the procedures and routines for assigning and collecting work. Distribute any related handouts, making sure that students understand how they can monitor their own assignments. Be clear when explaining that work will be due at the beginning of the class period on the day it is due. Explain any consequences for late assignments.

Step 6: Explain your grading system.

Pass out the handouts on assignments and grading. Explain in detail how students will earn their grades. Tell students to show the information to their parents. You may wish to have students bring back parent signatures indicating they have been informed of your grading system and of your expectations for the semester. This is an excellent way to document that your students are informed.

A FIVE-STEP PROCESS FOR TEACHING STUDENTS HOW TO BEHAVE

For every subsequent class activity during the first couple of days, implement the following steps. This process is useful for all activities from listening , to lectures, to passing out books, to excusing a class. The purpose of these five steps is to teach the students precisely what they should do to demonstrate that they are following the classroom rules. This will require some extra time the first few days of class, but will save time in the long run because students will more quickly begin to follow your rules and expectations.

Step 1: Get everyone's attention before you begin any class activity.

See Step 2 under "Tips on Conducting the First Ten Minutes of Class."

Step 2: Introduce each activity and describe exactly how you expect students to behave during that activity.

In describing how you want students to behave, provide as much detailed information as possible. Students have had many teachers over the years. Some allow talking, others do not. Some teachers want students to raise their hands, others do not. Each individual teacher must clarify his or her expectations. This is also how you will clarify any differences in how students are expected to behave during different activities in your classroom. For example, you would probably inform students before lectures and independent work times that they need to raise their hand if they have a question or something to say. However, during discussions you might allow them to speak without raising their hand as long as they do not interrupt someone who is speaking.

Provide explicit information on how you want students to interact with each other and with you. Introduce each activity by telling students whether they may talk to each other and if so, how loudly, about what topics, and for how long. Some students will talk during the entire period if they are told that talking is allowed. It is important to clarify exactly what you mean. The following examples are provided only as models of what might be said in this type of discussion. It is important for you to tailor your discussion to your expectations.

> Thank you for listening while we were discussing the grading system. The next thing we need to do is pass out textbooks. I need three people to pass out the books, and I will call on volunteers who raise their hands. Thank you. While they are passing out the books, you can work on finishing that form. If the form is finished, you may talk to someone sitting close to you or look at a book. If you choose to talk, it may only be to someone who is sitting immediately next to you on either side, or directly in front or in back of you. Talking may only be done in pairs, no three-way conversations. If you have a question for me, quietly raise your hand. When the books have been passed out, I will ask to have your attention, and at that time you will need to immediately stop your conversation and give me your attention.

After the books have been passed out, introduce the next activity by getting everyone's attention and then present your expectations for that activity.

> The next thing we are going to do is have a brief lecture. On most days, I will lecture for about half the period. If you have a question or comment about the lecture, it will be important for you to raise your hand and wait to be called on. There will be no other talking. During lectures, I will highlight information that will be on tests and give information about what to study from the textbook. I will try to prepare you as much as possible for all tests. I expect you to take notes on important information. If you have trouble with a test, I will ask to see your lecture notes. If anyone has questions about how to take notes or has questions about what information to put in their notes, feel free to ask during the lecture or to speak with me after class. Any questions?

Step 3: Provide students with positive feedback when they are meeting your expectations.

It is important for you to let students know they are on target. Students need to know that you appreciate their efforts. Simple matter-of-fact feedback will not embarrass secondary-level students. It tells them that you recognize their mature and responsible attitudes and actions. Examples of appropriate feedback statements to secondary students follow.

> I appreciate the way you give me your attention right away. It saves a lot of time when I don't have to repeat instructions.

> I noticed that everyone took notes when I said that the information on the three forms of matter was important. That's a good indication that everyone will be prepared for the first test.

For more information on the importance of positive feedback and for information on ways to provide feedback that will not be embarrassing to secondary-level students, see Chapter 3, *Teacher-Student Interactions*.

Step 4: Provide immediate feedback when students are not meeting your expectations.

Use a gentle verbal reprimand when students engage in minor misbehavior. A gentle verbal reprimand involves a matter-of-fact statement telling a student or students what they should be doing. For example, you may have a rule stating that students must raise their hand if they have a question or comment during lectures. If a couple of students begin whispering during a lecture, you might walk over to them and say, "Remember, if you have something to say during a lecture you are supposed to raise your hand and wait to be called on. If you do not wish to share your thoughts with the class, you should not be talking." It is critical that the gentle verbal reprimand be delivered very calmly and quietly. Emotion weakens the procedure. Your manner should imply that the students probably did not fully understand your expectations. You will therefore give them more direct information so that they can improve their behavior. This reduces the likelihood that students will resent a reprimand. If you are harsh with this procedure the student may justifiably feel, "Well, I didn't know what was expected in this stupid class!"

Verbal reprimands should be private, brief, and as immediate as possible. The more private the reprimand, the less likely the student will feel that he needs to challenge your authority to save face in front of his peers. However, immediacy should not be sacrificed for privacy. If you wait until the end of the period to reprimand a student, others will think that the misbehavior was acceptable. Similarly, do not take the student into the hall for a reprimand because immediacy is lost and the interruption could prompt other behavioral problems in your classroom. Verbal reprimands are most effective when the teacher immediately walks over to the student or students and quietly tells them how they need to improve their behavior.

The only caution in using verbal reprimands is that they are only short-term interventions. If the misbehavior continues after you have used verbal reprimands several times, you must change your strategy. Chapter 7, *Using Punishment Consequences* and Chapter 8, *Classroom Consequences* provide information on establishing effective consequences for misbehaviors that persist despite the verbal reprimands.

Step 5: At the end of each activity, tell students how well they have met your expectations.

If students have been successful in meeting your expectations, they need to know that you are aware of their cooperation and effort. If there have been problems, go over the problems without naming names. Identify class goals for the next activity of this type. Let your class know that you have higher expectations than were demonstrated, but that they will have an opportunity to work on improving their performance. Following is an example of this type of feedback.

> Most of today's lecture went pretty well. However, I did have to give reminders several times about not talking and about raising your hands when you have something to say. We will have another lecture for about half the period tomorrow. I would appreciate it if you would work harder on meeting my expectation of not talking and of raising your hands.

CHECKLIST FOR TEACHERS NEW TO A BUILDING

If you are a first-year teacher or an experienced teacher new to a particular school, use the following list of questions as a guide to finding out critical information regarding school policies. You should be able to answer all the questions below before the students arrive for the first day of school.

- Do you have a copy of the school discipline policy?
- Are you expected to discuss these policies with students?
- What are the procedures for referring a misbehaving student to the office?
- What behaviors do the administrators feel should be referred to the office as opposed to those handled in the classroom?
- Do the administrators have expectations regarding student behavior in your classroom?
- To what extent are you expected to monitor the halls and restrooms?
- What are you expected to do if a student you do not know is misbehaving in the halls or in the restrooms?
- What sort of records are you expected to keep regarding student behavior, attendance, tardiness, and so on?
- What are the procedures for allowing students to use the library or computer center during class time?
- What are you expected to do regarding parental contacts?
- What behaviors are unacceptable to you, and what are the consequences for inappropriate behavior?

Chapter 2

EFFECTIVE GRADING SYSTEMS

Mrs. Allen teaches high school biology. She has always enjoyed teaching but finds working with unmotivated students very frustrating. Mrs. Allen knows that other staff members feel the same way, having heard others complain, "Every year it seems as if I get more and more students who just don't care about their grades. They make no attempt to pass my courses, and it really doesn't seem to matter to them when they do fail. I guess their parents don't care either."

Motivating students to achieve academic success is frequently a difficult job. Teachers often face a lack of parental support. They must work with students who have been neglected or abused. Drug problems, absenteeism, and general apathy about course content can make it seem as if student motivation is outside a teacher's control.

Certainly, many factors affecting student motivation are outside the teacher's control. You cannot control a student's home life or eliminate all drug use. You cannot make every minute of instruction fascinating for every student in your class. Some part of every course is going to be hard work. The one motivational factor that teachers have complete control over is the grading system. While a good grading system will not solve problems related to poor teaching or poorly designed materials, a good system at least can increase student motivation. If an effective grading system is paired with effective instruction and carefully sequenced teaching materials, even low-performing students are likely to be successful.

A well-designed grading system can help foster student motivation. The most unmotivated students are those who have consistently gotten poor grades. They view grades much as many people view lotteries or sweepstakes. It would, of course, be nice to receive $1 million. However, the odds are stacked heavily against winning, so why try? Every student would love to get an *A* or a *B*, but many know from experience that their efforts do little to change the odds. Though many students quit trying, few give up hoping. When teachers hand back tests or papers, it is rare to see a student who doesn't care enough to quickly check out his grade. Even the lowest-performing student will still care enough about grades to see if by some chance she's "gotten lucky" this time. An effective grading system can teach students that they do have some control over the odds. Your goal is to teach students that they can become more successful by working hard throughout the term.

The first part of this chapter discusses the features of an effective grading system that helps teach students how to earn better grades. The second part of the chapter gives you procedures for designing an effective grading system for your courses.

FEATURES OF AN EFFECTIVE GRADING SYSTEM

1. Evaluation should be based on clearly defined course objectives.

In an undergraduate history course, a college instructor assigns 1,200 pages of reading. Every three weeks students are to be tested on a 400-page section of the reading and on three weeks of lecture. The final grade will be based entirely on the three tests. Prior to the first test, students are not provided with any information that will help them prepare for the test. When students ask what information from the text will be important, they are told, "Everything will be important."

The first test is composed of one essay question covering a topic that has not been mentioned in class and has been discussed on only three pages of the text. Out of fifty students, one receives an *A*, three receive *B*s, fourteen receive *F*s, and thirty-two receive *C*s and *D*s.

Students complain that the test was unfair. "How could we know which three pages were important? There is no way to memorize four hundred pages of text." The instructor replies, "I tested you on those three pages, not because they were the most important, but because anyone who knew those three pages must have learned the material on the other three hundred ninety-seven pages." On hearing this reply, half the students drop the class before the second test.

The true illustration above serves to demonstrate how courses seem impossible when important objectives are not clear to the instructor and students. Even sophisticated college students will choose not to play the game when there are overwhelming odds against knowing what to study. The instructor made a common error in assuming that it was the students' responsibility to identify important objectives. He felt that his job was primarily to give information. This misconception not only made it impossible for students to know how to study, it also resulted in the testing of random pieces of information.

In most cases, academically successful students are able to figure out critical objectives. If testing is on random bits of information, they still have a chance to succeed because they are fairly adept at remembering those pieces of information. Less capable students will have difficulty sorting out critical objectives. They will have less of a chance at remembering unconnected bits of information. In order to increase motivation for all your students, you will need to clarify your instructional objectives and then evaluate students on the basis of those objectives.

The major percentage of your final grade should reflect each student's mastery of the course objectives. A failing grade should indicate that a student has not mastered the objectives. Students who master the objectives should receive a *C*, and students who exceed the objectives should receive an *A* or a *B*. Grading on the basis of student mastery of objectives means that every student has the opportunity to pass the class.

This implies that you should avoid grading students based on a normal curve. Grading on a normal curve or a variation of a curve means that grades will be distributed according to the percentages below:

2% of the students will receive an *A*

14% of the students will receive a *B*

68% of the students will receive a *C*

14% of the students will receive a *D*

2% of the students will receive an *F*

Grading on a curve takes all incentive away from lower-performing students. They soon realize that their grades have little to do with how well they master course content. They must "beat" higher-performing students to succeed. No matter how hard they work, their performance will always be evaluated relative to that of higher-performing students.

However, if students can pass a course because they have mastered course objectives, they soon learn that they can succeed regardless of their relative position to other students. Your goal will be to provide instruction that results in as many students as possible receiving a *C* or better. You will not be giving away passing grades regardless of student performance. Student grades will reflect their demonstrated mastery of course objectives.

One of the benefits of organizing a course and the grading system around specific objectives is that it eliminates the need for students to "second guess" what they are supposed to learn. Many secondary students do not know enough about a given subject to identify the important things to learn. Trying to second guess the teacher is a no-win situation for most students. When students know the teacher's objectives, they know what they are supposed to study. This will increase the likelihood that students will put forth the effort to study. At the same time, use of course objectives will make it easier for you to evaluate student performance fairly and objectively.

2. Class lectures, projects, assignments, and tests must be clearly related to course objectives and evaluation procedures.

Miss Henry's Modern Problems course involves teacher lectures, guest lectures, panel discussions, films, and use of the district text. While all of Miss Henry's classroom activities focus on topics related to the text, her grading system is based solely upon unit tests provided by the textbook publisher. At the beginning of the term, a fair number of Miss Henry's students take notes during class activities. During the third unit of study Miss Henry invites a number of guest lecturers to speak. In observing her class, she is dismayed to find that very few students are actually taking an active interest in the information presented. Several students are obviously daydreaming. Mary Jane is sleeping in the back of the room. John is passing a note to Carlos.

Poorly designed evaluation procedures will frequently discourage motivation instead of encourage motivation. In the foregoing illustration, Miss Henry has failed to integrate her class activities with the textbook information, and she has failed to demonstrate how class activities will affect student grades. If she chooses to use guest lecturers, part of the students' grades must be based upon the information they have learned from these guests. For example, when Miss Henry first contacts her guest speaker, she should determine the general nature of the information that will be covered. When introducing the guest, Miss Henry can give her students some guidelines and a short assignment that will help them integrate the new information with information already covered in the course.

Our guest today is Susan James. She was a member of the Peace Corps. Her assignment took her to El Salvador, where she lived for two years. Miss James will be sharing the slides that she took in El Salvador and discussing her observations of the people she lived and worked with. As Miss James is talking, think about the economic conditions that we have been reading about in our unit on Latin America.

Your assignment this evening will be to write two paragraphs. The first should describe the way of life in El Salvador. You will want to listen to Miss James very carefully and observe her slides very closely. Your second paragraph should discuss your hypothesis concerning the underlying causes of the problems in El Salvador today. This assignment will be worth twenty points, and it will be due tomorrow. We are very lucky to have Miss James with us. She has indicated that she will be happy to answer any questions that you might have.

A failure to integrate course activities, assignments, and tests teaches students that grades are part of an unrelated and mystical system. The more you are able to integrate your activities, assignments, and tests, the more students will learn how daily effort results in a successful overall learning experience.

3. A percentage of the final grade should be based on daily participation and effort.

Mr. Nakamura teaches several sections of math. His fourth-period class is a sophomore geometry course. Mr. Nakamura has designed his course to include class discussions, lectures, and assignments on Mondays through Thursdays. Each Friday, students are given a quiz on the material that has been covered during the week. Class discussions and lectures typically focus on assignments that students were to complete the night before. Mr. Nakamura has followed this type of schedule to allow students to work on problems independently and then to resolve any difficulties as a group.

During class activities, only some of the students work hard. The other students do not seem to care whether they learn how to do the problems or not. These students are not working up to their potential because they are spending so much of their time goofing around. While behavior never gets completely out of hand, many of the students are not learning how to solve problems that will be on their tests.

Highly motivated and academically successful students know that their daily performance has a cumulative effect on their grade. These students know that each day's work will affect how much they learn, which in turn affects their test performance and eventually their final grade. Academically motivated students recognize that their daily efforts really will affect their future schooling options and job opportunities, whereas lower-performing and immature students do not understand these relationships. They do not realize that the reason they are not passing is because they do not work and listen during class.

Most grading systems in the secondary school are structured similarly to college grading systems. Attendance and the degree of student participation do not in themselves affect the grade. The grade is based solely on assignments, tests, quizzes, and so on. Unfortunately, in this type of system, there is no immediate accountability for "goofing off." By the time a student fails a test or fails a course, it is too late to make improvements. The delayed consequence is too weak to be effective.

An effective grading system at the secondary level must teach less sophisticated students the skills that sophisticated students learn on their own. The grading system must demonstrate that daily work and attention have a cumulative effect on a final grade. Less motivated students in the typical secondary classroom must be taught how to evaluate the long-term consequences of their daily actions. This can be done by basing a percentage of the grade on participation and effort. Students will learn appropriate classroom behavior, and they will learn that what they do in class each day is an important part of earning their final grade.

Some districts have a policy that prohibits teachers from using behavior in class as a criterion for grading. If this is the case, follow your district's guidelines. However, you might look at that policy closely. First, find out if the intent of the policy is to restrict you from lowering a student's grade because he has misbehaved. If so, you might still be able to use a system that bases part of the grade on behavior. The concern of many districts is that a teacher should not deduct points from a student's tests and assignments because of misbehavior. This does not prevent the teacher from saying that students will earn between 0 and 20 points each week based on how hard they work and how well they behave.

Frequently, you can justify basing a portion of the grade on behavior by saying that your class objectives involve teaching students the overall behaviors they need to be successful in any educational setting. For example, in a home economics class the ability to stay on task, to follow directions, and to follow safety rules are critical behaviors for being successful. This same argument could be used to justify grading on participation and behavior in more traditional academic classes like English or history. Students must learn more than just the information and concepts covered in class. By including participation and effort as a part of your grade, you will be demonstrating to students that learning independent study skills, knowing how to listen, taking responsibility for assignments and materials, staying on the appropriate task, attending regularly, and arriving on time do have a direct relationship to success and good grades. Learning these behaviors will be necessary for all future educational and professional endeavors and are therefore important objectives. Your district may agree that since these behaviors represent sound educational objectives, it is reasonable to base a percentage of each student's grade on these behaviors.

4. The grading system will need to include a monitoring system that gives students immediate and continual feedback on their daily performance and efforts.

In an urban high school the P.E. department bases 50 percent of each student's grade on participation and effort. They give this grade at the end of the term by averaging a student's grade from tests and performance scores with a grade they assign for participation. This participation grade is not given or discussed with students until the end of the term. The teachers are aware that this participation grade does not seem to have a motivating effect on student behavior.

One of the keys to making a grading system effective is the degree to which students feel their performance is being monitored and fairly evaluated. With 100 to 180 students passing through the typical secondary classroom each day, it is likely that several students go through the entire year getting feedback about their classroom behavior only at the end of the term. Because the feedback is so delayed, students cannot know what the grade is based upon. They have no way of knowing whether it is important to work hard only at the end of the term or whether effort each day makes a difference. Not knowing what a grade is based upon results in teachers and students feeling that participation and effort grades are subjective. Moreover, the grade does little to help a student learn academically successful behaviors. It will be critical to demonstrate that grades are based on actual daily performance.

Each day students must see that you are monitoring and recording information about student behavior and motivation. Each week students must see that this information has been used to determine a weekly participation grade. The weekly participation grade will help you demonstrate that daily behavior is reflected in the student's grade. If a high-performing student is not working up to potential, the teacher can reduce the weekly participation grade. If a low-performing student is having difficulty with course work but working very hard, you can encourage the student's efforts by assigning a high-participation grade.

An effective monitoring system can be designed to keep track of large amounts of information regarding student behavior, without interfering with other teaching responsibilities and without creating a lot of extra work. Recording, evaluating, and communicating the weekly participation grade to students can be done in as little as five minutes per class. Details on how to set up and implement a system of this type are discussed in detail in the next section of this chapter.

By including a participation and effort grade, your marking system will become more than a simple evaluation tool. It will become a systematic monitoring device that demonstrates to students that they are accountable for their efforts each day, and that effort each day will result in a better grade at the end of the term.

5. Effective grading systems must include relatively immediate feedback on written assignments and tests.

Joe is a high school sophomore who has had difficulty with school since the first grade. Though Joe has learned to read, it has been a struggle from the start. Joe has never been identified for special classes but every assignment is difficult. Joe has very supportive parents and two older sisters who have done well in school. Periodically, Joe gets a pep talk at home and studies very hard. Because studying is difficult, Joe also gets discouraged fairly frequently and gives up.

At the beginning of the term, Joe has gotten fired up again and has vowed to do well in science. The teacher is excellent, and Joe finds that this class is a little more interesting than some of his others. Joe studies hard for the first test. The test is fairly lengthy. The teacher is busy preparing for the new unit of study, and a couple of weeks pass before Joe finds out that he has passed the first test. In the meantime Joe has failed an English and a math exam and is feeling very discouraged again. When the second science test is administered, Joe forgets to study. He's feeling pretty good about science, though, because he knows he has a passing grade.

Joe's parents have helped him structure homework time, so Joe has also turned in all his written assignments. He has forgotten that half the assignments were only partially completed because he typically ignores questions he doesn't understand. By the time these assignments are graded, Joe only remembers all the time he has spent doing his science assignments, having forgotten that many of them were incomplete.

This process continues throughout the term. When Joe receives a failing grade in science, he is surprised and angry.

Frequently, immature students are not motivated by grading systems because they do not understand the relationship between their efforts on written work and their final grade. When there are delays between a student's effort and the reinforcement of a good grade, or between his failure to study and the consequence of a poor grade, the student's own inconsistent behavior will tend to make him think that grades are spurious. They are mysterious and sometimes just the whim of the teacher. Low-performing students tend to remember the times they worked hard and forget the times that they gave up. When grades are poor but the student has worked hard sometimes, the student may tend to think that effort doesn't make a difference. If you can arrange to give students almost immediate feedback on their efforts it will reduce the number of students who become confused and discouraged.

In addition to returning work with relative immediacy, it will also be important to communicate to students how they can improve a grade. In the foregoing example, Joe doesn't know why his science assignments haven't helped his overall grade. All he knows is that he has failed and doing homework didn't do any good.

6. An effective grading system will encourage students to keep track of their own grades.

In the foregoing situation, Joe has become discouraged because feedback on his work was so delayed. Joe also has difficulties because he views his grades as an unchangeable phenomenon. "My grades are bad, and they will always be bad. Even when I do well on assignments, I still flunk." Students like Joe lack the ability to keep records of their cumulative grade. If you ask a highly motivated student what her current grade in English is, you are likely to find that the student has a clear idea of how she is doing. "I have a B, and if I do well on the next test and on the term paper, I can push the grade up to an

A. However, if you ask a low-performing student the same question she may say, "How am I supposed to know what my grade is? Grades don't come out until three weeks from now." Low performers have rarely learned to keep track of their own grades. Part of an effective system involves encouraging students to record their own progress and to be continually aware of their current status in the class.

7. Grades should be based on points so students understand the relative weight of assignments, tests, participation, and so on.

Many students have never learned that different assignments may have different values. They may think that an *A* on a homework assignment will make up for an *F* on a test. Grading systems based on points make it easier for students to understand that some tasks are worth more than others.

Grading systems based upon points will make it easier for students to continually track their own grades. Point systems also provide a means for communicating the criteria you will use for evaluating each test and assignment and demonstrate to students how each test and assignment affects the final grade.

For example, if Joe had known the number of points that each item on an assignment would be worth, the teacher would have demonstrated that failing to complete some items affected Joe's grade. Compare the following instructions for an English paper:

1. Your assignment is to write a one-page editorial comment on an article you find in today's newspaper. Your assignment will be due tomorrow.

2. Your assignment is to write a one-page editorial comment on an article you find in today's newspaper. Your assignment will be due at the beginning of tomorrow's class. The total points possible for this paper will be 100 points. The breakdown of points for your editorial comment is listed on the board.

CONTENT, LOGIC, ORGANIZATION	50 points
PUNCTUATION AND SPELLING	20 points
CORRECT USE OF GRAMMAR	20 points
NEATNESS	10 points

The second teacher communicated to students exactly how the assignment would be weighted and the criteria used for grading. The first teacher gives students a graded paper, but they have no basis for determining how the paper was evaluated or how the paper will affect their final grade. Because the second teacher has clearly stated her expectations with her grading systems, students will be able to identify what can be done to improve a grade or what can be done in the future to maintain a grade.

DESIGNING AN EFFECTIVE GRADING SYSTEM

The steps outlined in the remainder of this chapter will help you design a grading system that teaches students to be more self-disciplined and motivated. It is important to establish a grading system that provides immediate feedback to students without interrupting instruction. This section gives an example of a grading system that incorporates all the features of an efficient and effective grading system. You may wish to design your own system, make modifications in the suggested system, or implement the following steps.

Step 1. Establish a percentage of the grade for classroom performance.

To teach students that daily effort affects a final grade, establish a percentage of the final grade for classroom performance. The exact percentage will vary from class to class according to the following factors.

Maturity and self-motivation: If you are working with students who are not yet sophisticated with grading systems, you must base a relatively large percentage of the grade on class performance. This includes students in the middle and junior high school and students of any age who have academic or behavioral problems. Highly motivated classes consisting of mature students do not need a very high percentage of the grade to be based on performance in class.

Type of subject: Some subjects must have grades that are based heavily on competency. For example, students in a ninth-grade writing class must demonstrate competency in basic writing skills to pass the course. If too high a percentage of the grade is based on participation and effort, a student could potentially pass the class without demonstrating mastery of the basic course objectives. For this type of class, you would not want to assign more than 15 percentage points for participation and effort. On the other hand, if you have a tenth-grade chorus class, it would be appropriate to have as much as 50 percent of the grade based on participation and effort. This would give credit to students who do not have outstanding voices, but who work very hard.

Course level: The level of student experience in a given subject area should also affect how much of a grade is based on participation and effort. Students beginning a new skill should have a higher percentage of the grade based on classroom performance than more advanced students. Any time students acquire a new skill, effort will determine whether students move beyond the beginning stages. It is during this time that students

Figure 2–1   Differing Percentages for Participation and Effort

TYPE OF CLASS	ESTIMATED STUDENT MATURITY	PARTICIPATION AND EFFORT %
Introductory woodshop	Mixed	50%
Advanced composition	Highly motivated Excellent skills	10%
Remedial English	Poorly motivated Low performing	20%
Biology	Mixed	20%
Intermediate band	Some mix, primarily motivated	30%
Advanced art	Highly motivated	20%
7th-grade social science	Mixed, many without interest in subject area	30%
12th-grade world history	Mixed	10%

need the most encouragement. As students gain proficiency in any skill area, the related tasks become more reinforcing in themselves. For example, beginning string students need encouragement as they learn to read and play notes. However, advanced string students are able to enjoy their own ability to play and interpret music. Figure 2–1 provides several examples of different types of classes and the kinds of percentages that might be reasonable to assign for participation and effort.

Determine a percentage of the final grade that your students should earn for daily participation and effort in class. Through the term, you will monitor and record student behavior. At the end of each week, students receive classroom performance points. These points represent a percentage of the final grade for daily participation and effort.

Step 2: Design an efficient system for monitoring and recording daily classroom behavior.

To demonstrate how daily performance affects a final grade, students need to see that their daily behavior is being monitored and recorded. Figure 2–2 shows an example of a monitoring and recording sheet that can be used to quickly note any information related to a student's classroom performance.

This Weekly Record Sheet is a class list that provides space to code each student's behavior every day of the week. This single form can be used to record attendance, assignments, behaviors that demonstrate above or below average classroom performance, and weekly point totals for classroom performance. Determining the number of points students can earn each week is discussed later in this chapter.

The Weekly Record Sheet should be kept readily accessible at all times. Some teachers wish to keep forms for each class on a clipboard, while others prefer to use a notebook. The Weekly Record Sheet should be kept close to wherever you work—on your desk, propped on a podium or chalk tray, or you may wish to carry it around with you.

At the beginning of each class, students should see that you have the record form ready to take attendance. If any assignments are due, you can record papers that are handed in on time while simultaneously taking roll. Through the remainder of the period, students should see you periodically using the record form. If a student walks into class late, you can quickly mark a *T* for tardy. If a student needs to be reminded to get to work, simply note an *O* for "off task" next to the student's name. Immediate coding of these negative behaviors will teach students that they are accountable for their actions each day. (See Figure 2–3 for a partially filled-in sheet.) When students excel, you can record an *E* for excellence or a *C* for cooperation. If immediate coding of positive behaviors would be embarrassing to students, code your notations of extra effort while students are getting out assignments or any time prior to your next class. Then, privately, let the students know that you have acknowledged their extra effort. For additional information on giving students positive feedback without causing embarrassment, see Chapter 3, *Teacher Student Interactions.* Using the Weekly Record Sheet daily will provide valuable information for evaluating student performance at the end of the week.

Step 3: Determine approximate number of total points students may earn for tests, assignments, and class projects during the term.

Count the topics or units of study you hope to cover during the term, possibly working from the district text or from a district curriculum guide.

Next, using the number of units you hope to cover, estimate the number of tests, assignments, and projects students will be accountable for during the term. Though you are projecting what you hope to accomplish during the term, these preplanning steps will

Figure 2–2   Weekly Record Sheet

WEEKLY RECORD SHEET

Date _____   Reminders _____

Class period _____   _____

STUDENT	MON.	TUES.	WED.	THUR.	FRI.	TOTAL

CODE: EXCELLENT WORK = E +2   OFF TASK = 0 −1   ABSENT = A
         COOPERATIVE = C +2   DISRUPTIVE = D −1   UNEXCUSED
         BONUS POINTS = B   LATE WORK = L −1   ABSENCE =
                                                       UA −4
                                                       TARDY = T −2

Figure 2–3   Partially Filled-In Sheet

WEEKLY RECORD SHEET

Date _Sept. 14-18_   Reminders _____

Class period _4_   _____

STUDENT	MON.	TUES.	WED.	THUR.	FRI.	TOTAL
Agner, Donna		✓ E			✓	18
Amato, Lee		✓			✓	16
Anderson, Dan	0	✓		T-6	✓	13
Baumbaugh, Gary		—	0		✓ E	16
Buckee, Cheryl		✓ 0			✓	15
Carpenter, Dustin	0 0 0	✓			✓	13
Crossett, Gelia		✓			✓ E	18
Deane, Russ		A (B+4)	A (B+4)		✓	16
Dorns, Jan	E	✓		0	✓	17
Edwards, Lanny		✓ 0			✓	15
Felch, Yvvette		✓			✓	16
Franklin, Lavar		✓			✓ E	18
Godon, Randi	A (B+4)	✓ 0	E		✓	17

not lock you into an inflexible system. By estimating the number of tests, assignments, and projects students will be graded on, you are merely setting the stage so students will have a general idea of how their performance will be evaluated. You do not have to preplan the specific assignments or write all your tests for the term. Adjustments in the actual numbers of assignments and tests can be made as you work to meet the needs of your students.

Assign point values to the tests, assignments, and class projects. The actual point value of different types of work will vary according to the organization of your course and how heavily you wish to weigh different types of work. Once you have assigned point values to student work, add all the points together. This gives you an approximate number of "work points" that students may earn during the term.

Planning for a history class might look something like the following example:

```
7 units covered in the nine-week term
7 tests . . . . . . . . . . . . . . . . . . 100 points each . . . 700 points
7 quizzes . . . . . . . . . . . . . . .  20 points each . . . 140 points
18 homework assignments . .  10 points each . . . 180 points
1 term paper . . . . . . . . . . . . . 200 points . . . . . . . 200 points
```
TOTAL WORK POINTS   1220 points

Preplanning for a beginning woodshop class might look something like the next example:

```
5 tests on power tools . . . . . .  40 points each . . . 200 points
5 performance checkouts . . .  20 points each . . . 100 points
2 wood identification tests . .  40 points each . . .  80 points
Book rack project . . . . . . . . 200 points . . . . . . . 200 points
Candle holder project . . . . . 200 points . . . . . . . 200 points
```
TOTAL WORK POINTS   740 points

Step 4. Determine the total number of points students may earn for participation and effort during the term and establish a weekly point total for class performance.

This percentage of the grade will be referred to as class performance points. In this step, you determine the actual number of performance points students may earn for their effort and participation each week. For a class of thirty-five students, you need approximately five minutes at the end of the week to assign these points.

To determine how many points students can earn in a week, you must do a little math. If you are not a math major, don't panic. Figure 2–4 is designed to help you. Following the directions on the table, begin with Step A, then follow the column labeled

Figure 2–4   Total Points and Weekly Participation Points

A. Put the total "work points" (from step 2) in this box . . . . [ ]

Put the "participation percentage" (from step 3) in this box . . . . [ ]

DESCRIPTION	DIRECTIONS	SAMPLE	SAMPLE	YOUR CLASS
B. Determine the percentage of the grade based on "work points": Take the "participation percentage" and subtract it from 100 to determine the "work percentage."	100% −Participation percentage Work Percentage	100% −10% .90	100% −40% .60	100% − %
C. Determine the total number of points for the term: Divide the "work points" by the "work percentage."	Work Points ÷ Work Percentage Total Points for Term (approx.)	1220 ÷.90 1355.5	740 ÷.60 1233.3	÷ .
D. Determine the approximate number of points for participation: Subtract the "work points" (rounded off) from the "total points for term."	Total Points for Term − Work Points Total Participation Points (approx.)	1355 −1220 135	1233 −740 493	−
E. Determine the number of points students could earn each week for participation: Divide the total "participation points" by the number of weeks in the term.	Total Participation Points ÷ Number of Weeks in Term Weekly Participation Points	135 ÷ 9 15	493 ÷ 9 54.7	÷
F. Round off the weekly participation points to the nearest whole number. Note: if the "weekly participation points" came out a whole number do not do steps 7 and 8. If rounding was necessary, the total points must be adjusted.			55	
G. Adjust the "total participation points": Multiply the "weekly points" times the number of weeks in the term.	Adjusted Weekly Participation Points × Number of Weeks in Term Total Participation Points	×	55 × 9 495	×
H. Adjust "total points for term": Add the "total participation points" to the "work points."	Total Participation Points + Work Points Total Points for Term	+	495 +740 1235	+

(From step H) Total points for term _____
(From step A) Work points _____
(From step F) Weekly participation points _____

"Directions." Even if you do not understand the procedures, you will arrive at the right numbers. The table will give you the following information.

Step F. Number of weekly performance points possible

Step G. Total number of performance points for the term

Step H. Total number of work and performance points for the term

You may feel that the procedure is more complicated than it needs to be. However, each step is necessary to award points in whole numbers. Without the additional steps you could end up having to assign students 54.7 weekly participation points, or you could end up with performance points and work points that do not equal the total points for the term.

Your total number of work points remain the same through the computations. If you end up adjusting the number of assignments or tests during the term, your total possible points may be slightly different than your initial planning detailed, but your participation percentage will still be close enough to work effectively.

Note on low-performing students: If you are working with low-performing students in a resource room or remedial setting of any type, you may want to consider setting up daily student performance points for participation and effort as opposed to weekly performance points. This increased immediacy of feedback will frequently help motivate students who have given up. The major disadvantage of daily grades is the amount of time required to manage the system. Daily grades should be used only with class sizes of fifteen students or less. With the smaller class size, assigning and recording daily performance grades takes two to three minutes at the end of each period.

Step 5. Establish the criteria and point values for earning class performance points.

In this step, you determine how specific behaviors will affect students' weekly performance points. Students must see a direct relationship between the behaviors you record on the Weekly Record Sheet and the number of points they are awarded at the end of each week.

Average student performance should automatically earn approximately 80 percent of the possible weekly performance points. If it is possible to earn a total of 40 points each week, students would earn 32 points for average performance. Some teachers make a big mistake by awarding the total points possible to any students who did not get in trouble during the week. Students must see that they can earn the full points only by being highly motivated throughout the week. Once you have determined the number of points students will earn for average classroom performance, list the types of behaviors that average students typically demonstrate in your classroom. You can use this information to inform students how to earn the "average" number of points.

Other factors automatically lower or raise a student's weekly performance points. Factors that automatically raise a student's grade should be those behaviors that you feel demonstrate excellence in participation and effort. These factors vary among teachers and also vary depending upon the type of class you have. If you have difficulty identifying behaviors that demonstrate above average student participation and effort, compare the behavior of *A* students with *C* students. Try to identify classroom behaviors that typically differentiate these students. This part of a student's grade is subjective. Your job is to teach students the kinds of behaviors you subjectively feel are a demonstration of excellence.

Factors that automatically lower a student's grade should be behaviors that would not be acceptable in a work situation. These include such things as tardiness, disruptiveness, and late work. Several of these behaviors are listed below with guidelines for determining the number of points that should be deducted from an "average" participation grade. The suggested points would be for a class where 20 points per week could be earned for class performance.

Breakdown of Reduced Points	% of Weekly Total	Example
Any disruptive behavior	5%	1 point
Any reminders needed about class rules or staying on task	5%	1 point
Tardiness	10%	2 points
Late work	10%	2 points
Unexcused absence	20%	4 points
Excused absence (made up with extra credit assignment)	20%	4 points
Sent out of class	20%	4 points

Disruptive behavior: Students will lose points for any disruptive behaviors. Behaviors that result in a loss of class time should logically affect the student's classroom performance grades. This automatic consequence allows you to respond unemotionally and predictably, and students learn that they are accountable for their behavior at all times.

Reminders about following class rules or staying on task: Occasionally, students need to be reminded of rules or they need to be reminded to stay on task. A loss of points in these areas tells students that they must remember to be self-disciplined.

Tardiness: A loss of points for tardiness demonstrates to students that they can earn points for their performance once they are in class, but that being late for class affects their overall evaluation. Students who have not learned to arrive on time will have difficulty maintaining a job.

Late work: A loss of points for late work is a clear demonstration to students that they are accountable for turning in work at a specified time. Students should automatically lose the designated points for the day, plus have only a percentage of the points possible on the assignment. For example, the student might lose two participation points for failing to have the assignment ready on the day it was due as well as lose 10 percent of the assignment's value.

Unexcused absences: If students have an unexcused absence, they obviously have not taken advantage of the opportunity to earn points. Therefore, students earn no participation points and are given no opportunity to make up the points.

Excused absences: If students have an excused absence, they will be allowed to earn the credit they have missed. Note that they will not automatically earn performance points on the days they are gone. Instead, they will have an opportunity to do extra credit to make up the lost class time. This procedure is not designed to penalize students who are ill. It is designed to demonstrate that class time is valuable. When class time is missed, less learning takes place. Thus, a small extra-credit assignment must be completed to compensate for the lost time. Students will learn that they are accountable for making up class time and that absences are only worthwhile when unavoidable.

This procedure should also apply to students who miss class due to involvement in sports, student government, and other extracurricular activities. Students should understand that participation in these activities is legitimate, but that they are still accountable for class time.

If at any point you have a student who has a serious illness, exceptions should be made. If a student is out of class over an extended period of time, award performance points as regular work is made up.

Some administrators object to this procedure of requiring make-up work to be able to earn the participation points. Be sure to clear this procedure with your district administration before implementing this aspect of the grading system. If you are not allowed to require make-up assignments for missed class time, you will simply have to give the full points to any students with excused absences.

Sent out of class: If a student is sent out of class, she has lost the opportunity to earn performance points for the day and has been penalized for the severity of the disruption.

Figure 2–5 is an example of how an eighth-grade history teacher might award points. Figure 2–6 is a blank copy of this form for your convenience. Follow the form or implement the following suggestions:

a. Note the participation and effort percentage.

b. Note the total weekly performance points.

c. Identify the types of behaviors that demonstrate average student performance and determine the number of points students will earn for average performance (80 percent of total points).

d. Identify the types of behaviors that demonstrate excellent participation and effort and determine the number of additional points earned.

e. Identify any behaviors that will result in failure to earn points and determine the number of points that will not be earned.

f. Identify factors that will result in bonus points and identify the number of bonus points earned.

Step 6. Assign weekly performance points.

At the end of the week, your Weekly Record Sheet will have all the information you need to determine the student's performance points. Simply follow these steps.

a. Begin with the number of points students can earn for average performance.

b. Add the appropriate number of points for each notation of excellence.

c. Subtract the appropriate number of points for each notation of inappropriate behavior.

d. Record the total number of points earned on the weekly record sheet.

Figure 2–7 shows the Weekly Record Sheet that was filled out based on the criteria identified in this list. In looking at the filled out form, it may appear to require a lot of work to use the form and determine the point totals. The first week of using the form will be like learning to do any new task. Initially it may be difficult but with use it will become more automatic and easier. With practice, all the coding of behavior becomes a habit that requires no additional time or effort in your teaching day, and awarding the points at the end of the week will take no more than five minutes.

Figure 2-5   Identifying Point Values and Criteria for Specific Performance Points (Sample)

IDENTIFYING POINT VALVES AND CRITERIA
FOR SPECIFIC PERFORMANCE POINTS

SUBJECT _U.S. History_

GRADE __8__

a. PARTICIPATION AND EFFORT PERCENTAGE _10%_

b. TOTAL WEEKLY PERFORMANCE POINTS   _20%_

c. Behavior that demonstrates average student performance
Follows rules
Follows directions
On task most of the time
Prepared for class

Average student performance = 80% of total possible points
= _16_ points

d. Behavior that demonstrates excellent student performance and cooperation
100% on task
Contributes to discussion
Asks relevant questions
Positively assists other students if asked

Each notation of cooperation and excellence for a given day =
10% of the total possible points
= _+2_ points

e. FAILURE TO EARN POINTS
(subtracted from an overall excellence or average in student performance for the week)

Any disruptive behavior	(−5% of weekly total)	− _1_
Any reminders needed for following class rules, or for staying on-task .	(−5% of weekly total)	− _1_
Tardiness	(−10% of weekly total)	− _2_
Late work	(−5% of weekly total)	− _1_
Unexcused absence	(−20% of weekly total)	− _4_
Excused absence.	(−20% of weekly total)	− _4_
(Made up by completing extra credit assignment)		
Sent out of class	(−20% of weekly total)	− _4_
_____ .	(− % of weekly total)	−___
_____ .	(− % of weekly total)	−___
_____ .	(− % of weekly total)	−___

f. BONUS POINTS
Peer tutors   _+2_ points
Significant improvement in behavior   _+2_ points
or attitude

28

Figure 2–6   Identifying Point Values and Criteria for Specific Performance Points

IDENTIFYING POINT VALVES AND CRITERIA
FOR SPECIFIC PERFORMANCE POINTS

SUBJECT _____

GRADE _____

a. PARTICIPATION AND EFFORT PERCENTAGE _____

b. TOTAL WEEKLY PERFORMANCE POINTS _____

c. Behavior that demonstrates average student performance

_____
_____
_____
_____
_____

Average student performance = 80% of total possible points
= _____points

d. Behavior that demonstrates excellent student performance and cooperation

_____
_____
_____
_____
_____

Each notation of cooperation and excellence for a given day =
10% of the total possible points
= _____points

e. FAILURE TO EARN POINTS
(subtracted from an overall excellence or average in student performance for the week)

Any disruptive behavior	(−5% of weekly total)	−____
Any reminders needed for following class rules, or for staying on-task .	(−5% of weekly total)	−____
Tardiness	(−10% of weekly total)	−____
Late work	(−5% of weekly total)	−____
Unexcused absence	(−20% of weekly total)	−____
Excused absence	(−20% of weekly total)	−____
(Made up by completing extra credit assignment)		
Sent out of class	(−20% of weekly total)	−____
_____ .	(− % of weekly total)	−____
_____ .	(− % of weekly total)	−____
_____ .	(− % of weekly total)	−____

f. BONUS POINTS

_____   _____ points
_____   _____ points

Figure 2–7   A Completely Filled-In Weekly Record Sheet

WEEKLY RECORD SHEET

Date _Sept. 14-18_   Reminders _____

Class period _4_   _____

STUDENT	MON.	TUES.	WED.	THUR.	FRI.	TOTAL
Agner, Donna		✓ E			✓	18
Amato, Lee		✓			✓	16
Anderson, Dan	O	✓		T-6	✓	13
Baumbaugh, Gary		—	O		✓ E	16
Buckee, Cheryl		✓ O			✓	15
Carpenter, Dustin	O O O	✓			✓	13
Crossett, Gelia		✓			✓ E	18
Deane, Russ		A (B+4)	A (B+4)		✓	16
Dorns, Jan	E	✓		O	✓	17
Edwards, Lanny		✓ O			✓	15
Felch, Yvvette		✓			✓	16
Franklin, Lavar		✓			✓ E	18
Godon, Randi	A (B+4)	✓ O	E		✓	17
Green, Christopher		✓			✓	16
Hammon, Matthew	E	✓			✓	18
Johnson, Charlene		✓			✓	16
Jones, Jesse		✓ C		O	✓	17
Kemp, Lonnie		✓	O		✓ O	14
Kuntzmann, Dana	UA	UA			✓	8
MacKight, Todd		✓			✓	16
Mezick, Chanya		✓ O			— O	13
Nelson, Wendy	C	✓			✓	18
Owen, Travis		✓			✓	16
Potesta, Sam		✓	E		✓	18
Quince, Bonnie		✓			✓	16
Robinson, Eddie	D	✓		E	✓	17
Schmidling, Ruth		—	A		✓	11
Semolke, Gail		✓			A	12
Sumida, Marilyn	O	✓			✓	15
Taylor, Danny		✓	E		✓	18
Timmons, Jay	E	✓		C	✓	20
Van de Veer, Steve		✓ O O			✓	14
West, Shaun		✓			✓	16

CODE: EXCELLENT WORK = E +2   OFF TASK = 0 −1   ABSENT = A
COOPERATIVE = C +2   DISRUPTIVE = D −1   UNEXCUSED
BONUS POINTS = B   LATE WORK = L −1   ABSENCE =
        UA −4
        TARDY = T −2

Step 7. Design a procedure for giving students their weekly classroom performance grade.

Before students leave on Friday, they should be given their weekly performance points. If students do not receive feedback about their classroom performance until Monday, the time delay may weaken the procedure. Students need frequent and consistent feedback.

Towards the end of the period each Friday, plan to spend five minutes figuring out student performance points. During this time, students should be engaged in an independent task. Once you have determined each student's weekly performance points, there are several different ways to give students their points. The major consideration is that students have an opportunity to see how their grade was determined.

a. Post the Weekly Record Sheet so that students can see their performance marks and the point totals for the week. The major advantage of this procedure is that weekly performance points do not have to be transferred to another sheet, and students can see exactly how their performance points were determined. The major disadvantage is that everyone's performance points are visible to everyone in the class. This lack of privacy can result in teasing, or may result in some students bragging about poor performance grades.

b. Provide students with identification numbers. Post the Weekly Record Sheet, but cover students' names with another sheet listing the corresponding identification numbers. This procedure ensures privacy and also does not require any transferring of points or performance marks. The major disadvantage is that it will take some time to organize the system so that students know their numbers. However, once the system is set up, a single cover sheet can be used week after week with all your classes. An example of a posted Weekly Record Sheet is shown in Figure 2–8.

c. Students can be given individual forms showing the breakdown of their total weekly performance points. This option provides students with very direct and private information. Students who have difficulty in school will benefit from this feedback. However, this procedure is obviously very time consuming for the teacher. This option will be realistic only if you have very small classes. Figure 2–9 shows a sample form.

Step 8. Design a form for students to record their own grades.

Some students need to be taught how to keep track of their grades. This can be accomplished easily by providing students with a grade sheet. In Step 3, you identified the approximate number of tests, assignments, and class projects students would complete during the term and the number of work points each was worth. List this information on a Student Grading Sheet with spaces for students to record work points, weekly performance points, and point totals. A sample is shown in Figure 2–10.

The maturity and level of sophistication of students will serve as a guide for determining how much prompting you must give students to record their grades. A typical seventh-grade class will have many students who must be taught how to track their grades. Each time students receive a grade, require students to record their grades. It may also be necessary to inform students that you will conduct periodic spot checks to make sure they have all kept their grading sheets up to date. Very immature students may need to be additionally reinforced for recording their grades by awarding bonus points.

If your students are fairly sophisticated, the grading sheet will still be a useful tool. Simply hand out the sheet at the beginning of the term and let students know that you

Figure 2–8   A Posted Weekly Record Sheet

WEEKLY RECORD SHEET

Date _____   Reminders _____

Class period _____

STUDENT #	MON.	TUES.	WED.	THUR.	FRI.	TOTAL
1		✓ E			✓	19
2		✓			✓	16
3	0	✓		T–6	✓	13
4		—	0		✓ E	15
5		✓ 0			✓	15
6	0 0 0	✓			✓	13
7		✓			✓ E	19
8		A ⟨B+4⟩	A ⟨B+4⟩		✓	16
9	E	✓		0	✓	17
10		✓ 0			✓	15
11		✓			✓	16
12		✓			✓ E	19
13	A ⟨B+4⟩	✓ 0	E		✓	17
14		✓			✓	16
15	E	✓			✓	19
16		✓			✓	16
17		✓ C		0	✓	17
18		✓	0		✓ 0	14
19	UA	UA			✓	11
20		✓			✓	16
21		✓ 0			— 0	14
22	C	✓			✓	18
23		✓			✓	16
24		✓	E		✓	19
25		✓			✓	16
26	0	✓		E	✓	16
27		—	A		✓	12
28		✓			A	14

will occasionally check to see that they are recording their grades. For all students, the grading sheet will be a useful tool for illustrating your grading system at the beginning of the term. Though adjustments may be made as you work through the term, students will be given a clear idea of what type of work they are going to be doing and the relative point values for different types of tasks.

Step 9. Teach students how your grading system works.

Plan to spend part of the first class period teaching students how your grading system works. Use the Student Grading Sheet as a basis for discussion. Plan to present and explain the following topics.

Figure 2-9   Weekly Participation Grade Sheet

WEEKLY PARTICIPATION GRADE

STUDENT _____   DATE _____

MONDAY   TUESDAY   WEDNESDAY   THURSDAY   FRIDAY   TOTAL POINTS

E = EXCELLENCE (2 POINTS)   D = DISRUPTIVE (−1 POINT)
C = COOPERATIVE (2 POINTS)   O = OFF TASK (−1 POINT)
I = IMPROVEMENT (1 POINT)   L = LATE WORK (−1 POINT)

A = ABSENT (−4 POINTS)
M = MAKE UP CREDIT (5 POINTS)
T = TARDY (−2 POINTS)

- Relative point values of assignments, tests, papers, and other student work
- Percentage of the grade based on participation and effort in class
- Procedures for monitoring and recording daily performance to determine the weekly performance grade
- Procedures for tardiness, excused absences, and unexcused absences
- Use of Student Grading Sheets for students to record their own grades
- Procedures for late work
- Extra credit procedures and procedures for improving grades on tests or papers

As the term progresses, encourage students to keep track of their grades. When you notice students falling behind, try to meet with them early in the term. Go over the grading sheet and emphasize things that students can do to improve their grades.

Step 10. At the end of the week, log the class performance scores into your grade book and file the Weekly Record Sheet.

When you have assigned point totals for class participation and informed students of their grades, transfer the information from the Weekly Record Sheet into your grade book. You may want to lay out the entries in the grade book so that all the class performance scores are together. This can allow for an easy visual reference regarding any student's behavioral performance throughout a term. This summary of class performance can be very useful when students or parents have questions about a grade.

When you have logged the performance score into your grade book, file the Weekly Record Sheet. Keeping these records on file can be useful for several reasons, the most important being to provide answers to any questions about a student's grade. The record sheets provide detailed information about a student's behavior and motivation. This information is useful in conferences with students, with parents, and with administrators. It can also be useful for determining a "special education" placement or for any formal hearings or meetings about a particular student.

Figure 2–10   Student Grading Sheet

CLASS PERIOD _____

STUDENT _____

TESTS:
        1 Score _____/100 points
        2 Score _____/100 points
        3 Score _____/100 points
        4 Score _____/100 points
        5 Score _____/100 points   Total _____/ 500 points

QUIZZES:
        1 Score _____/ 20 points
        2 Score _____/ 20 points
        3 Score _____/ 20 points
        4 Score _____/ 20 points
        5 Score _____/ 20 points   Total _____/ 100 points

TERM PAPER:
        Score_____/200 points   Total _____/ 200 points

HOMEWORK:
        1 Score _____/ 10 points
        2 Score _____/ 10 points
        3 Score _____/ 10 points
        4 Score _____/ 10 points
        5 Score _____/ 10 points
        6 Score _____/ 10 points
        7 Score _____/ 10 points
        8 Score _____/ 10 points
        9 Score _____/ 10 points
      10 Score _____/ 10 points   Total _____/ 100 points

WEEKLY PARTICIPATION:
        Week 1   _____/ 20 points
        Week 2   _____/ 20 points
        Week 3   _____/ 20 points
        Week 4   _____/ 20 points
        Week 5   _____/ 20 points
        Week 6   _____/ 20 points
        Week 7   _____/ 20 points
        Week 8   _____/ 20 points
        Week 9   _____/ 20 points   Total _____/ 180 points

FINAL SCORE _____/ 1080 POINTS

Keeping the Weekly Record Sheets on file can also provide useful information to you about revising your teaching methods with a particular group. For example, you may be concerned about off-task behavior in your seventh-period class. Looking at the record forms for the last four weeks will give detailed information about the extent of the problem. If there are many *O*s marked on the sheet, it is a good indication that your concerns are warranted. This would indicate that you should do something to make the students more accountable for staying on task. You could use this book, another reference, or talk to other teachers about ways to teach students to be more on task. The record sheets will help you identify where class behavior needs to improve.

Step 11. Design all class activities, assignments, tests, and papers around unit objectives.

Your final job will be to design your course or units of study around specific instructional objectives. At the beginning of each unit, identify your objectives and communicate them to your students. Students should receive a passing grade if they master these objectives. If you have difficulty identifying objectives, begin planning your instructional unit by designing the final test. For the most part, your unit of instruction should be based on the information and concepts on which you will test students.

CONCLUSION

An effective grading system is more than an evaluation tool; it is also an instructional tool and a motivational tool. If designed and implemented well, a grading system can encourage students to try their best each day. An increase in daily motivation increases the chance that students will keep up with the work and learn how to demonstrate mastery of course objectives. When a student discovers she can be successful in your class, she will remember her success. This will increase the likelihood that she will try to succeed in subsequent classes.

Section II
SELF-DISCIPLINE AND MOTIVATION

One phrase has become very popular with educators. "We have to get students to be more responsible for their own behavior." This statement represents an important educational goal, but you must realize that a teacher cannot "make" a student become more responsible. Students who have not yet learned to be personally responsible and independent must be taught these traits.

This section is designed to help you implement strategies that will increase student responsibility and self-discipline. Chapter 3 will help you monitor and evaluate the types of interactions you are having with students. Modifying the types of interactions can result in a significant increase in student motivation. Chapter 4 covers goal-setting procedures as a strategy for getting students to be more aware and concerned about their own behavior. If students become aware of behavioral goals, they will sometimes try to reach that goal without any structured reinforcement system being set up. Chapter 5 examines classroom reinforcement systems that can be helpful with immature groups of students. Chapter 6 focuses on the "high-risk" student. Procedures are introduced that may help you assist specific individuals who are headed for trouble.

While consequences for misbehavior are an important part of any classroom discipline plan (see Section III), the major emphasis must be on teaching students to be responsible for their own behavior. The chapters in this section are designed to help you accomplish that goal.

Chapter 3
TEACHER-STUDENT INTERACTIONS

This chapter will explore how to help students grow, mature, and learn to be more responsible for their own behavior. The current stress on discipline in the schools tends to imply that teachers need only to design effective consequences for misbehavior and the natural result will be self-disciplined students. While consequences for misbehavior are a necessary part of an effective discipline plan, punishment will result only in a short-term reduction of unacceptable behavior. Punishment does not teach self-discipline as the teacher, not the student, controls behavior. This chapter will focus on how to increase student motivation by working on positive interactions with students on a day-to-day basis. Powerful teachers carefully orchestrate interactions in their classrooms and set a tone that encourages student responsibility.

At the secondary level, it is easy to assume that teachers should no longer have to make a special effort to encourage and motivate students. This is partially true. The most confident students enter the secondary school with years of continual reinforcement behind them. These students enjoy learning for the sake of learning. They take pride in their accomplishments and complete their assignments with a sense of self-satisfaction. To heighten this sense of self-motivation, successful students are continually recognized for their efforts by teachers and peers. The following is an example of such a student.

Kristin is a high school senior who has just been nominated by her peers for the school's "Girl of the Year" award—a fine example of student maturity and self-discipline. Take a look at Kristin growing up.

Like all young children, Kristin's favorite things were doing what adults were doing. When the TV was on, Kristin was encouraged to identify objects and imitate new sounds. When Kristin played quietly, she was given praise for her independence. When she was out of sorts, she was left on her own.

When Kristin was two, her parents separated and her mother returned to a full-time job. Kristin was cared for by a woman with a baby of her own. Kristin was a helpful addition to this daytime home. She helped fold diapers and entertain the baby. When Kristin's mother picked her up, Kristin completed her day by helping her mother shop and clean. While they were completing their daily routine, Kristin and her mother had a lot of time to talk because Kristin worked right alongside her mother.

By the time Kristin began kindergarten, she knew most of the kindergarten curriculum and had been identifying colors and playing with pens and pencils from the age of 18 months. Kristin's teacher was always delighted with Kristin's papers and art work. As Kristin continued through grade school, assignments were rarely difficult, so Kristin had the time and energy to do a really nice job.

Since the eighth grade, Kristin had held an elective office every year. Though Kristin is not one of the most visibly popular students, she is well respected and liked by her peers. Kristin has a scrapbook filled with *A* papers, certificates of merit, and momentos from state conferences. Kristin remains a relatively quiet student. Yet, when she does take part in a class discussion she is given the teacher's undivided attention and respect. Kristin, not unlike most adolescents, will remember high school as a somewhat painful time. She will be happy to graduate from high school. But Kristin is one of the lucky ones. With a 3.8 GPA, Kristin will leave high school with a well-developed sense of self-confidence and motivation.

Positive attention naturally falls to those who do well. On the other hand, negative attention naturally falls to those who have problems. The primary difference between motivated and turned-off students is not the need for attention, but in the way they have learned to get attention. Compare Kristin's experience with Justin's, in the following example.

> Justin is a high school sophomore. He is the son of loving, concerned, and hard-working parents. Justin has a younger sister who does very well in school. Justin, on the other hand, does poorly and always seems to be in trouble.
>
> Justin's parents report that he's always been difficult, from the moment he was born. Justin was one of those colicky babies who never seemed to outgrow his fussiness. By the time Justin was one, he threw tantrums throughout the day.
>
> In first grade, Justin's mother recalls being called to school very early in the year because Justin refused to follow the classroom rules. When the teacher asked the students to line up, Justin, a defiant child, always remained at his desk, and when Justin was supposed to be working on a coloring sheet, he was playing with blocks.

In looking at Justin's early history, you see a pattern developing. During the early months, Justin cried continuously because he was colicky. His exhausted parents learned to grab a much needed moment of rest when the baby was quiet. As Justin outgrew his colic, his parents continued to hold and rock, walk and comfort him when he cried and, tragically, to ignore him when he was quiet. As Justin grew older, he learned that playing independently meant that attention went elsewhere; however, if he hit his sister, screamed, or threw something, he was sure to get someone's attention. In the first grade, Justin learned that doing what the teacher told him to do meant that he would be ignored, but if he did something else he always got attention. The worse his behavior, the more intense the attention.

As a secondary student, Justin misbehaves habitually. He rarely has positive interactions with adults, and he almost seems to get high on intense emotional confrontations. Justin knows himself as a "bad kid." When he is asked why he behaves the way he does, Justin just shrugs his shoulders, "I don't know. I guess I was born that way." Though Justin spends most days not caring or being obnoxious, he really doesn't want to be "bad." Like most kids in trouble, Justin even has days when he vows that he is going to try harder. Look what happens to Justin on one of those rare days.

> During first period, Justin is ready to pay attention and work hard. After the teacher takes roll call, he lets the students have a fifteen-minute free period. Not having many friends, Justin just sits for a while and eventually ends up rolling little spit balls and throwing them into the lights, to which the teacher says, "Justin, can't you even behave yourself during free time? I can't have that kind of behavior in this class. I'll be calling your parents this evening."
>
> In second period, Justin finds himself wondering what's going to happen when his parents hear from his first-period teacher. Justin sits brooding quietly at the back of the room. He leaves class without hearing that he has a homework assignment the next day.
>
> In third period, Justin works very hard at being a good kid again. The period goes by and the only recognition Justin gets is his name being called during roll call.
>
> In fourth period, Justin is still trying to do better. In spite of being insecure and afraid of looking stupid, Justin raises his hand to volunteer an answer. The only comment the teacher makes is, "No, Justin, that's wrong. Sally, can you tell us the right answer?"

Although Justin is probably not consciously seeking attention, he is an insecure individual in need of feedback and interactions with the adults around him. However, he is shown daily that the only way to get that attention is through misbehavior. His academic efforts are never good enough to earn the kinds of grades needed for extra attention. The only thing that Justin excels in is living up to his past reputation. To compound Justin's problems, his academic skills are very poor. The difference between Justin and Kristin is heightened by the simple fact that Kristin reads well and Justin reads poorly.

> In fifth-period English class, students are given a fifteen-minute period of sustained silent reading each day. Two book reports are expected by the end of the term, but no other requirements are given. Kristin is deeply involved in a P. D. James mystery. It is light reading but Kristin finds it difficult to put the book down. Being a very able reader, Kristin takes full advantage of the fifteen-minute reading period. She has always had trouble finding enough hours in the day to complete an enjoyable book. At night, Kristin's mother must frequently remind her that she had better quit reading and go to bed.
>
> Justin also has a fifteen-minute reading period each day; however, it is the slowest fifteen minutes of his day. Sometimes he takes a nap. Occasionally, he flips through a magazine or book. Most of the time he just sits, and sometimes he gets into trouble. Justin has never finished reading a book in his life. Anything of interest is too difficult for him to read. By the time he makes a mistake on every fifth or sixth word, nothing makes sense. Reading is boring.

Able students are often intrinsically rewarded by academic tasks. They are motivated by a combination of success, enjoyment of academic tasks, and self-satisfaction. Unfortunately, only a small percentage of each class will be made up of students who excel. Average and low-performing students desperately need to hear that their efforts are also recognized and count for something. Their best efforts may bring only mediocrity and perhaps continued failure. These students must receive respect and attention for making improvements. Teachers can teach students that it is worthwhile to do one's best. While Chapter 1 helped you set up an effective learning atmosphere, the following strategies will help you maintain a high level of student motivation and self-discipline.

IMPROVING STUDENT-TEACHER INTERACTIONS

Step 1. Establish clear behavioral expectations for students.

Student-teacher interactions can be improved only when you have established clear expectations for student behavior. Students cannot be self-disciplined if they do not know what is acceptable and what is not acceptable. Clear expectations will allow you to respond consistently to behavior, and it will give students a chance to demonstrate their willingness to cooperate. If you are not sure whether you have established clear borderlines between appropriate and inappropriate behavior, read or reread Chapter 1.

Step 2. Design consequences for misbehavior.

This step is discussed in detail in Chapter 8, *Classroom Consequences*. It is, however, an important step in improving student-teacher interactions. Students must know that you will respond consistently and unemotionally to misbehavior.

While demonstrating that you do not tolerate misbehavior, your effective consequences will also remove whatever is reinforcing the misbehavior. If a disruptive student is reinforced by the one-to-one attention she receives, an appropriate consequence to misbehavior must include giving the student as little attention as possible. If the student is reinforced for misbehavior by experiencing a sense of power by getting the teacher angry, it will be important to implement consequences to misbehavior unemotionally. If the student is reinforced by feeling important enough to be talked to, the consequence to misbehavior must not include a lecture.

Use Chapters 7 and 8 to determine how you will handle misbehavior. Keep in mind that any behavior that occurs repeatedly is being reinforced.

Step 3. Reinforce appropriate student behavior and academic efforts by initiating positive student-teacher interactions.

To effectively motivate an entire classroom of students, effort must be acknowledged more frequently than inappropriate behavior. Where student effort is not acknowledged, classrooms are often chaotic or there is an atmosphere of oppression where nagging and punishment dominate. If you accept each student as he is and acknowledge effort, even the most unmotivated students will learn that there are benefits for behaving maturely. Effective teachers initiate numerous positive interactions prior to the time students have an opportunity to initiate negative interactions.

What does it mean to "acknowledge" or "reinforce" appropriate student behavior and effort at the secondary level? It is easy to conjure up images of teachers shoving candy down the throats of students who are yelling, "What do I get if . . . ?" Or, it is easy to imagine teachers gushing over students with praise or trying to buy them off with bribes. While external tangible reinforcers and praise may have their places, these are really very primitive ways of trying to motivate students. Providing students with positive student-teacher interactions means that you will take the time to initiate contact with any student who puts forth effort. When an average-performing student is working hard on an assignment, you may stop by his desk and briefly discuss his assignment with him. When a lower-performing student is listening to a class discussion, you may ask a very easy and direct question of her. If a student is frequently disruptive, you may have him staple papers for you the moment you see him take his seat appropriately. These are all examples of natural positive interactions. As your classroom becomes dominated by positive interactions, students will learn to take a chance in your classroom and put forth a little effort.

Positive feedback is also a powerful tool in providing students with positive student-teacher interactions. However, at the secondary level it is easy to embarrass students by using praise inappropriately. The following guidelines will help you to provide students with constructive praise.

GUIDELINES FOR PROVIDING EFFECTIVE POSITIVE FEEDBACK

Step 1. Positive feedback must be highly contingent on student behavior.

Contingent positive feedback tells students that you are aware of their performance, individually and in a group. Contingency implies that you will give feedback to the best performance of every individual. High performers will receive recognition for assimilating information and for analyzing new situations and demonstrating that they are exerting some effort. Average performers will receive attention for taking part in class discussions and asking pertinent questions. Low performers may need attention for simply staying on task, for listening attentively, and for completing assignments. A student who typically misbehaves will need recognition for cooperating and having the maturity to try changing his behavior. When positive feedback is contingent, you will not make students feel babyish by praising them for behaviors or skills they take for granted. Contingent feedback results in students knowing that you accept each student as she comes to you and acknowledge each student's steps towards maturity and growth.

Step 2. Positive feedback should be given in a matter-of-fact manner.

While flowery, emotional praise may embarrass secondary students, calm, quiet, matter-of-fact statements will give students the recognition they need. Positive feedback should not imply that you are treating students any differently from the way you would treat an adult. A journalist would be complimented if his boss said, "Nice job on the restaurant article." An accountant would not be insulted if a client said, "Thanks for getting my tax returns done so quickly." Students will also appreciate statements that communicate you have recognized their efforts.

Step 3. Use descriptive rather than evaluative statements.

Descriptive statements briefly tell students what was worthy of comment. "Ralph, you should be pleased with your participation in our class discussion. Your comments were very pertinent to the topic." These kinds of statements provide students with recognition for a job well done, and they also help teach students behaviors that are compatible with learning.

Nondescriptive or evaluative feedback simply tells students that they did a nice job, but the statement fails to communicate exactly what was worthy of comment. "Keep up the good work, Ralph." Evaluative statements may be effective when students know exactly what you are referring to but may result in students' feeling that praise comments are also spurious. The following is an example of nondescriptive praise.

> Carlos is an immature student in Mrs. Elders' freshman math class. He frequently doesn't turn in papers, is often late to class, and is rarely on task. On Monday, Carlos manages to sneak into class late and fails to turn in an assignment. He doesn't pay attention as problems are being discussed, but in a burst of energy Carlos does extremely well on a timed fact test. As Carlos leaves the room, Mrs. Elders makes it a point to say, "You worked hard today, Carlos!"

Though Carlos worked hard on his time test, he did not deserve praise for the entire class period. The nondescriptive praise is noncontingent. Carlos worked hard only on his time test, yet he was given recognition for the whole period. This tells Carlos that it is okay to goof around if you work hard part of the period. Evaluative statements are most effective when paired with descriptive feedback. "Carlos, nice job on your time test! Your accuracy is improving."

Step 4. Positive feedback to individual students should be relatively private.

Secondary students can be embarrassed by positive feedback because they do not want to be singled out as "teacher's pets." While some positive feedback can be given very naturally in front of the class, "Pat, that was an astute observation," other comments will lose their power simply by the fact that you need to give the student attention for behaviors that should have been learned in grade school.

Due to time limitations, you will have to utilize a variety of opportunities for giving students positive comments in private. Conferences can be held before class, after class, and during independent work times. You can also have relatively private discussions with individual students while passing by their desks. If a student is likely to be embarrassed by any kind of feedback in front of her peers, positive feedback can be given via a note. If you are working on improving a specific problem that you have discussed with the student, feedback can be given in the form of a nonverbal signal—a nod, a lift of your hand, a smile. When paired with periodic conferences, the nonverbal signal can be effective even though it is nondescriptive feedback.

Step 5. Provide feedback to groups of students whenever possible.

Acknowledging the efforts of an entire group of students helps establish a sense of cooperation and community within the classroom. Group recognition is also a comfortable way for secondary students to accept praise and take pride in their accomplishments.

Group praise should be used frequently, but it also must be used contingently. It is easy to fall into the pattern illustrated here.

> Mr. Saunders' English class has had a difficult time with the district spelling program. To encourage students to master word lists, Mr. Saunders has set up a home-study routine and established rehearsal patterns for breaking down difficult lists of words. Initially, a third of the class had gotten Ds and Fs on the tests. Half of the students had gotten Cs and a handful of students had gotten As or Bs. After two weeks of working on the new spelling system, most students have made remarkable improvements. Only two students continue to flunk the tests. Mr. Saunders is very pleased and tells his class, "You have really made remarkable improvements in spelling. I must commend the students in this class for their commitment to our new study routine. It is really paying off."

This group praise is noncontingent to the two students who continue to get Fs on their spelling test. Because they are also a part of the positive comment, praise becomes nonmeaningful to these students. In this instance, most but not all of Mr. Saunders' class deserved to have their efforts recognized. Mr. Saunders might have said, "I am pleased with the improvements that I am seeing on spelling tests. Those of you who have made a commitment to our new study routine are doing much better on your tests. It is really paying off."

Group praise must communicate that all students are expected to do well. If student behavior during independent work time has improved with the exception of one student, group praise will tell the class that you expect only "most" of the class to do well. However, when used contingently, group praise will help foster the positive learning atmosphere that encourages student motivation.

Avoid group praise that specifically excludes one or two individuals. It would be inappropriate to say, "All but one of our class members worked hard today." This does not serve as praise to the ones who worked. It only gives attention to the one person who did not. If you want to acknowledge the performance of the students who did work, target several of those students each day and provide individual feedback.

Step 6. Eliminate pauses after giving positive feedback.

It is natural to follow a positive comment with a pause. In interactions with other adults, this is the normal pattern. "Sandy, I really like your new haircut." This statement would be followed by a pause, as you wait for the person to respond. However, this same interaction pattern in a classroom can cause problems. If you tell a student that she has done a particularly nice job and then pause, the student will feel that she must respond. If the student says something acceptable, she may feel that everyone will think she is "brown nosing." Instead, many students will respond with embarrassment or with a wisecrack. If praise is following by a pause, your comment may actually be punishing to the student.

This problem can be eliminated by giving positive feedback and then immediately shifting the focus to another topic or student. "Henry, your essay was very creative. Class, your homework assignment for tonight will be . . . " By shifting the focus from the student who has been praised, you eliminate the pressure that positive feedback potentially puts on students.

Step 7. Be persistent.

Some students feel uncomfortable with positive feedback because they have had so little. You may wish to meet privately with these students and discuss ways that they can respond to positive comments. Overall, be persistent. Every student needs to learn that he has enough self-worth to accept recognition from someone else.

You may encounter a few students who misbehave immediately following a positive comment. These students view themselves as troublemakers. Though they take pride in efforts noticed by a teacher, they also tend to panic. "Now, I'm expected to be perfect." Fear often leads this student to misbehave, his way of of saying, "I am the same problem student that I have always been." Misbehavior creates a safe environment. These students need a lot of feedback for appropriate behavior. Minor misbehavior will not deter you from expecting and recognizing success. If you run into a student who also persistently holds onto failure, see Problem 21, "Being Embarrassed by Praise or Not Liking Praise," in Section IV.

GAINING SOPHISTICATION WITH EFFECTIVE STUDENT-TEACHER INTERACTIONS

Though peer approval and attention are vitally important in the secondary school, effective teachers recognize that teachers orchestrate the amount of attention that is given to appropriate and inappropriate behavior. The quality of student-teacher interactions determines the amount of self-control exhibited in the classroom. This explains why a student may be totally disruptive in one room and at least tolerable in another.

Because students and teachers are all individuals, every teacher will encounter a particular class period of the day, a particular group of students, or a particular student who does not measure up to expectations. Because a particular student or group is challenging your ability to set the tone, it is very easy to find that negative interactions begin to overpower the effect of your positive interactions. For this reason it is useful to periodically monitor and evaluate your interactions with students. The easiest and most reliable way to monitor interactions is with the use of a cassette tape recorder. Self-monitoring can provide many insights into the way you are interacting with your students.

Once every month, identify the class period where student behavior seems to be the least mature. Tape at least thirty minutes of the class period when behavior seems to be at its worst. Place the tape recorder close to where you spend the majority of your time. Once it is running, conduct your class as normally as possible. If you are unnerved by having a tape recorder going, run the tape recorder several times every week until it becomes more natural to you.

Place the tape recorder in an unobtrusive spot. If students are likely to see what you are doing, tell them that you are taping the class so that you can improve your teaching. You do not need to specify that you will be listening for positive and negative interactions.

Plan to listen to your tape during a free period or a time at home when you will not

Figure 3–1   Monitoring Interactions with Students

MONITORING INTERACTIONS WITH STUDENTS

1. Use a cassette tape recorder to tape the class period where the most behavior problems occur. Listen to the tape and evaluate your interactions by following the steps outlined below.

2. Count every evaluative interaction between you and your students. If you are interacting with a student because of something positive that student has done, make a mark in the Positive Feedback column. If you are interacting with a student because of something negative that student has done, make a mark in the Negative Feedback column.

Positive Feedback	Negative Feedback

Try to achieve a ratio of at least three times more positive feedback than negative feedback.

3. Adjust the count based on your estimate of the nonverbal feedback that would not be recorded on the tape.

4. Evaluate whether your positive feedback was highly contingent on student behavior.

5. Evaluate the sincerity of your positive feedback.

6. Did your positive feedback have variety? Did you describe the positive behavior that led you to give the student(s) feedback?

7. How was the positive feedback distributed among:
   __ High performers   __ Middle performers   __ Low performers
   __ Males   __ Females
   __ Mature students   __ Immature students
   __ Students in the front of the room   __ Students in the back

Establish a plan for changing student behavior by changing the type and quality of the feedback you give to students. Work on that plan for the next month and then tape the same class period again.

be interrupted. Use the monitoring form shown in Figure 3–1 to evaluate your interactions with students. Detailed steps for using the form follow it.

Step 1. Count every interaction you have with students.

Listen for any interaction you have with a student or students. If you are interacting with a student when she has engaged in appropriate classroom behavior, make a mark in the positive column. If you are interacting with a student because of negative behavior, make a mark in the negative column.

It is sometimes difficult to determine whether your interaction should be counted in the negative or positive column. The following examples are provided to help you analyze your interactions with students.

Comment	In Response to:	Positive/Negative
Sandra, quit goofing around.	Off-task behavior	Negative
Sandra, don't forget that time is running out.	Off-task behavior	Negative
Jessica, how is your assignment going?	On-task behavior	Positive
Jessica, how is your assignment going?	Off-task behavior	Negative

The critical difference between positive interactions and negative interactions is not whether your comment is friendly or punitive in tone. The difference between positive and negative interactions is whether your interaction is the result of appropriate or inappropriate student behavior.

Negative interactions must occur. Even academic corrections will be considered negative because they are in response to something you would like to see less of. "Jean, you need to work harder on subject-verb agreement." However, you will also be marking any encouraging comments about academic endeavors in the positive column. "Sonja, your introductory paragraph provided very clear information about the topic of the paper."

Do not feel that your goal is to reduce interactions in the negative column to zero. Interactions in the negative column are an integral and important part of the teaching process. If you have more negative feedback than positive, however, you are demonstrating to students that it is easier to get your attention through negative behavior than through positive behavior.

Your goal is to have at least three interactions marked in the positive column for every mark in the negative column. Thus, in a class of immature and unmotivated students where academic corrections and gentle verbal reprimands may be necessary, you should provide a lot of positive feedback to students when they are working hard. If you are working with a group of high-performing students, you will have fewer academic and behavioral corrections and therefore less of a need to have a high number of positive interactions.

Step 2: Evaluate whether your positive feedback is contingent on student behavior.

Positive feedback will be an effective motivator only if it is contingent. As you listen to the positive feedback, put yourself in the place of the students. "Is the feedback relevant?" "Does it relate directly to something you have done?" "Are you proud of the accomplishment the teacher commented on?"

Contingency must not be used as an excuse to provide positive feedback only to the "best" students in class. Contingency means that feedback is given to the best performance of "each" student. One student may be given feedback for advanced writing skills, and another student may be given feedback for getting his homework in on time. When comments are relatively private, students will rise to the occasion.

Step 3: Evaluate the sincerity of positive feedback.

You may occasionally feel that your comments sound contrived or phony. Certainly, the best positive feedback is feedback that is given naturally. However, if feedback is contingent, students will value your feedback regardless of how you sound. Keep it up!

Step 4: Determine whether there was variety in your positive feedback.

Did you describe the positive behavior that led you to comment on a student's behavior or work? One of the most common mistakes in providing positive feedback is to use a set phrase over and over again. If you notice the same phrase four or five times on one tape, it is being overused. If a phrase is overused students quit hearing it. This can be avoided by focusing on the use of descriptive comments. If you want to, you can leave out evaluative comments such as "terrific," "wonderful," and "fantastic" altogether. Secondary students are more likely to respond to comments like the following examples:

> Class, the questions you asked while the guest speaker was here were very sophisticated.
>
> 84 percent, that's a big improvement, Willie.
>
> A very creative idea—thanks for remembering to raise your hand.
>
> Your report was organized and followed a logical sequence.
>
> This was a very productive work period. I see several people were able to complete their assignment.

Step 4: Determine how your positive feedback was distributed.

What was the distribution among high-, middle-, and low-performing students? Low performers should have the most positive interactions, and the highest performers should receive the least amount. High performers will continually evaluate their own performance. Motivation will naturally come from succeeding and from the intrinsic reward of academic tasks. Low-performing students may need positive feedback and encouragement two or three times during a class period, and average performers must not be forgotten. It is easy to completely overlook the average student who never does outstanding work and never has significant academic or behavioral problems to worry about. Every student must be given recognition. If you are concerned about the distribution of your attention, use a class list and count your interactions with individual students.

You may also have to look at the distribution of your feedback based on the sex of the students. Though no teacher intends to, some teachers inadvertently notice all the positive things that female students do and all the negative things that male students do. Some teachers do exactly the reverse. Either pattern is a mistake. Every student should have access to positive interactions with teachers.

Examine the distribution between the front of the room and the back of the room. If the majority of negative interactions are going to the back of the room, it might be wise to make seating assignments. Disperse throughout the room those students who frequently choose to sit at the back of the room. Students who are the most immature should be assigned seats close to where you spend the majority of your time. Once seating arrangements have been made, work on distributing your positive attention to students in all parts of the room.

Finally, establish a plan for improving interactions based on your evaluations. Focus on one class period. If you try to change your interactions with every class throughout the day, you will find yourself exhausted. When you discover the power of positive interactions, it will be easy to generalize your skills to other classes. Powerful teachers rely on positive interactions rather than intimidation. Your efforts to increase positive interactions will result in a more restful and enjoyable day as problems diminish. Though you may initially feel as if improving positive interactions with students diminishes your teaching time, teaching time will actually become more efficient and productive. Positive interactions take only a few seconds now and again throughout your day, while negative interactions are often time consuming, exhausting, and disruptive to your entire day. It is much more productive to "catch" a student doing something right than it is to wait until he misbehaves to get your attention. Keep in mind that every human relationship requires attention. Students must continually put themselves on the line to be evaluated by you. They will meet their potential only when they know that you recognize their best efforts.

Chapter 4
GOAL SETTING

Solutions to student problems will vary because every student is an individual. Resolving problems is frequently a process of trial and error. When increasing student-teacher interactions and effective grading systems fail to reach a misbehaving student, goal setting is sometimes an effective tool. The teacher and student work together to identify goals, define behaviors that will interfere with reaching the goal, and set up student responsibilities that will help the student obtain his objective.

> Martin is a reasonably capable and likeable student. However, his grades are never what they could be because he frequently fails to turn in papers. Martin's biggest problem is poor use of time. He never bothers anyone; he just sits and does nothing much of the time. Martin is severely penalized in classes where grades take into account class participation. Grades, increasing positive interactions, and classroom consequences seem to have little effect, so many teachers find themselves resorting to nagging and lecturing Martin. He is always agreeable, but he never changes.

Martin has potential, but the system has failed to reach him. Martin needs to learn that he is capable of taking responsibility for himself. Goal setting will give Martin an opportunity to help himself learn how to be more successful.

> Candy is a fourteen-going-on-twenty-seven year old. Life has undoubtedly shown this girl scenes beyond the eyes of most adults. Physically mature and attractive, Candy gets around. There is obviously no supervision at home. Candy seems to be free to do whatever she wishes, whenever she pleases. As a ninth grader, Candy continues to do well academically. She typically pulls a 3.0 GPA. However, teachers wonder what will happen to Candy when her older friends are no longer in school. She is frequently seen around town with people who have already dropped out.

Candy is also a student who might benefit from goal setting. Her grades indicate that she is responsive to the system. Her willingness to work indicates that she cares about school. Her problem is simply a lack of direction and support for her efforts. Goal setting may be a tool for demonstrating that she can have high ideals. Goal setting can teach Candy that she does have control over her life.

Goal setting is frequently a useful tool because it sets formal expectations for the student. It provides a vehicle for discussing relevant issues, and it lets the student know that someone at school cares enough to help the student achieve her potential.

Step 1: Select a goal-setting form applicable to the student with whom you are working.

The forms in Figures 4–1 and 4–2 may be useful. The first form would be used for students who have no specific behavioral problem, but could benefit from establishing some direction. The second form would be more useful for specific behavioral problems. If neither form is applicable, feel free to design your own.

Step 2: Work through the form before meeting with the student.

This step is to help you get a handle on the problem prior to meeting with the student. You will eventually work through a blank form with the student and encourage her participation in the goal setting. However, working through the system yourself prior to meeting with the student will help you give the process direction.

Figure 4–1   Goal-Setting Form 1

GOAL-SETTING FORM 1

Student _____

Class _____

Goal _____

_____

_____

Student responsibilities for achieving the goal

_____

_____

_____

_____

Teacher support responsibilities

_____

_____

_____

_____

Evaluation procedure _____

_____

Date of goal evaluation _____

Student's signature _____

Teacher's signature _____

Figure 4–2   Goal-Setting Form 2

GOAL-SETTING FORM 2

Student _____

Class _____

Description of the problem _____

_____

Goal _____

_____

Student responsibilities for achieving the goal

_____

_____

_____

_____

Teacher support responsibilities

_____

_____

_____

Evaluation procedure _____

_____

Date of goal evaluation _____

Student's signature _____

Teacher's signature _____

First, if applicable, identify the problem that is interfering with student success. If the student will need to abandon unacceptable behaviors, clearly specify the borderlines between acceptable and unacceptable behaviors.

Next identify a positive goal. A positive goal requires a student to "do" something. When students have problems it is very natural to think of goals that will help the teacher rather than the student. "Don't bother others" requires nothing of the student and helps only the teacher. An example might be as follows:

My goal is to:
   Turn homework and class assignments in on time
   Raise my grade from a *D* to a *C*
   Learn to get along with others

With some students you may need to help identify long-range goals and then follow the long-range planning with short-term planning.

Long-range goal:
   Get a good-paying job

Short-term goal:
   Complete high school
   Go to college
   Get a part-time job
   Earn a scholarship

Once the goal has been established, identify what the student can do to achieve the goal. These are student responsibilities. Student responsibilities or expectations place a demand on the student. If the student has severe problems, expectations need to be within the immediate range of the student's capabilities.

Next determine what you can do to help the student achieve her goals. This is very important because it demonstrates to the student that you are concerned enough to put forth effort. Some of the things the teacher might do are:

- Reduce the amount of nagging
- Tell the student more frequently when work is done well
- Be more objective in evaluating work
- Observe the student more frequently in class
- Contact the student's parents when behavior improves
- Help the student keep records of current grades
- Help the student learn how to respond to different situations by role playing

Step 3: Identify ways to evaluate progress.

It will be important in most cases to have a measurable way to determine whether the student is making progress.

Self-counting is a procedure that teaches the student that he can learn to take responsibility for his own behavior. In some instances, this works best by taking baseline data and comparing behavior over time. In other cases, it may be advantageous to have the student count mutually incompatible behavior. For example, if the student were working on becoming more positive about himself, you might have him counting positive and negative comments about himself. Self-counting procedures can also be used to create opportunities for the student to work on appropriate behaviors. Every time the student does something that is negative, you might require that he practice doing something positive.

Evaluation may also involve determining whether a series of student responsibilities have been completed. For example, if the student's goal is to eventually work in an office, her responsibilities might include interviewing the school secretary and one other office worker to determine what kinds of qualifications she will need to meet her long-range goal.

Finally, evaluation may be as simple and informal as the student and teacher meeting every week to discuss how things have gone.

Step 4: Meet privately with the student at a neutral time.

Explain your objectives. Some examples follow:

I know that school has been difficult for you and I would like to help you set some goals that might make it easier.

I'm concerned about your grade in this class. In checking through your current grades, I see that you have a *D*. I really think that's a shame because your grades would average a high *C* if you had turned your papers in on time.

I thought we might get together to talk about some of your future options. Your papers are of very good quality, demonstrating that you have a good mind. Have you thought about what you would like to do when you complete high school?

Step 5: Work on short- and long-range goals. To identify short-range goals, have the student imagine what school or your classroom would be like if he were really successful. To work on long-range goals, have the student imagine enjoying himself on a normal autumn day following graduation.

Help the student identify goals from the situation he describes and then fill in the form. The goals you have in mind may help guide the discussion, but work as much as possible from the student's ideas.

Step 6: Help the student identify student and teacher responsibilities that will help her reach her goal.

You may be able to help the student identify what she needs to do by asking her exactly what she sees herself doing when she imagines being successful in school. Student responsibilities must be structured so that the student can actively reach her goal. Share some of the ideas that you have. Jointly fill in the form. Next work on things that you can do to help her out.

Step 7: Set a date to evaluate whether the student is meeting a goal.

Initially, the goal should be evaluated within a relatively short period of time. With all students, this should be no longer than one week. If you are working on a behavior problem, the short term of evaluation forces the teacher and student to be aware of their patterns of interactions.

If you are helping a student with long-range planning, the short evaluation period will help the student recognize that his daily efforts will create a longer-range goal.

Step 8: Sign the goal-setting form.

Signing the goal-setting form is simply a formality that highlights the importance of your plan. If the student does not choose to make an effort in reaching her goal, you should probably explore the more structured individual motivational plan in Chapter 6, *The High-Risk Student.*

Step 9: Follow through on your responsibilities.

Make an obvious attempt to carry out your responsibilities. Frequently, students will wait to see whether the teacher is making an effort to meet her responsibilities before the student will make an effort to meet her own responsibilities.

Recognize student efforts. Provide her with feedback. Feedback needs to be very adultlike and discreet. A nod, quietly making an appropriate comment to the student at her desk, a note on an assignment, and greeting the student at the door are examples of ways you can provide appropriate positive feedback without potential embarrassment.

Step 10: If the student engages in unacceptable behavior, follow through with any consequences that have been set up.

Avoid acting disappointed or disgusted. View the student's misbehavior as a momentary setback. Imply that you still expect the student to be able to meet positive expectations.

Step 11: Evaluate student progress.

On the date of evaluation, the student and teacher should discuss whether the student is meeting her goal. You should discuss together what is working and what is not working. If the first goal is working well, you may be able to help the student continue experiencing success by filling out a new goal-setting form that is a duplicate of the first. The second evaluation would take place over a longer span of time.

If things are not going well, the student and teacher may decide that they need to modify the responsibilities of the teacher and the student or that they need to set up an individualized reinforcement system. For example, the teacher may be able to help with a talking problem by assigning seats to students. The following conversation would occur in a private setting.

> Joe, I've noticed that you are really making an effort to cooperate in class but that Tammy is very hard for you to ignore. I think that I can help by assigning everyone to a specific seat. In this way I can make it easier for you to reach the goal by placing your assigned seat away from Tammy's.

A completed goal-setting form is shown in Figure 4–3 to give you an idea of what the process may be like.

GOAL SETTING WITH AN ENTIRE CLASS

Goal setting is a useful activity for any student, not just students who have problems. You may wish to do some basic goal-setting activities with your entire class. Students often don't realize that they do have some control over their own destiny. Goal setting is a particularly useful activity for students who seem to lack direction or maturity.

Goal setting will need to be taught in a structured lesson. The first session should emphasize the benefits of goal setting and present some examples of people who have reached a goal. You might want to read a short biographical sketch of someone who has reached a goal and have students trace the steps taken by the person to reach the goal. Help students recognize that being successful usually means that a person has had goals.

Figure 4–3   A Completed Goal-Setting Form

STUDENT: Martin Schroeder
CLASS: U.S. History

PROBLEM: Poor use of class time and problems with handing papers in on time

GOAL: Martin will raise his grade from a *D* to a *C*

STUDENT RESPONSIBILITIES:

1. Martin will come to class with a sharpened pencil, his textbook, and notebook paper.
2. When an assignment is given, Martin will immediately write down the assignment on the top of a clean sheet of paper.
3. When the teacher tells students to begin working, Martin will immediately open his book and begin the assignment.
4. If Martin has questions, he will raise his hand to get help.
5. Martin will stay on task to the best of his ability.
6. Martin will give his best effort to keeping up with ten-minute pacing intervals that he and Mr. Johnson set up.
7. Martin will complete unfinished work at home and turn work in on time.

TEACHER RESPONSIBILITIES:

1. Mr. Johnson will periodically check to see that Martin has all needed materials when he enters the classroom.
2. As soon as he has time, Mr. Johnson will check to see that Martin has written down the assignment correctly.
3. Once the class has started work on the assignment, Mr. Johnson will help Martin break the assignment into parts that could probably be completed in ten-minute periods.
4. Mr. Johnson will periodically check to see whether Martin needs any help.
5. When Martin is working hard, Mr. Johnson will walk by his desk and comment on his work.
6. Mr. Johnson will immediately check off work handed in on time at the beginning of each class period.

EVALUATION: At the end of one week, Martin and Mr. Johnson will go over the gradebook and count the number of assignments completed on time versus the number of assignments completed on time the week before.

EVALUATION DATE: Friday, 3:00

STUDENT SIGNATURE _____
TEACHER SIGNATURE _____

Success rarely grows out of chance. Opportunities may present themselves by chance, but successful people have cleared the way for themselves by working on one goal after another.

Have students brainstorm possible goals. Tell students that you will write their ideas on the board. Tell them not to worry about stating their own goals, just to share goals that anyone might have. Outline brainstorming rules. "Suggest anything you can think of. Keep your evaluations of the goals to yourself. We will try to write as many goals as we can in the next ten minutes. I'll begin by writing a few that I've thought up."

Pass English class

Own my own car

Get a good-paying job

Make more friends

Try out for rally squad

When students have helped generate goals, help the students separate long-term from short-term goals. A short-term goal is anything that can be accomplished in the next few months. A long-term goal will generally take six months to several years to accomplish.

Next, help students analyze different types of goals. Break long-term goals into several short-term goals. Then help students identify specific things that would need to be done to reach the short-term goals. Here is an example:

Long-term goal: own a car

Short-term goals:
Pass driver's test
Get a part-time job
Determine how much money it will cost to own a car

What I need to do:
1. Study the driver's manual 15 minutes every night
2. Set up a schedule to practice driving with parents
3. Begin checking car ads
4. Determine how much gas will cost to drive____miles each week
5. Check on insurance costs
6. Determine the cost of owning a car
7. Check job ads every evening
8. Spend one afternoon each week looking for a job

When students have had practice breaking down several different goals, have each student fill out a copy of the Goal-Setting Form shown in Figure 4–4. Tell students that they can work with someone else or get help from you if they wish; however, let students know that this is a private exercise designed to help them become more aware of what they want and how they can get it. They need to understand that they are not required to share this information with the class and they will not be asked to turn in the Goal-Setting Form to you.

The Goal-Setting Form in Figure 4-4 can be used as part of a lesson with the entire class on goal setting.

Figure 4–4   Goal-Setting Form 3

GOAL-SETTING FORM 3

Date _____

Long-range goal _____

_____

_____

Short-range goals _____

_____

_____

_____

Things I will do in the next week to begin reaching my goals

_____

_____

_____

_____

_____

Evaluation

_____

_____

Have students work on their goals for a week, and then have them write a self-evaluation. Begin the process again, having students set new goals or continue working on the same goal. This activity may sound time consuming, but once students have learned the basics, it may take as little as five minutes every two or three weeks.

Many times, students view the teacher's efforts to improve behavior as if the teacher is doing something to them. Goal setting is one way to communicate that students should have a say in their own direction and some control over their own future.

Chapter 5

CLASS-WIDE MOTIVATIONAL SYSTEMS

A classroom reinforcement system is any formalized set of procedures designed to motivate the majority of students in a classroom. While a classroom motivation system may help teach individual students to behave more appropriately, its specific aim is to help improve the behavior and motivation of all students.

The effective grading system suggested in Chapter 2 is an example of a classroom reinforcement system. In most cases, this type of grading system, paired with positive student-teacher interactions, will reach the great majority of students in the secondary school. However, there are instances where these procedures are not strong enough to be effective. When 10 to 15 percent of your students are not motivated by an effective grading system and positive student-teacher interactions, it is time to look at setting up a different or an additional classroom reinforcement system. This may occur in the following instances:

1. In communities where education and therefore grades are of too little value to sufficiently motivate students
2. In classes that are too large to effectively monitor individual participation and effort
3. In classes of high-performing students where good grades can be earned with very little effort and where motivation needs to be increased
4. In classes of low-performing students where student behavior must be turned around before an effective grading system can become motivating

Classroom reinforcement systems can be designed to reduce tardiness, reduce disruptive behavior, and increase academic effort. Classroom reinforcement systems can be used to increase motivation for following rules, to increase on-task behavior, and to teach basic work skills in vocational settings.

The following illustrations are designed to give you an idea of how classroom reinforcement systems might be productive under different circumstances. In the first illustration, the teacher manipulates the grading system to place a higher emphasis on effort in class. The second illustration shows how the teacher sets up a grading system for a large group of unmotivated students in a setting where it would be difficult to monitor individual effort. The third example shows a classroom motivation system that might be used for a group of students who are not motivated by grades.

ILLUSTRATION ONE

Problem: Students fail to use class time efficiently, but they consistently earn good grades because they turn out high quality work. The current grading system does not motivate students to make better use of class time because they earn good grades regardless of their classroom performance.

Description: Mr. Hayes has an advanced woodworking class composed of fifteen students. All the students are highly skilled craftsmen in their fourth year of woodworking. Students take great pride in their workmanship and consistently earn *A*s. While students produce work of superior quality, Mr. Hayes is concerned about the amount of class time that is wasted. When Mr. Hayes takes data, he finds that students spend approximately 70 percent of class time off task. Mr. Hayes has tried verbal reprimands, but finds that students work for only a short time before they are goofing around again.

Designing the classroom reinforcement system: Mr. Hayes decides that teaching students to establish good work habits must be a priority. His students have reached a point where good craftsmanship is reinforcing in itself, but where poor work habits may limit what they can accomplish. To begin setting up a classroom reinforcement system, Mr. Hayes defines on-task behavior as looking at a tool, working with a tool, briefly talking with another student about a project or tool (thirty seconds), working with a tool, or waiting to use a tool. He defines off-task behavior as sitting and doing nothing, talking about anything other than a woodworking project, or talking with another student for more than thirty seconds.

Mr. Hayes decides to manipulate his grading system to reinforce students' on-task behavior. His advanced students care about their grades, as they have always been successful. Mr. Hayes realizes that the quality of the student projects will always be excellent. Students take a great deal of pride in their work. For this reason, he has decided to base only 10 percent of the students' grades on the quality of their work, while 90 percent of the grade will be based upon on-task behavior.

Mr. Hayes designs a grading system where each student can earn six points per day. Five points are earned by working hard and staying on task. One point is earned for actively participating in clean-up. Mr. Hayes decides to keep track of student points on the Weekly Record Sheet. He will keep the Weekly Record Sheet with him on a clipboard. At unpredictable intervals, he will scan the classroom and record anyone who is off task. To keep track of the times he has monitored students each day, Mr. Hayes will keep a tally of his monitoring. Each off-task behavior will be noted with a check mark next to the student's name. Any student who does not participate in clean-up will also receive a check mark next to his name.

At the end of the period, Mr. Hayes will assign points. Every student will have had an opportunity to earn six points, and any student with no checks will receive the six points. Any student with check marks will have six points, minus any check marks. The Weekly Record Sheet in Figure 5–1 shows one complete week recorded using this system.

Each student will have an opportunity to earn thirty on-task points per week and a total of 270 points for the term. Thirty points will be awarded for class projects. Students will be told that projects will receive the full thirty points if the present quality is maintained and they are turned in on time.

Once Mr. Hayes has outlined his new grading system, he explains the system to his students. He lets students know that he will be monitoring their behavior at different times throughout the period. Mr. Hayes describes the behaviors he will be looking for and what kinds of behaviors will not be acceptable. Mr. Hayes also acknowledges that there will be times when he may record off-task behavior inaccurately, but that students will need to accept his calls the way an umpire's judgment must be accepted. There may be times when he will record someone as being off task when the student is actually thinking about his project. On the other hand, there will be times when a student might be thinking about the football game or his girlfriend when Mr. Hayes thinks he is actually on task.

Mr. Hayes also describes his recording system. He informs the students that he will tell them when they have gotten checks for off-task behavior during the first week of the new system. After that, students will be expected to be aware of their own behavior. Stu-

Figure 5–1   A Filled-In Weekly Record Sheet

WEEKLY RECORD SHEET

Date _Nov. 4–9_   Reminders _____

Class period __7__   _____

STUDENT	MON.		TUES.		WED.		THUR.		FRI.		TOTAL
Audiss, Will	√√	4	√	5		6	√	5	√	5	25
Ballin, Jerry		6	√	5	√	5		6		6	28
Brukin, Rod		6		6		6		6		6	30
Draper, Ginnie	√	5		6		6		6		6	29
Dysert, Lee	√	5	√√	4	T√√√	1	√	5	T√	3	18
Epstein, Eric		6		6		6	√	5		6	29
Felt, Paul	√√√√	2	√	5		6		6	E	7	26
Greenhill, Greg	A	⊕6	A	⊕6		6		6		6	30
Guarthreg, Theresa		6		6		6		6		6	30
Iturra, Cliff	√	5		6	UA	0		6		6	23
Kennedy, Chris		6	√	5		6	√	5	√	5	27
Miller, Lee	√	5		6	√	5		6		6	28
Shulze, Ken		6		6		6	A		A		
Turner, Kyle		6	√	5		6		6		6	29
Warnke, Todd		6		6		6	√	5		6	29

CODE: EXCELLENT WORK = E   OFF TASK = √ −1   ABSENT = A
UNEXCUSED
ABSENCE =
UA −3
TARDY = T −2

dents are told that they will always be welcome to look at the Weekly Record Sheet after class.

Finally, Mr. Hayes makes sure that students are fully aware of how the on-task points will be translated into their final grade, along with the points for their final projects. Throughout the discussion, Mr. Hayes impresses on his students the importance of learning to work efficiently.

In the weeks to follow, Mr. Hayes frequently scans his room at unpredictable intervals. Students never know when he is recording and when he is just observing. By systematically monitoring and documenting student behavior, Mr. Hayes teaches his students the importance of being on task during work times.

ILLUSTRATION TWO

Problem: Students need to learn that participation and effort in class will affect their mastery of new skills. While the teacher thinks that a participation-and-effort grade would help students learn to work hard during class time, the class is too large to effectively monitor each student individually. The problem of large classes is common for band, chorus, drill-team and some other elective subjects.

Description: Mrs. Garrity teaches a beginning band class of forty-five students at the junior high. A few of her students are very motivated. They take private lessons and are learning to play and enjoy music. Unfortunately, the majority of Mrs. Garrity's students are not so motivated. Students want to play well, but they lack the discipline and motivation needed to master their instruments. During school practice sessions, students waste ten minutes every day talking and fooling around while they get their instruments out. Once in their seats, Mrs. Garrity finds that she has to repeat instructions several times. While students are not overtly disruptive, they frequently play around with their instruments and turn the pages of their sheet music while Mrs. Garrity is talking. When Mrs. Garrity begins conducting a piece, she often finds that several students aren't ready and she frequently has to start over again.

Designing a classroom reinforcement system: Mrs. Garrity decides to use a classroom reinforcement system to motivate students to cooperate and make better use of classroom time. With 45 students, it is very difficult to keep track of individuals. Grading students on individual skill development is difficult enough, so Mrs. Garrity decides that a group motivational system will be the most manageable.

Mrs. Garrity begins by listing appropriate and inappropriate behaviors:

Appropriate behaviors

Students are in their seats with instruments and music ready one minute after the final bell.

Students listen and follow directions.

Students begin playing the correct music when the conductor raises her baton.

Students wait quietly and follow along while others are playing or talking.

Inappropriate behaviors

Students talk and fool around after the final bell.

Students play, tune, and adjust instruments while the teacher and class discuss procedures and techniques.

Students fail to attend to directions and demonstrations.

Next, Mrs. Garrity decides that she can use her grading system to more effectively motivate students. Up until this time, grades have been based upon individual performance assignments, home practice time, and class effort. Mrs. Garrity recognizes that the effort grade has been vague to students. She has never specified how the grade is earned and students are basically unaware of how they are doing until the end of the term.

Mrs. Garrity decides that the class-participation-and-effort grade will represent 60 percent of the students' total grade, of which 20 percent will be based on home practice time and 20 percent upon individual performance assignments. The class-participation-and-effort grade will be a class grade, represented by points earned for the following behaviors:

2 points	All students will be in their seats, quietly waiting, with instruments ready one minute after the final bell rings.
0–5 points	Students will follow all directions and attend to instruction.
0–3 points	Students will wait quietly while other students play their instruments or discuss procedures and will always be ready to play their instruments.

During the term, students will be able to earn 450 class performance points, 150 points for home practice, and 150 points for individual performance assignments, for a total of 750 points. Mrs. Garrity also specifies that any individual student may be fined individual points for blatant misbehavior.

Mrs. Garrity decides to the use the Weekly Record Sheet to keep track of class points. She will keep the record sheet on her music stand so that she can immediately award points as students are ready to begin class. If students fail to earn points during the class session, Mrs. Garrity will quietly note the problem on the record sheet. Just before class is dismissed, Mrs. Garrity will tell students how many points they have earned. Once Mrs. Garrity has fully designed her system, she discusses it with students. Mrs. Garrity explains the specific behaviors that she is watching for and tells students that she is confident that they can learn to behave like professional musicians.

ILLUSTRATION THREE

Problem: The classroom is noisy, and students are disruptive. Students are frequently tardy. They do not listen, and they are careless about getting their homework in.

Description: Mr. Bell's seventh-grade math class is chaotic. This group of low-performing students is very immature. They frequently come running into the classroom, acting more like first graders than seventh graders. When Mr. Bell gives instructions, half the students don't listen. Mr. Bell frequently reminds students to get to work, to follow directions, to raise their hands if they have questions; and when things get too out of hand, he has to yell at them to get them to sit down and work.

Designing a classroom reinforcement system: Mr. Bell decides that enough is enough and begins reorganizing his classroom. First of all, he revamps his grading system to include daily classroom participation and effort as part of his grading system. Though he carefully follows the procedures outlined in Chapter 2, Mr. Bell accurately assesses that things have gotten too far out of hand to quickly turn behavior around by only manipulating the grading system. Mr. Bell also recognizes that the students in this math class will have difficulty being motivated by the grading system because they will have difficulty believing that they actually have much of a chance to change their grades. Mr. Bell will need a stronger reinforcement system to teach the students the behaviors needed to earn daily participation-and-effort grades.

Mr. Bell begins to develop a classroom reinforcement system by defining behaviors that are inappropriate and appropriate. Once this list is completed, Mr. Bell begins outlining a reinforcement system. He decides that students should be given the opportunity to earn points for the following behaviors. Note that these are group points, not points given to each individual.

Every student comes to class on time.	1 point
All students follow rules during the first half of the class period.	1 point
All students follow rules during the second half of the class period.	1 point
Students work independently and quietly.	1 point
Every student turns in homework on time.	1 point

Next, Mr. Bell asks students to help him brainstorm things for which they would like to work. Once a long list is on the board, Mr. Bell and the students eliminate all suggestions that are not feasible. When the list has been pared down, students vote on the reinforcers for which they would like to work. Students vote for as many items or privileges as they would like. When the voting is complete, Mr. Bell tallies the points and lists the most popular choices. Students will be able to earn points toward each of the reinforcers in the order of their preference.

Overnight, Mr. Bell determines the number of points students must accumulate to earn each reinforcer. The next day Mr. Bell posts the reinforcement schedule and explains very clearly what students must do to earn the points. He tells students that points will be accumulated. Once they are earned, they will not be taken away. Points can be earned over whatever period is necessary and do not have to be earned consecutively. The students' reinforcement schedule looks this way:

15 points	Music played during independent work times for one week
15 points	15 minutes of free time
15 points	Class outside one period

Mr. Bell also discusses the new grading system, explaining how individual grades will be based on effort and participation and on specific assignments and tests. Students are given a grading sheet so they can keep track of their grades. Mr. Bell tells students he is confident that they can learn the behaviors that are important for success in school. Before ending the discussion, Mr. Bell shows students his recording system and lets them know that he will be happy to answer any questions throughout the term.

During the first week, Mr. Bell finds that one student is going to misbehave to keep the rest of the class from earning points. This student is told that he is no longer a part of the group reinforcement system. He is put on an individual reinforcement system. Mr. Bell works out a consequence for the types of misbehavior the student is exhibiting. After discussing the problem with the student, Mr. Bell begins imposing a classroom isolation consequence for any misbehavior. In addition, Mr. Bell works on actively increasing student-teacher interactions and institutes an individual reinforcement plan. When the student is able to complete a full week without being isolated, he will earn the right to become a part of the classroom reinforcement system.

Classroom reinforcement systems can be powerful tools for changing the behavior of a group of students. These systems are effective when teachers provide consistent and supportive feedback for appropriate behavior.

BASIC STEPS FOR SETTING UP A CLASSROOM REINFORCEMENT SYSTEM

Step 1: Define behaviors you are concerned about and establish boundaries between unacceptable and acceptable behaviors.

In establishing a class-wide reinforcement system, it will be important for the class to know exactly how you expect them to behave. If you are concerned about students being off task, you must define exactly what student behaviors will be considered on task, as well as exactly what constitutes off-task behavior. If you are concerned about students' following class rules, you should examine your class rules and identify specific acceptable and unacceptable behaviors. If you are concerned about students' being tardy, you must define exactly what will be considered "on time."

Step 2: Identify a reinforcer.

If students can be motivated by grades, you may need to manipulate your grading system. Base a higher percentage of the grade on the behavior that needs to be improved. However, if students do not seem to be motivated by grades, you may need to manipulate your grading system and establish an extra incentive to improve behavior and effort.

The easiest way to select an additional incentive is to have a class brainstorming session. Tell your class about the problems they are having and how these problems are affecting their academic progress. Explain to students that you are going to have a brainstorming session to identify things they might enjoy working for as a group. They will have ten minutes to suggest as many things as possible. You will write all suggestions on the board. Tell students that no idea is stupid. Their goal is to make as along a list as possible, without any discussion of the ideas.

At the end of ten minutes, lead students through the list, eliminating any suggestions that are not realistic. When the list has been reduced to items that are possible, have students vote. Let each student vote for as many ideas as they would like. Tally the votes and arrange the list in order of preference. The first item on the list will be the first goal, the second item the second goal, and so on.

A list of reinforcers that might be used if students are unable to generate their own list follows.

Five minutes of free time at the end of the period

A free class period

A field trip

Music heard during study time

Two to three days without homework

Class held outside

A movie

A party

Pizza delivered to school

Step 3: Set up a reinforcement schedule and specify what students must do to earn the reinforcers.

If, for example, you are dealing with a class problem of tardiness, you might tell students that the class will earn one point every day that no one is late. When the class earns four points, they will have five minutes of free time.

Step 4: Set up a record-keeping system.

It will be important for students to see that you are monitoring and recording the behavior that needs improvement. The Weekly Record Sheet can frequently be used to help you with record keeping. If your group is very immature, you may want to keep information on a chart that the class can see.

Step 5: Discuss the reinforcement system with students and keep them informed of their progress.

Once you have established your schedule of reinforcement and set up a record-keeping system, discuss the plan with students. Tell students exactly what they must do to earn points toward the reinforcement and the number of points they must earn. Explain your record-keeping and monitoring system. Once students have begun working toward a goal, keep them informed by providing positive feedback. "You have just earned one more point. That gives you eighteen points out of twenty. You are working very hard and will reach your goal with two more points."

Step 6: If one student misbehaves to keep the whole group from earning points, work to change that individual.

Some students are so hooked on negative feedback that they misbehave to keep the whole class from earning a reinforcement. If you have a student who enjoys this kind of attention, carefully explain why the student misbehaves and that the whole class needs to work on ignoring any misbehavior designed to disrupt the class.

You will also need to define the inappropriate behavior and set up a consequence. Since this student enjoys class attention, you may need to set up a classroom isolation consequence. When the student misbehaves to keep the group from earning a point, the student immediately goes to an isolation area in the classroom. He will need to spend a set period of time sitting and working quietly in isolation before he is allowed to rejoin the class. When the student behaves appropriately, it will be important to provide him with attention for cooperating. For example, you may give him the privilege of recording a class point because he has worked so hard to help the class earn it.

If these steps do not reduce the student's misbehavior, the student will need to be excluded from the class-wide reinforcement system. If this is the case, the student's behavior will no longer affect classroom efforts. The student's misbehavior will not count against the rest of the class, and the student will not be allowed to participate in any reinforcer earned by the group. This alternative should be avoided if at all possible. If the student forces you to exclude him from the group effort, set up an individual reinforcement system that will allow him to earn the right to become part of the group again.

CONCLUSION

Classroom reinforcement systems can be good tools for teaching a group of careless and unmotivated students to care about their behavior. These systems should be used only when effective grading systems fail and when a large number of students are having problems. If only one or two students are unmotivated, look at an individual reinforcement system.

The classroom reinforcement system, like all management tools, will be successful at changing student behavior only if the teacher is consistent, supportive, and has an effective grading system. This tool can teach a group of immature students to monitor their own behavior and work together toward a common goal.

Chapter 6

THE HIGH-RISK STUDENT

Gloria is a sophomore who is continually teased by many students in the school. She is overweight and unattractive due to hygiene problems. Gloria is called a number of names, and she is the focus of many jokes. Students make fun of Gloria in the classroom, but most of the harrassment takes place in the halls and cafeteria. When Gloria is teased she usually reacts by yelling, "Shut up." Gloria's teachers have begun noticing that she is becoming more and more isolated. School is a very painful place.

Bill is a seventh-grade student—a little bantam rooster, ready to put his fists up at the slightest provocation. Bill has been referred to the office for taunting other students. He has been suspended a number of times for fighting and once for carrying a switchblade. Bill is obviously a bright boy. His tongue is sharp and his answers are witty. Surprisingly, Bill is always in school. His grades are just good enough to get by. He usually gets low *C*s and an occasional *D*. Teachers frequently find themselves thinking, "If only Bill would put some of that energy into school work. . . . Unfortunately, he is more likely to end up in jail or cut up on some back street."

Mark is a high school junior—barely. Upon checking through his records, it can be found that Mark has been absent an equivalent of two-and-a-half school years. When he is in school, Mark is quiet and almost sullen. When work is turned in, it is of very poor quality. Though Mark is failing in most of his classes, no one knows much about him. He is the phantom student.

And then there is Jennifer! Most teachers wish she would stay home. Frequently angry and confrontational, Jennifer in class is like an unexploded keg of dynamite.

Gloria, Bill, Mark, and Jennifer are all high-risk students. High-risk students are "turned off," disruptive, chronically tardy, chronically absent, and often referred to the office for misbehavior. These are students who are the most likely to drop out of the school system. Approximately 25 percent of all students drop out of school prior to graduation. These are usually young people in trouble. They are likely to be failures. They are headed toward prison, welfare, prostitution, drug addiction, isolation, chronic unhappiness, or any combination of these. Certainly, the ideal situation would be to have loving and skillful parents take the time to turn these students around. Unfortunately, most of these students are in trouble because their parents haven't found the time or had the skill or love to help them in the first place.

Salvaging a high-risk student is possible. Everyone has heard stories of the troubled adolescent who made it because of a caring teacher. While it is obvious that most high-risk students will not live to be famous writers, actors, or politicians, individual attention from a caring teacher can change the odds for students who will otherwise fail before they reach the age of twenty.

This chapter focuses on suggestions for helping high-risk students. Strategies are provided for schools or individuals who care enough to go the extra thousand miles to salvage a high-risk student.

A SCHOOL-WIDE PLAN FOR SALVAGING HIGH-RISK STUDENTS

With limited contact and regular teaching responsibilities, teachers cannot realistically expect to provide every high-risk student with the kind of one-to-one attention that will be required to make a difference. Every teacher will need to cooperate, but the high-risk student will need one special person who takes the time to support and encourage small successes. Therefore, a school-wide support system pairs a faculty member with one high-risk student. That support person will keep in touch with classroom teachers to see how the student is doing, help set up peer tutoring when needed, make parental contacts, set up individualized motivational systems, and take part in staffings to help plan for the student.

Each school will need to set up its program for salvaging high-risk students with the recognition that they cannot help every targeted student. However, if fifty teachers work to help fifty children and only half are successful, twenty-five students will have learned that they can be part of a system that cares. For an individual, a high-risk program may mean the difference between living successfully in society or being another person on the fringes—in jail, on the streets, or living on welfare.

Step 1: Present to the faculty the school-wide plan for salvaging high-risk students.

Discuss the drop-out rate and failure rate of your school. Explain that high-risk students are kids who have little chance of succeeding without intervention. The high-risk plan will attempt to salvage at least a few lives each year. This plan will benefit students and may also benefit the school as students learn to work more cooperatively within the system. Explain that the high-risk program will pair a volunteer staff member—teacher, administrator, counselor, or other school personnel—with one student. The staff member will serve as a special counselor, student advocate, and support person through the school year. Briefly explain the student identification process and the training program. Ask staff members to think about the plan over the next few days, to ask questions, and then to make a decision as to whether they will take part in the program.

Step 2. Identify high-risk students.

While staff members are determining whether they will take part in the high-risk program, begin the process of identifying students. Ask every teacher to submit the names of their two highest-risk students and the name of a third student who would benefit from one-to-one support. Ask teachers to write a brief descriptive paragraph about the three students they identify. Also identify students who have been referred to the office for misbehavior, tardiness, and absenteeism. With the list of students identified by teachers and the list of office referrals, you will have a complete list of the students who are in the greatest need of assistance.

Step 3: Meet with volunteer faculty members and match one high-risk student with each volunteer.

Probably the easiest way to match teachers with students is to circulate the list of high-risk students and ask each volunteer to choose a student with whom he or she would be willing to work. Since the volunteer will be serving as a type of advocate for the student, it might be best to suggest that the volunteers choose students who are not currently in their own classes. However, if a teacher feels that he has already established a special rapport with a student who is in his class, allow the teacher to work with that student.

For the remainder of this chapter, the volunteer teacher will be referred to as an advocate. This label is not intended to imply that the teacher will serve as a legal advocate. It simply means that the volunteer will have a special interest in helping the student learn to function successfully in the school system.

If there are only ten volunteer advocates and fifty high-risk students, forty students will not have an advocate. In this situation, some staff members may volunteer to work with more than one student. Try to discourage this. Serving as an advocate may be time consuming. if an advocate becomes overburdened, the chance of success with each student will dwindle. While a one-to-one program may mean that several students will not be included, help will be available to students who were not helped in the past. As the program proves itself, you may wish to begin recruiting additional staff members.

When the pairing process has been completed, provide each advocate with any information that can be made available—teacher descriptions, information about truancy, and office referrals. This information can help the advocates begin to learn more about their students' needs.

Step 4. Train advocates to work with high-risk students.

The initial training session should emphasize that the efforts of the individual teacher may or may not salvage the child. The high-risk plan is a last-ditch effort, but a worthwhile one. Remind teachers that their individual attention will be remembered even by those students who do not seem to succeed. Outline the responsibilities of the teacher:

- Get to know your student's past history and outline areas of concern. Identify behaviors most in need of change to succeed in the system.
- Ask the student's teachers to fill out current academic progress reports.
- Set up a parent conference to discuss academic and behavioral problems. Explain that you will always be available and will keep in touch with the parent on the student's progress. Determine whether you can rely on parental support.
- Meet with the student and set realistic behavioral and academic goals.
- Set up an individualized motivation system if necessary.
- Set up a staff meeting if necessary to enlist the help of classroom teachers.
- Meet regularly with the student, and monitor progress.
- Explore other resources that may provide information on helping the student. Chapter 4, *Goal Setting,* and the remainder of this chapter may be especially useful. Section IV, *Trouble Shooting,* may be useful for giving information about handling specific behavioral problems. The final section of this chapter provides an example of salvaging a high-risk student.
- Be persistent. Keep in mind the magnitude of the behavioral change you are asking the student to make. The bigger the change, the more difficult the problem.

Step 5. Meet with volunteer staff members every four to six weeks.

The purpose of these meetings is to discuss how their students are doing, to share ideas, and to provide support. Working with the high-risk student will not be easy. If it were easy someone would have helped this student long ago. Changes may take time and may be very frustrating. Talking with other advocates about their successes and failures can provide a feeling of support and purpose. The meetings will help advocates learn about things to avoid and new things to try. Periodic meetings can result in renewing the energy that is needed to reach the high-risk student.

DESIGNING AN INDIVIDUALIZED MOTIVATIONAL SYSTEM

There are strategies that can be used by any staff member who wishes to help an individual student learn to succeed within the system. The individualized motivational system is designed for students who do not respond to improved student-teacher interactions, effective grading systems, and goal setting. The individualized motivational system is used when classroom consequences and motivational systems are too broad for the needs of an individual student.

The individualized motivational system is the most powerful behavior change tool. Because the student has not responded to less structured tools, the individualized plan offers the student alternative benefits for cooperating and trying to function within the school system. If the plan works, the student will initially work because of the extra incentives but will eventually learn that success has benefits of its own. As the student becomes motivated by passing grades and teacher encouragement, the reinforcers of the individualized plan can be faded and dropped. With each individual student, it is difficult to predict whether a plan will work or not. It is safe to say that unless something special is done for these students, however, they will never be motivated by the system itself. These students are high-risk students.

The following steps are the basic components of an individualized system. Variations must be made for every student, depending on the individual's needs. No two problems will be exactly alike. You are working with human beings. Some individualized plans may involve only goal setting. Adjust the steps, the order of the steps, and the strategies to work for the student.

Step 1. Identify problems that interfere with student success in the school setting and determine where problems typically occur.

Example: John Weatherby

Problems:
    Antagonizes other students
    Fights
    Tardy
    Temperamental, easily frustrated, gives up if task is difficult
    Needs to improve academic progress (currently failing most courses)
    Doesn't pay attention during class
    Doesn't turn in assignments

Problem areas:
    Classrooms, halls, cafeteria

Step 2. Write positive expectations for student behavior.

Define what the student is expected to do and how he is expected to perform in each identified setting. If the student's difficulties are centered in classrooms, you must talk with the student's teachers to determine specifically what the student needs to do to succeed in each class. The more detailed the expectations, the more likely the student will be able to succeed.

You may wish to circulate a form similar to the completed examples in Figures 6–1 and 6–2 if the student will need to make behavioral improvements in all classes. A blank copy of this form is provided in Figure 6–3.

Figure 6–1   Request for Behavioral Expectations (Sample)

REQUEST FOR BEHAVIORAL EXPECTATIONS
(Sample)

STUDENT: John Weatherby
TEACHER: Mrs. Jesse   PERIOD   1   SUBJECT: Basic Math II

BEHAVIORAL EXPECTATIONS:

1. Before the final bell rings, socialize in a quiet voice, and keep negative thoughts to yourself.
2. Be seated at 8:30 with math book, paper, pencil, and completed assignment.
3. Raise your hand and wait to be called on if you have a question.
4. Focus on each task and try your best.
5. Work quietly and independently during study times.
6. If you have difficulty, raise your hand and ask questions.

COMMENTS: My greatest difficulty with John is his interaction with other students. He always manages to antagonize them.

Include behavioral expectations for areas outside the classroom when applicable.

Step 3. Group the expectations and identify the borderline between acceptable and unacceptable behavior under different conditions.

Acceptable	Unacceptable
• Being in your appropriate place when the final bell rings, with all needed materials.	• Reaching your seat as the bell rings Arriving without any of the articles identified by each teacher, including a sharpened pencil
• Walking while in the school building.	• Running or jogging in the halls, cafeterias, locker rooms
• Treating every person with respect.	• Making a comment or calling a name that would anger someone
• Listening to and follow directions in class.	• Talking to someone else when directions are given Playing around with any object while the teacher talks Turning around in chair while directions are being given
• Making an appointment with the teacher or raising your hand if you have difficulty with an assignment or problems with a referee in P.E.	• Stopping work Playing with books and objects Making loud noises with objects Arguing
• Keeping your hands and feet to yourself.	• Jostling, wrestling, pushing, or nudging

The more severe the student's problems, the more specific you will need to be in identifying appropriate and inappropriate behavior. If the student has a very difficult time, it may be important to define borderlines for every class and setting.

Figure 6–2   Request for Behavioral Expectations with Letter to Teacher (Sample)

REQUEST FOR BEHAVIORAL EXPECTATIONS
WITH LETTER TO TEACHER
(Sample)

Dear _____,

We are currently working on an individualized motivational plan for a student in your class. We need your cooperation in identifying specific behaviors that are important for success in your classroom. Please write positive statements of your behavioral expectations for the student and return the form to my box by Jan. 10. We will use these statements in setting up a contract and will need to have your help monitoring these behaviors while the student is in your classroom. When the Student Assistance Plan has been drawn up, I will be in touch with you for a staff meeting. Thanks for your cooperation.

REQUEST FOR BEHAVIORAL EXPECTATIONS

STUDENT: John Weatherby
TEACHER: Mr. Benton   PERIOD: 2   SUBJECT: P.E.

BEHAVIORAL EXPECTATIONS:

1. Be dressed and in the gym by 10:25.
2. While in the locker room, handle only your locker, gym clothes, and towel.
3. Keep your hands and towel to yourself.
4. Walk in the locker room.
5. In class, listen to directions.
6. Accept all the calls by referees.
7. Talk respectfully to fellow students and teachers.

COMMENTS:

Include behavioral expectations for areas outside the classroom when applicable (halls, cafeteria, school fields, walkways, and restrooms):

1. Keep negative thoughts and comments to yourself.
2. Keep your hands and feet to yourself.
3. Walk in the halls.

Step 4. Determine how appropriate behavior will be monitored and counted.

In some instances, the motivational system will count the amount of time the student has been successful. In others, the system will count student output. For example, if the student is disruptive in class, the system will count the amount of time the student behaves appropriately. If the student has difficulty completing assignments, the system will be based on the amount of work the student completes. Some systems will count both time and the amount of work a student completes. Always begin with a simple sys-

Figure 6–3   Request for Behavioral Expectations with Letter to Teacher

Dear _____,

We are currently working on an individualized motivational plan for a student in your class. We need your cooperation in identifying specific behaviors that are important for success in your classroom. Please write positive statements of your behavioral expectations for the student and return the form to my box by _____. We will use these statements in setting up a contract and will need to have you help monitor these behaviors while the student is in your classroom. When the Student Assistance Plan has been drawn up, I will be in touch with you for a staffing. Thanks for you cooperation.

STUDENT _____

TEACHER _____ PERIOD _____ SUBJECT _____

BEHAVIORAL EXPECTATIONS:

COMMENTS:

tem that focuses on the problem behaviors that are most likely to cause the student to fail. As the student becomes successful in a particular area, the system can be expanded.

Once you have determined what you will be counting, determine the increment that will be counted. For example, if the student has difficulty turning in homework assignments, will you count homework for each class, each day, each week, or the term? If you are counting the amount of time a student behaves appropriately in class, will you count ten-minute time intervals, one class period, half days, a day, or a week? The more severe the problem, the smaller the increment must be. Smaller increments increase the likelihood that the student will be able to look at his behavior and recognize that he can be successful. Smaller increments mean the student will receive frequent feedback on his efforts throughout the day. It also means that classroom teachers will need to deal with the high-risk student at frequent intervals. If the student has difficulty with homework assignments, homework assignments must be monitored on a daily basis. A one-week assignment will need to be broken into daily tasks.

Next, design a form that will monitor and record the appropriate behavior increments. The Daily Report Card is one system that can be used for monitoring appropriate student behavior. Figure 6–4 shows a monitoring system for time increments and for the amount of student work. A blank copy of the Daily Report Card is provided in Figure 6–5.

An even simpler monitoring form is the Behavioral Record (Figure 6–6). This monitoring system can be used for a problem that occurs primarily in one class.

The Daily Report Card or the Behavioral Record is carried by the student throughout the day. Initially, the student will report to the advocate, counselor, school psychologist, or special teacher each afternoon. The afternoon meeting would focus on successes

Figure 6–4   Daily Report Card (Sample)

DAILY REPORT CARD
(Sample)

John Weatherby _____   Jan. 15 _____
STUDENT NAME   DATE

Teachers:

1. Sign the card to indicate that the student was in class and presented the card to you at the end of the period.
2. Initial the first space if the student followed the set of rules that we have designed with you.
3. Initial the second space if the student showed improvement, cooperation, and effort in class.
4. Initial the third space if the student turned in the assigned homework. (If there was no homework, also initial the space.)

PERIOD	SIGNATURE	RULES	EFFORT	WORK
FIRST	_____	_____	_____	_____
SECOND	_____	_____	_____	_____
THIRD	_____	_____	_____	_____
LUNCH	_____	_____	_____	_____
FIFTH	_____	_____	_____	_____
SIXTH	_____	_____	_____	_____
SEVENTH	_____	_____	_____	_____

STUDENT MONITORING: You will be responsible for monitoring your own behavior in the halls and cafeteria. At a private time, check each time period that you were able to be successful at following each of the rules below.

1. Keep negative thoughts and comments to yourself.
2. Walk away quietly from anyone who behaves immaturely.
3. Keep hands and feet to yourself.

_____ Before school   _____ Between fifth and sixth
_____ Between first and second: _____ Between sixth and seventh
_____ Between second and third   _____ After school
_____ Lunch

Figure 6–5   Daily Report Card

DAILY REPORT CARD

_____   _____
STUDENT NAME   DATE

Teachers:

PERIOD	SIGNATURE	RULES	EFFORT	WORK
FIRST	_____	_____	_____	_____
SECOND	_____	_____	_____	_____
THIRD	_____	_____	_____	_____
LUNCH	_____	_____	_____	_____
FIFTH	_____	_____	_____	_____
SIXTH	_____	_____	_____	_____
SEVENTH	_____	_____	_____	_____

STUDENT MONITORING: You will be responsible for monitoring your own behavior in the halls and cafeteria. At a private time, check each time period that you were able to be successful at following each of the rules below.

_____ Before school   _____ Between fifth and sixth
_____ Between first and second   _____ Between sixth and seventh
_____ Between second and third   _____ After school
_____ Lunch

and allow the student and staff member to discuss how problem areas could be handled more appropriately.

The final monitoring system to discuss is the Weekly Record Sheet, described in Chapter 2. If you have set up a motivational system for an individual student in your classroom, you can also use the Weekly Record Sheet to monitor the individual behavior

Figure 6-6 Behavioral Record

Behavioral Record

STUDENT NAME Janetta Jones

TO: Mrs. Celeste	Mon	Tue	Wed	Thu	Fri
Please initial one space for every class period	___	___	___	___	___
that Janetta successfully meets the expectations	___	___	___	___	___
we have discussed. If Janetta fails to meet	___	___	___	___	___
expectations, please explain the problem so	___	___	___	___	___
Janetta can make improvements the next day.	___	___	___	___	___

of a student. The sample record sheet in Figure 6-7 shows how a record sheet might look at the end of a week. Note that Dana Kuntzmann is on an individualized system. The initials "RC" are the teacher's initials and represent that the student had a successful day of following the rules.

Your monitoring system will be built to suit the needs of your student. Feel free to be creative. The illustration beginning on page 69 provides a number of different monitoring systems designed to meet the needs of an individual student.

Step 5. Meet with the parents.

Once you have identifed problems and defined expectations for the student, meet with the parents. Explain that you would like to act as a special support person for their child. If they agree, your role will be to try to monitor the student's behavior and teach her skills that will help her survive in school. Define some of the behaviors that have interfered with the student's success in the past. Tell the parents that you recognize school may not hold a lot of interest for their child and that you would like to put the student on an individual plan that will help her become more interested. Try to determine how much support you will be able to count on from the parents. Regardless of the outcome of your conference, let parents know that you will keep them informed. Let them know that someone at school is on their child's side.

Step 6. Identify possible reinforcers toward which the student might be motivated to work; then meet with the student to discuss the plan, expectations, and reinforcement.

Determining what will motivate a turned-off student is difficult because the student has not been interested in anything the school has to offer. Occasionally, the best reinforcer is what happens to the student when he improves his behavior. For example, the best reinforcer for a student who is chronically teased may be getting students to stop teasing her. Or, the reinforcer may be something as simple as free time. However, in most high-risk cases, the reinforcer will need to be something more powerful such as money, cosmetics, car parts, computer time, or food. Remember, the greater the change you are asking for, the more powerful the reinforcer must be.

If the parents seem very supportive of your efforts, have them help suggest some things the student might work for. This could include responsibilities such as use of the family car or a later curfew on weekends. If the parents mention something that costs money, try to determine with great sensitivity whether they could provide the reinforcer.

Figure 6–7 A Filled-In Weekly Record Sheet

WEEKLY RECORD SHEET

Date _Sept. 14-18_   Reminders _____

Class period _4_   _____

STUDENT	MON.	TUES.	WED.	THUR.	FRI.	TOTAL
Agner, Donna		✓ E			✓	18
Amato, Lee		✓			✓	16
Anderson, Dan	0	✓		T-6	✓	13
Baumbaugh, Gary		L	0		✓ E	16
Buckee, Cheryl		✓ 0			✓	15
Carpenter, Dustin	0 0 0	✓			✓	13
Crossett, Gelia		✓			✓ E	18
Deane, Russ		A ⊕(B+4)	A ⊕(B+4)		✓	16
Dorns, Jan	E	✓		0	✓	17
Edwards, Lanny		✓ 0			✓	15
Felch, Yvvette		✓			✓	16
Franklin, Lavar		✓			✓ E	18
Godon, Randi	A ⊕(B+4)	✓ 0	E		✓	17
Green, Christopher		✓			✓	16
Hammon, Matthew	E	✓			✓	18
Johnson, Charlene		✓			✓	16
Jones, Jesse		✓ C		0	✓	17
Kemp, Lonnie		✓	0	✓ 0		14
Kuntzmann, Dana	RC	RC ✓	0 0	RC E	✓ RC	15
MacKight, Todd		✓			✓	16
Mezick, Chanya		✓ 0			L 0	13
Nelson, Wendy	C	✓			✓	18
Owen, Travis		✓			✓	16
Potesta, Sam		✓	E		✓	18
Quince, Bonnie		✓			✓	16
Robinson, Eddie	D	✓		E	✓	17
Schmidling, Ruth		L	A		✓	11
Semolke, Gail		✓			A	12
Sumida, Marilyn	0	✓			✓	15
Taylor, Danny		✓	E		✓	18
Timmons, Jay	E	✓		C	✓	20
Van de Veer, Steve		✓ 0 0			✓	14
West, Shaun		✓			✓	16

CODE: EXCELLENT WORK = E +2   OFF TASK = 0 −1   ABSENT = A
COOPERATIVE = C +2   DISRUPTIVE = D −1   UNEXCUSED
BONUS POINTS = B   LATE WORK = L −1   ABSENCE =
UA −4
TARDY = T −2

The primary concern is to try to find some things that the student has really wanted. Most parents can help with suggestions.

Initially, do not worry about how you are going to obtain the reinforcers. Meet with the student. Explain that you would like to help the student learn to enjoy school and experience more success. Tell the student you are working on a system that will help him be more successful in school. Let him know that you will be asking him to do things that may be difficult for him, so he may work for something he would really like to have. You can suggest some of the things his parents may have mentioned. Next help the student brainstorm some ideas. You may use the list below to help you if you get stuck.

Tokens for a video arcade

Tickets to:
    roller rinks
    movies
    sporting events
    school functions
    fashion shows
    car races
    concerts

Lessons:
    driving
    swimming
    piano
    dance
    gymnastics

Things:
    car parts
    video cartridges
    gift certificate for clothes
    records or tapes

Responsibilities:
    office assistant
    later curfews
    peer tutoring
    correcting papers
    working in library

Time:
    on school computer
    in metal- or woodshop
    for home economics
    in art room
    in weight training room

Once you have developed a list, evaluate the items with the student. Some of the items may not be realistic, but they may provide ideas for modification. For example, buying a motorcycle may not be feasible, but you may be able to rent a motorcycle from a local shop. You may not be able to provide a horse, but you may be able to provide horseback-riding lessons. Try to identify two or three things the student seems interested in. The initial reinforcer should be powerful, but not so costly that the student will have to work for it over a long period of time.

Step 7. Secure the reinforcer.

If parents are supportive and seem to have the resources to help out, call the parents to make a final determination on the reinforcer. Let them know that you will keep them informed on how the student will finally be expected to earn the reinforcer. If the parents are not a resource or cannot be relied upon to follow through, you may need to be creative in finding access to the reinforcers. Contact a local merchant to see if he would donate the item. You may be able to offer to have the merchant's business mentioned in the school paper or parent newsletter as a patron and supporter of the school and youth of the area. Another resource might be a service or community group interested in supporting your efforts. If you are working as part of a school-wide high-risk program, the administration may choose to help you out by securing community sources or grant money to help support your endeavors. In obtaining any help, the names of individual students should always remain confidential.

Step 8. Once the reinforcer has been identified and secured, determine the number of increments that will earn the reinforcer.

Look at the magnitude of behavioral change you are expecting from the student. If it is a relatively large behavioral change, the system should be designed so that a relatively small amount of success leads to the reinforcement. Determine the number of increments or points the student can earn in a day. Next, determine how many points the student will need to earn the reinforcer. Your goal is to set up a system that will make the student feel, "Oh, yeah. I could do that. If I do well, I could earn that by Thursday. Not bad." Keep in mind that if you require too much, the student will feel that he has no hope of earning the reinforcer, and the system will fail.

Look again at the system for John Weatherby in Figure 6–4. Each day John would have fifteen opportunities to earn recognition for appropriate behavior from teachers and seven opportunities to monitor his own appropriate behavior. Translated into points, John can earn a total of 22 points each day. To determine the number of points the student will need to earn his reinforcer, you may decide that three days is a sufficient time period. Therefore, you might tell John that he will earn the reinforcer when he has accumulated 60 points. This leaves John a little leeway. With effort, he should be able to earn his reinforcer easily within the first week.

When setting up the reinforcement schedule, try to avoid systems that require consecutive increments, such as "When you have had four good days in a row . . . " These systems are weak because the student is punished for good days along with the bad. He may have three good days and one bad day. Requiring consecutive increments means that the student has earned nothing for the days that he tried. Many students will give up with this type of system.

Finally, avoid setting up systems that require the student to demonstrate appropriate behavior within a given time limit, such as "If you have four successful days a week, you have earned . . . " This system is weak because the student will have no incentive to work if he has two bad days at the beginning of the week. The incentive is also removed for working hard on Friday if he has already had four days of appropriate behavior.

Step 9. Call a meeting of all teachers working directly with the student.

Present the plan. Discuss the positive expectations for behaviors. Go over what the student will need to do in order to behave appropriately. Discuss borderline behaviors and help teachers arrive at a firm understanding of appropriate and inappropriate behavior. Ask teachers to make a conscious effort at acknowledging student effort and improvement. Let them know that for a high-risk student something as simple as sitting quietly may be an effort. Arrange a nonverbal signal the student can watch for indicating that he is behaving appropriately.

Give everyone copies of the Weekly Record Sheet. Explain the procedures. Let teachers know that you appreciate their efforts in making this attempt at salvaging the student. These kinds of efforts will surely make everyone's job easier in the long run. Explain that the effort will take patience on everyone's part.

Step 10. Design or discuss consequences for unacceptable behavior with staff members.

No matter how well you design the motivational system the student will test to see how teachers are going to react to inappropriate behavior. There will be bad days. Everyone will need to be prepared to act unemotionally and consistently. Try to prepare teachers and yourself to react to any possible misbehavior by imagining all the things the student might possibly do in class. Place these behaviors into one of the four categories listed below:

1. Acceptable behavior: Behavior the teacher will encourage to happen more often in the future and that will therefore lead to recognition and to the reinforcement.

2. Unacceptable, attention-getting behavior: Behavior that will be ignored such as failing to raise his hand, chronic complaining, argumentative statements. (See Chapter 8.)

3. Unacceptable behavior that leads to a mild classroom consequence such as time out in the classroom, or time owed. (See Chapter 8.)

4. Unacceptable behavior that warrants office referral: This should be a very limited category of behaviors such as physical violence and direct defiance. (See Chapter 9.)

Step 11 (Optional). Set up a written contract.

In most individualized systems, a formal written contract is laid out between the student and any teachers involved in the system. The written contract adds formality to the system—both for the student and the teachers. It emphasizes the responsibility that the teachers and student have to uphold their respective parts of the contract, and it requires teachers to summarize their role. This helps to clarify the system.

In setting up the contract:

a. Make a brief overall statement of the student goal.

b. Specify what the student should do.

c. Specify how behavior will be evaluated and monitored.

d. Specify the reinforcer.

e. Specify the teacher's responsibilities.

The example in Figure 6–8 is for John Weatherby. As his behavior will be evaluated by six different teachers, the contract has been written to include the expectations and responsibilities of all involved.

The contract should be signed by all staff members. It can be laid out during the staff meeting.

Figure 6–8   Behavioral Contract

Behavioral Contract

The following contract between John Weatherby and his teachers is designed to help John learn to get along with and enjoy peers and to develop behaviors that will help him become more successful in school.

STATEMENT OF STUDENT RESPONSIBILITIES

1. John will arrive to all class periods on time with all needed materials and completed assignments. He is to be in his assigned place when the final bell rings.
2. John will keep all negative comments and thoughts to himself.
3. When John has difficulty with an assignment, he will quietly raise his hand and wait for help.
4. When John feels angry he will turn away and walk to another part of the room. He will go back to working on another part of his assignment, or he will count until he is calm.
5. John will keep his hands and feet to himself at all times.
6. John will give every assignment his best effort.
7. John will follow all class rules.
8. John will wait quietly at the end of each period to have his Daily Report Card signed.

STATEMENT OF TEACHER RESPONSIBILITIES

1. Each teacher will work hard to notice and acknowledge John's efforts at making improvements in his behavior and academic progress. Each teacher will remember to let John know that he is aware of his efforts by giving him an occasional nod.
2. At the end of each period, each teacher will evaluate and complete John's Daily Report Card. If John has been successful, the teacher will give him recognition for his efforts and initial his Daily Report Card. If John has had difficulty, the teacher will calmly explain to John what he needs to do to earn his point the next day.
3. If the teacher is held up for any reason after class and John has to wait to get his Daily Report Card signed, the teacher will write a pass for John to get into his next class.

STATEMENT OF STUDENT ADVOCATE RESPONSIBILITIES

1. Mr. Arnez will collect the Daily Report Card and issue a new card immediately after school.
2. Mr. Arnez will help John identify ways that he can earn any point that was missed. If a problem has occurred, he may help John role play ways to handle similar problems in the future.
3. Mr. Arnez will help John keep track of his cumulative points.
4. Mr. Arnez will provide John with gas tickets and time tickets as John earns his credits.

AGREEMENT

Each teacher initial and student check mark will equal one point. 30 points will equal a ticket for one gallon of free gas and 15 minutes' use of the family car.

Teachers' Signatures

_____	_____
1st Period	6th Period
_____	_____
2nd Period	7th Period
_____	_____
3rd Period	Advocate
_____	_____
5th Period	Student

Step 12. Meet with the student to discuss the final plan.

Explain the entire plan to the student. Go over the specific expectations for all classes and settings when applicable. Discuss the borderline between inappropriate and appropriate behavior. Let the student know that all his teachers will work together to try to deal with him fairly and consistently. Go over monitoring forms and then present the student with the contract. Let the student know you hope he will give the system a try. He has nothing to lose and everything to gain. Tell him that the contract is designed to let him and all of the teachers know his responsibilities. During this session, you may wish to do some role playing to help the student learn to deal with situations that have been difficult in the past.

The following illustration of a plan for a high-risk student demonstrates the kind of support some students may need.

Description: Gloria was the high school student who was overweight and unattractive because of hygiene problems. She is called names and is the object of many jokes. Most of Gloria's problems take place in the halls and cafeteria, though staff members have overheard the rude student comments. Gloria's standard reaction is to get red in the face and to yell, "Shut up." Faculty members notice that the harassment has not abated, and if anything, it has gotten worse. Over the course of the year, teachers also notice that Gloria has become more and more withdrawn.

Contributing factors: Students tease someone like Gloria because of her reaction. While students who harass another student demonstrate immaturity and insensitivity, this type of teasing is generally not the result of maliciousness. Students who tease maliciously, tease many students. They do not focus on only one student.

When one student is habitually teased, the major problem is usually the student's reaction and her inability to initiate any other kind of interaction with peers. Students who are chronically teased in the secondary school have probably been teased from the time they were very young. This pattern will be difficult to change.

The student's appearance is also a factor in teasing. However, helping the student change her physical appearance alone will not eliminate the problem. Students will continue to tease the student as long as she reacts to the harassment.

Problem solving: The following steps should alleviate Gloria's harassment.

Step 1: Determine who will be able to work with the student on a daily basis.

Because this is a severe and difficult problem, it will take a long time to resolve. It will require the support and encouragement of all the student's teachers, and it will also require that someone work with the student ten minutes every day for at least a month. Since classroom teachers probably cannot provide this help, the school counselor or psychologist needs to be the support person in this plan. The student must work with someone who is patient and firm in uninterrupted daily lessons. These lessons will be designed to teach the student to control her behavior.

Step 2: Discuss the problem with the student to determine whether she wants to eliminate the teasing by making a commitment to changing her behavior.

Tell the student that you would like to help her eliminate the teasing she has to face. Explain that punishing students who tease her may work momentarily, but as soon as teachers aren't around, she will be teased again. Tell the student you would like to help her get rid of the problem and learn to behave in ways that will not encourage others to give her a hard time. Explain that students who are teased all the time generally do things to keep the teasing going. Tell the student that you can help her change that, but admit that it will take a lot of work and willpower on her part.

Emphasize that you cannot make the other students stop teasing her by punishing them. Explain to the student that teachers are dismayed when this happens, but the only thing that will effectively stop the teasing will be her changing her own reactions. Explain that teachers will begin ignoring all incidences of her being teased. Tell the student you are not leaving the student in the cold. Teachers will no longer intervene for her because they understand she is the only one who can really control whether the teasing continues.

Ask the student if she is willing to work with you. If she is unwilling, remind the student that other teachers will no longer intervene when she is teased. If the student continues to be reticent, ask her if there is someone else she would feel comfortable working with. If the student does not want to try to change her interactions with other students, let her know that she can come to see you if she ever changes her mind.

Step 3: Discuss the student's problem at a weekly staff meeting.

Briefly describe the student's difficulties and explain that teachers are being asked to ignore all incidences of the student being teased. Explain that you will, or hope to, work with the student so she may learn to deal more effectively with the teasing.

Also ask that teachers help the student build a better self-concept. This student has failed to learn how to interact positively with others because she has a poor self-image. Ask teachers to matter-of-factly greet her with a simple smile, to occasionally stop to chat with her in the halls, and to take an active interest in her academic progress. Explain that the student will be working with you to learn to ignore teasing and to gradually improve her appearance.

Step 4: In the daily training session, teach the student to ignore teasing through modeling and role playing.

The easiest and most effective way to eliminate chronic teasing is to completely ignore it. During the first training session explain to the student that immature students will tease her to see her reaction. It isn't any fun to tease someone unless you get a reaction. That is the whole point of teasing. Explain to the student that when she reacts to teasing she is rewarding her tormenters. If she can learn to ignore them, she will learn to punish them by refusing to give them what they want.

Have the student make a list of any names or comments that have bothered her. Go through the list and tell the student what you would do to ignore the students in each instance.

During the next several sessions spend approximately five minutes out of ten on role playing. For the first couple of sessions, have the student call you names. Demonstrate how to respond appropriately. As the student becomes more comfortable with these situations, reverse rolls. Tell the student that you are going to call her names and see if she can unemotionally ignore them. Begin with the names and comments that bother her the least. Gradually work in the more offensive comments. Try to set up situations that are as similar as possible to encounters with other students. As the student grows more comfortable with these sessions, you may even want to bring in another adult. Much of the student's reaction to teasing will be embarrassment in front of others. Role playing should be designed to help the student learn to cope with as many situations as possible. Conduct a role playing session only if the student wants to participate.

Step 5: Provide the student with a system for monitoring the number of times she is teased and her reaction each time.

The student should be taught to record incidences of teasing and her reactions so she can see that progress is being made. This monitoring system will also help the student become more aware of her behavior and what needs to be done in daily practice sessions.

Provide the student with a card similar to the one in Figure 6–9.

Teach the student to record each teasing incidence by coding her reaction. She should keep the card with her at all times in a notebook or folder. Tell the student that she should record each incidence as soon as possible after it occurs.

Step 6: Teach the student to chart the percentage of times she is able to ignore teasing and the number of times she is teased.

First the student should chart the percentage of times she was able completely to ignore teasing. To determine this percentage, divide the number of times the student ignored teasing by the total number of times she was teased.

Number of times teasing ignored ÷ Total times teased each day

The student should understand that her goal is to be able to chart that she ignored teasing 100 percent of the time. A sample of the type of chart you will need is shown in Figure 6–10.

Next, it will be critical for the student to chart and record the actual number of times she was teased each day because it may be difficult for the student to see that any progress is being made. If the student is being teased an average of fifteen times a day, going to an average of ten times a day in two weeks is a marked improvement. Because the student is still being teased fairly frequently, she may have difficulty seeing that ignoring is paying off. Stress to the student that the problem will not stop immediately. If the number of times is going down, progress is being made. A sample chart for recording the number of times the student has been teased is shown in Figure 6–11.

Step 7: Work to help the student improve her self-concept.

Students learn to ignore teasing or to laugh it off when they have a good self-concept. In addition to learning to ignore teasing, a student like Gloria needs to build self-confidence through improved interactions, academic success and improved appearance.

As the student becomes fairly adept at role playing, gradually shorten the amount

Figure 6–9   Reaction Card

Week of _____				
Mon.	Tues.	Wed.	Thur.	Fri.

Code: I = Ignored   R = Reacted a little
       U = Got upset

Figure 6–10   Behavioral Percentage Chart

Behavior being monitored: <u>% of Times Teasing Was Ignored</u>

%	Week 1 M T W T F	Week 2 M T W T F	Week 3 M T W T F	Week 4 M T W T F	Week 5 M T W T F
100					
90					
80					
70					
60					
50					
40					
30					
20					
10					

of time spent on role playing and work on making suggestions for improving appearance. Work on one thing at a time. Begin with things that will be the easiest and will make the most obvious change. Then help the student set a schedule for taking care of her appearance. Use the Personal Schedule calendar in Figure 6–12 to help the student develop better hygiene habits. If you suggest that the student needs to take a daily bath or shower, have the student look at the calendar to select a time that will be best. You may have to suggest that the student get up earlier, or she may need to shower in the evening if it is hard to get into the bathroom in the morning. Help the student set a schedule for washing her hair. If she has very oily hair, the schedule should include washing her hair at least every other day. Help the student set a specific time to work on personal care skills and the specific days they should be accomplished. The student should have a copy of the Personal Schedule calendar, and you should keep one. During each daily meeting, check off the things the student was able to keep up with. If the student has a number of excuses for why she was not able to get something done, help her rearrange her time schedule. For example, if the student fails to bathe on Wednesday nights because of a favorite TV program, suggest that she take her bath before the show. After several weeks, the Personal Care calendar might look something like Figure 6–12. A blank copy of the Personal Care Calendar is provided in Figure 6–13.

As the student's basic appearance improves—laundry is done on certain days, hair is washed, and so on—you can begin thinking about getting the student to work on an appropriate diet and exercise course. As the results will be much more difficult and slow to achieve, improvements in this area should be approached only after the student has made significant improvements in other areas.

Continue to work with other staff members to improve student-teacher interactions. Every few weeks, inform teachers of the student's progress and remind staff members that the student still needs a little extra encouragement. As the student works on personal hygiene, ask that staff members make small comments about how nice she looks.

Figure 6–11   Behavioral Frequency Chart

Behavior being monitored: <u>Daily Record of Teasing</u>

	WEEK 1	WEEK 2	WEEK 3	WEEK 4	WEEK 5
	M T W T F	M T W T F	M T W T F	M T W T F	M T W T F
25					
24					
23					
22					
21					
20					
19					
18					
17					
16					
15					
14					
13					
12					
11					
10					
9					
8					
7					
6					
5					
4					
3					
2					
1					
0					

Figure 6–12   Personal Schedule (Sample)

Behavior being monitored: _Personal Care_

Week of _Jan. 21-25_

Time	Mon.	Tues.	Wed.	Thur.	Fri.

6:30 _Get up_ →
6:45 _Shower and wash hair_ →
7:00 } _Eat breakfast_ →
7:15
7:30 _Brush teeth, dress, get school materials_ →
7:45 _Leave for school_ →
8:00

SCHOOL

4:30 _Arrive home_ →
4:45 _Fix snack_ →
5:00 } _Choose clothes for tomorrow and put clothes in wash if necessary_ →
5:15
5:30
5:45 } _Relax_ →
6:00
6:15 _Help prepare dinner_ →
6:30
6:45 } _Eat dinner_ →
7:00
7:15 _Clean up dishes and put clothes in dryer_ →
7:30
7:45
8:00 } _Homework_ →
8:15
8:30
8:45
9:00 } _Relax_ →
9:15
9:30
9:45 } _Make sure clothes are ready for next day_ →
10:00
10:15 } _Go to bed_ →
10:30

Figure 6-13   Personal Schedule

Behavior being monitored: _____

Week of _____

Time	Mon.	Tues.	Wed.	Thur.	Fri.

6:30 _____
6:45 _____
7:00 _____
7:15 _____
7:30 _____
7:45 _____
8:00 _____

SCHOOL

4:30 _____
4:45 _____
5:00 _____
5:15 _____
5:30 _____
5:45 _____
6:00 _____
6:15 _____
6:30 _____
6:45 _____
7:00 _____
7:15 _____
7:30 _____
7:45 _____
8:00 _____
8:15 _____
8:30 _____
8:45 _____
9:00 _____
9:15 _____
9:30 _____
9:45 _____
10:00 _____
10:15 _____
10:30 _____

Step 8: When the student has been able to consistently ignore teasing for two consecutive weeks, begin meeting less frequently with her.

When the student has been successful at ignoring teasing for two consecutive weeks, and when teasing does not occur more than once or twice a week, schedule meetings for Monday, Wednesday, and Friday. Eventually, drop to a Tuesday–Thursday schedule. Each time you reduce the number of times that you meet with the student emphasize how well she is doing. Eventually, meet with the student once a week. This should be continued for the remainder of the school year. The student must know that you have a continued interest in her success.

Step 9: Help the student become involved in extracurricular activities.

As the student's self-confidence grows, it will be important for her to become involved in activities with peers. Help the student select a school club to join. If the student is very unsure of herself, you may wish to set her up with a student sponsor for the first few meetings.

MODIFYING A SYSTEM THAT IS NOT WORKING

The previous illustration demonstrates ways that a high-risk student might be helped. It incorporates the applicable strategies identified in this chapter and also stretches to meet the individual needs of the student. if your system is not working, explore the following possibilities:

1. Have you given the system enough time to work? Sometimes students will spend two or three days misbehaving before settling into a more positive routine. Give the system at least a week before you begin making revisions.

2. Can the student help to identify why the system is not working out? If the student can provide information, adjust the system accordingly. Try to let the student know that the goal of the system is not to "force" him to change, but is rather an attempt to make the classroom a more tolerable place for the student and the teacher.

3. Are the student's peers reinforcing appropriate behavior? If the student's friends or other classmates laugh when the student misbehaves, talk about how "tough" the student is, or give the student attention for misbehavior, peer attention is probably interfering with the system. Talk individually with students who give attention to the misbehavior. If appropriate, let them know they are hurting their friend's chances of succeeding in school. Ask students to ignore misbehavior. Go over specific situations when students should ignore misbehavior. If this is not effective within a few days, impose mild classroom consequences for attending to the student's misbehavior. This might include failure to earn participation points or owed time.

4. Have you required increments of appropriate behavior that are too large? If the student is very immature, she may not be able to manage her behavior for the length of time that was set up. If your system measures appropriate behavior for a class period, you may need to divide each class period into two increments. If this is the problem, you do not have to change the reinforcement. The student needs more immediate feedback, not necessarily more immediate reinforcement. If a student needed five whole class periods to earn a football-game ticket, change the system so that she will need ten half periods to earn the ticket.

5. Is the reinforcement too delayed? When a student is expected to make a large behavioral change, the tendency is to choose a high-powered and expensive reinforcer.

Because of the cost, the system delays the reinforcer too long. The student may lose sight of the reinforcer and feel that he has no chance at success. It may be necessary to select less valuable reinforcers that can be earned over a shorter term. Prior to changing the system, though, it may be possible to keep the student going by emphasizing at periodic intervals how much closer the student is to the reinforcer. "You have already earned half the points that you need."

6. If the foregoing suggestions do not help you resolve problems and get the student going again, meet with the student and an objective third party. A school psychologist, counselor, or principal may help you identify weaknesses or drawbacks in the system you have designed.

7. If all the suggestions do not work, refer the problem to the school psychologist or to an appropriate professional. Provide information on all the things you have tried and be available to assist in any further planning for the student.

Section III
CONSEQUENCES FOR MISBEHAVIOR

This section is designed to help you implement calm consistent consequences for inappropriate behavior. Chapter 7 provides important information about how to use consequences effectively and how to avoid common traps teachers sometimes fall into while using punishment. Most misbehavior should be dealt with in the classroom setting. Chapter 8 presents consequences and procedures the teacher can use as alternatives to sending students to the office. Chapter 9 gives an overview of the features of an effective school discipline policy. While it is beyond the scope of this book to present full detail on how to set up policies, this chapter will at least provide specific information for evaluating strengths and weaknesses of the current policies in your school.

Chapter 7

PUNISHMENT CONSEQUENCES— GUIDELINES AND LIMITATIONS

Punishment techniques are a necessary part of an effective discipline policy. To use punishment procedures effectively, however, it is important to understand that they are only a small part of a broad plan to improve student behavior. This plan must include clear expectations, positive interactions with all students, and an effective grading system.

> Mrs. Meyen is presenting the safety rules for the next lab experiment. Therese responds with, "Yeah, yeah, yeah. Rules, rules, rules." This is the fourth or fifth wisecrack of this type from Therese today. In exasperation Mrs. Meyen angrily retorts, "Listen to me, young lady. I am tired of your comments. Don't say anything for the remainder of the class." Therese smiles and says, "Something, everything, ANYTHING!" At this point, Therese is sent to the office. This pattern between Therese and Mrs. Meyen is repeated two or three times each week.

In this example, the attempt to punish Therese's sassiness is ineffective. The pattern of misbehavior continues. Therefore, there are several adjustments the teacher needs to make if she is going to teach Therese to get along in her class. In order to understand why punishment is often ineffective with secondary students, it will be necessary to explore what punishment is and the misconceptions surrounding punishment. These considerations will help you determine when and how punishment can be used effectively. This chapter, then, will look at guidelines for implementing punishment effectively, and the next two chapters will explore specific classroom and school-wide consequences for misbehavior.

PUNISHMENT DEFINED

Punishment is a term that is frequently misunderstood. A consequence is only a punishment if it reduces the future frequency of a behavior. Grounding a child is a punishment only if it reduces how often the misbehavior later takes place. A punishment can be something the teacher does or says. It can be something other students do or say, or a punishment can be something the student thinks or feels himself. Punishments are not necessarily overt consequences such as time out, suspension, or some form of corporal punishment. A punishment is anything that results in a behavior taking place less and less often in the future. If a consequence does not reduce the future frequency of a behavior, it is not a punishment.

> Mrs. Hunt loves teaching and is a very conscientious teacher. Her class is working quietly on an assignment that most students are enjoying and taking seriously. However, Sandra keeps turning around and talking to the student in back of her. Every time Sandra talks, several students turn to see who is talking. This is very annoying, so Mrs. Hunt tells Sandra to stop talking. Sandra is quiet for a few minutes, but needs attention again after a few minutes. This time she begins drumming her fingers loudly on her desk. Mrs. Hunt does what has worked before. She tells Sandra to stop and Sandra stops. This pattern continues day after day.

Mrs. Hunt thinks that her verbal reprimands are punishing because Sandra always stops misbehaving immediately. However, Mrs. Hunt is giving Sandra exactly what she wants—attention. This is the "criticism trap." The attempt to punish has failed because the misbehavior continues. It will always be important to examine any technique that is designed to reduce or eliminate unwanted behavior. If the behavior continues, the procedure is not punishing.

No technique is universally punishing for every student. An effective punishment for one student may have absolutely no effect on another student. Each student, as an individual, will respond to different things in different ways. For this reason, it will be important to adjust techniques and strategies to determine which are the most effective in changing student behavior. If a commonly used consequence is not effective for a given student, it does not mean the student is hopeless or that he "just doesn't care about school." It simply means that this particular student does not find that particular consequence punishing.

> Rick is a second-grade student who is slightly below average in academic abilities and social maturity. Rick knows that he should always try to do his best in school, and he has tried. When Rick has been lucky, his teacher has noticed that he is working hard and tells him what a nice job he is doing. This means a lot to Rick because his teacher is very important to him. However, Rick has also learned that there is an easier way to get attention and feedback from his teacher. Working hard all day is a difficult job.

> Rick has learned that if he engages in a minor misbehavior like tapping his desk while the teacher is talking, he gets one-to-one attention. The teacher actually stops her lesson and asks him to stop tapping. Of course, Rick always obeys the teacher because he does want to please her.

Compare the two ways that Rick has learned to get the teacher to talk to him. On the one hand, he can work hard all day long, with the chance the teacher might notice and praise him. This requires a lot of effort and hard work with no guarantees that the teacher will notice what a nice job he is doing. On the other hand, he can tap his pencil. This isn't work at all, not a bit tiring, and it is guaranteed to get the teacher's attention.

Rick, whose performance is low academically and socially, is basically insecure. Consequently, he does need a lot of attention, and he will get it as efficiently as possible. He learns to frequently engage in a minor misbehavior so the teacher will look at him and tell him to stop. Rick does not like to be scolded. He does not intentionally try to annoy or bother the teacher. He simply needs attention so badly that the type of attention he receives is irrelevant. Rick probably does not know why he misbehaves and probably does not like being a "bad" boy. However, the longer the pattern goes on, the more Rick views himself as "bad."

Now let's look at Rick as an eighth grader. The only differences between Rick as a second grader and Rick as an eighth grader is that he has had six additional years of practice at getting attention through inappropriate behavior and six additional years of believing himself to be "bad." He is now more experienced and sophisticated at getting attention through misbehavior, and he is much better at it. Many secondary students misbehave for the attention they receive. Getting in trouble is habitual. It may be fun. It certainly is not punishing.

If a student is seeking attention through misbehavior, the teacher's attempts to punish may be exactly what the student wants to have happen. This does not mean that there should be no consequences for misbehavior. Schools have a limited number of consequences at their disposal, and these are not very powerful. This does not mean that consequences will not be used. It means that they will need to be chosen carefully to give the student as little attention as possible for misbehavior. The most powerful tool for changing behavior will come from increasing positive interactions for appropriate behavior.

COMMON MISCONCEPTIONS

Misconception 1: Punishment is a powerful strategy for changing behavior.

At the secondary level, punishment often lacks power because the most difficult students have become inured to any punishment procedure that can be used. Some students have been lectured to, yelled at, sent to the principal, sent out of the room, kept after school, suspended in school, and suspended out of school, and they simply no longer care. They have an attitude of, "So what?"

When punishment is effective, it is still weak because it reduces a behavior by establishing an avoidance response. Its weakness les in the fact that punishment alone fails to teach students to be responsible, motivated, and cooperative. Improved behavior at the threat of punishment simply means the cost of punishment outweighs the benefits. The student may change the way she behaves, but not change the way she "wants" to behave.

Misconception 2: If teachers would be tougher with students, students would learn to be more self-disciplined.

Punishment is effective only as long as the threat of punishment hangs over an individual's head. Punishment does not teach the *benefits* of changing behavior. Whenever students realize the threat of punishment has been removed, they are likely to begin engaging in the inappropriate behavior again. Exceeding the speed limit on the freeway demonstrates how ineffective punishment can be when a threat is removed. When police cars are visible, most people carefully stay within the speed limit. When it is unlikely that police are around, many people exceed the speed limit. These people are willing to take the chance that they won't get caught. Punishment procedures do in fact make the teacher a police officer in the classroom. Even the lowest-performing student will realize that it is the teacher who presents the threat of punishment. When the teacher is gone, or has his backed turned, students may engage in misbehavior with no consequence. This also means that punishment techniques will not help a student generalize better behaviors to other settings. The threat of punishment may control a student in Mr. Johnson's class, but have no effect on the way a student interacts with others.

Misconception 3: Students respect teachers who are tough.

This misconception probably grows out of the fact that we typically remember respecting teachers who consistently gave out fairly severe punishments for misbehavior. It seems logical that our respect grew out of the teacher's ability to punish effectively. However, we also remember teachers who used the same consequences and were laughed at. Why is it that students will cringe when one teacher sends a student out of class and smirk when another teacher does the same thing? The critical difference is not the use of punishment, but the teacher's ability to combine positive interactions with consistency, fairness, and high expectations. Consequences are taken seriously because they are imposed within the context of a positive environment. A less respected teacher may try to use the same punishments, but will use them inconsistently and too frequently to have impact.

Misconception 4: Classroom control is established through the use of punishment.

A common misconception regarding punishment is that a teacher's major means of classroom control is through the use of punishment. If the teacher attempts to establish control primarily by punishing misbehavior, he may actually create more problems than he solves. Because students are placed in an adversarial relationship with the teacher, they will often test to see how much they can get away with. The overuse of punishment will lead to students' feeling that the consequences are no big deal because they have been through them so many times before. The end result may be that students will actually be encouraged to engage in misbehavior.

A teacher who tries to "control" students through the use of punishment is in for a very frustrating experience. At best, the teacher will have a quiet classroom but lack students who are motivated to do their best academic work. Avoid trying to control students. The teacher's job is to teach and foster learning. This is accomplished by establishing a comprehensive management plan with a heavy emphasis on reinforcement to encourage student motivation.

GUIDELINES FOR USING PUNISHMENT EFFECTIVELY

A comprehensive management plan will include consequences for misbehavior. There are obviously times when punishment procedures are necessary. While you are teaching students to take pride in their accomplishments, it may be necessary to demonstrate that some behaviors are not going to be tolerated in your classroom. The following section presents guidelines for developing effective punishment procedures as part of a discipline plan. In implementing the procedures, you should remember that punishment procedures are essentially weak, even if all the guidelines are followed. Punishment has a low probability of successfully teaching a student with severe behavior problems to behave more appropriately. However, punishment procedures can be used to eliminate misbehavior on a short-term basis while more appropriate behaviors and attitudes are being taught and reinforced. Several guidelines to keep in mind when planning and implementing a punishment consequence follow.

Guideline 1: Define the specific behavior you are concerned about.

Identify the behavior that has been causing problems or interfering with the learning process in the classroom. For example, if there are problems in class with students being disruptive, define exactly what you mean by disruptive. If there is a problem with a student who becomes extremely hostile and angry, define what you mean by hostile. Hostile behavior could be defined in the following way:

Frances will be considered to be exhibiting inappropriate hostile behavior whenever she:

- Raises her voice beyond a normal speaking range
- Makes rude or sarcastic comments about the teacher, the class, or other students
- Makes threatening statements to the teacher or other students
- Clenches and shakes her fists toward the teacher or other students

Guideline 2: Clearly specify the borderline between acceptable and unacceptable behavior.

Students have to understand exactly what each teacher expects. Therefore, it is essential to make sure the student understands exactly how you will evaluate the things she does. A clear borderline increases the likelihood that you will be consistent in your implementation of the consequence. It also increases the chance that the student will learn quickly to avoid the unacceptable behavior because she will know exactly what behaviors lead to consequences and what behaviors are acceptable in class.

To draw a clear line between acceptable and unacceptable behavior, think of five different situations when the problem behavior might happen. For each of the five situations, identify three acceptable and three unacceptable ways the student could handle each situation. With this many examples, both you and the student should have a clear concept of the borderline between acceptable and unacceptable. With your examples, be sure to include things like tone of voice and body language that may affect your evaluation of the acceptability of a given behavior. An example of one situation that might be identified when defining the borderline for a student who talks back follows.

Situation: James is sitting and staring out the window. "James, please get started with your writing assignment."

Unacceptable Responses	Acceptable Responses
Says, "Screw you."	Says, "Okay."
Shouts, "All right!"	Says nothing but gets started.
Says, "I hate this stuff."	Asks, "Does this need to be done by the end of the period?

Guideline 3: Discuss beforehand the unacceptable behaviors, the borderlines between acceptable and unacceptable behaviors, and the consequences with the student or students involved.

Consequences for unacceptable behavior should never be a surprise to students. Imagine that the speed limit on an interstate highway has been changed, but no one has been informed. Even though no one knows of the change, traffic tickets are given to people who are not staying within the new speed limit. This would obviously be unfair. It is also unfair to punish students unless they know that the behavior is unacceptable and will lead to a consequence.

The discussion of consequences for a particular misbehavior should take place at a neutral time, not immediately after a misbehavior has occurred. A neutral time provides distance from the initial problem. It gives the teacher time to determine how the misbehavior should be defined and what consequences would be appropriate. The neutral time also gives everyone enough distance to discuss the problem calmly and rationally.

If several members of your class have been engaging in the misbehavior, you will want to discuss the problem and future consequences with the whole class. If only one or two students are having difficulty with this misbehavior, it is better to talk with them individually.

The discussion of consequences prior to putting them into effect is very important. If students are in the dark, they will not be intimidated by unknown consequences. To the contrary, many students will engage in misbehavior to find out what will happen. Keeping students guessing does not keep students on their toes. It simply challenges them to test you. Keep your students informed of rules and consequences.

Guideline 4: Be as consistent as possible in implementing consequences.

Some students have learned that what some teachers say and what they actually do may be two entirely different things. Given this, you can safely expect to be tested. Students need to find out whether you mean what you say. You must therefore be prepared to implement the consequences you have established. As students realize you are going to be consistent, they will abandon this inevitable type of testing behavior. Students do not have to test once they know what you are going to do.

It is also important to follow through with established consequences because many students have developed a sense of power from not getting caught, or from "beating the system." No matter how often they have gotten caught, or how severe the punishment has been, some students keep trying to beat the system if they know there is a chance to "get away with it." The reinforcement and the feelings of power that come from beating the system are much more powerful than the occasional punishment. Implement the consequence every time the unacceptable behavior occurs.

Guideline 5: Establish punishments for as few behaviors as possible.

Follow the foregoing procedures for only a few of the most intolerable misbehaviors. The use of punishment requires consistently applying consequences when a misbehavior occurs. If the list of misbehaviors is too long, there is no way that a teacher can be consistent. Any attempt to be consistent will result in the teacher spending most of the day monitoring and punishing misbehavior.

Much of the misbehavior that is seen in many classrooms can be eliminated by following the procedures identified in Chapter 1. Most students who understand rules and expectations from the start feel no need to experiment with misbehavior. Inappropriate behavior that is designed to get attention can frequently be eliminated by ignoring the misbehavior and creating a positive learning atmosphere. Many misbehaviors can be eliminated by teaching students the desire to succeed in school. This is far more productive than teaching students to behave through fear of punishment. See Chapters 3, 4, and 6 for additional information on teaching students to be self-disciplined.

Guideline 6: Always treat students with respect.

Punishment techniques must demonstrate to students that certain behaviors cannot be tolerated. There must be matter-of-fact consequences for inappropriate behavior. Punishments that severely embarrass students may be effective at eliminating misbehavior, but they will also destroy any possibility of a positive relationship between teacher and student. A student who has been humiliated by a teacher is unlikely ever to do well for that teacher again and will not do more than the bare minimum required to avoid being humiliated again.

Guideline 7: Implement punishment procedures unemotionally.

It is important to remain as unemotional as possible when following through with a punishment. Over the years, some students have learned that the ability to make a teacher angry or annoyed is reinforcing. Therefore, an emotional response from the teacher weakens the effectiveness of the punishment strategy.

Staying calm basically demonstrates to a student that power is not gained through misbehavior. Students who have many behavior problems are insecure individuals. They will frequently misbehave in an effort to have an impact on those around them. It will be important for the teacher to show these students that they do have power, but it comes through motivation and positive behavior rather than misbehavior.

In attempting to implement unemotional punishments, do not attempt to become an emotionless teacher, but emotion has no functional place in the meting out of punishments. If you have a tendency to become angry, ask what the anger has accomplished. Then remember that your anger has probably served to encourage the student to misbehave again. Try to remain calm the next time the misbehavior happens.

Guideline 8: Establish a plan to reinforce students for improved behavior.

Punishment in isolation has a low probability of encouraging a long-term change in student behavior. If an effective punishment has been established, it will result in a short-term improvement in the student's behavior. To ensure the improved behavior continues, it will be critical to reinforce the student for improved behavior. If reinforcement for appropriate behavior is not immediately available, the student will revert back to getting attention through negative behavior, and the punishment will have lost its effectiveness.

A plan to reinforce improved behavior can be as simple as occasional verbal feedback or as detailed as a formal reinforcement system. The sophistication of your reinforcement plan is dependent upon the severity of the misbehavior and the overall behavior of a student. For severe problem students, see Chapter 6 *The High-Risk Student.* For other problems, see Chapter 3, *Teacher-Student Interactions,* and Chapter 4, *Goal Setting,* for reinforcement ideas.

Guideline 9: At the end of two weeks, evaluate the effectiveness of your efforts to reduce misbehavior. Modify your plan if necessary.

If the frequency of the misbehavior has not been significantly reduced over the two-week period, change your plan. The first thing to look at is increasing the power and structure of your reinforcement system. Manipulate the reinforcement system at least two times before making changes in the punishment technique. A tendency is to first increase the severity of the punishment. Avoid this impulse. There is a good chance the more severe punishment will not work either. If you get into a pattern of accelerating the degree of punishment, it won't be long before the student must be suspended from school. If the student is not in school, you have no chance of teaching him anything. Twice as much effort goes into trying to get the student motivated than goes into trying to eliminate inappropriate behavior. With a focus on the positive, it is much more likely that you can reach even very difficult students.

Chapter 8
CLASSROOM CONSEQUENCES

Except for severe behavior problems such as student violence or blatant defiance, it is best to resolve problems within your own classroom. If you handle problems instead of referring them to the office, you demonstrate to students that you are willing to work with them and are capable of developing a mutually productive relationship. Use of classroom consequences also allows you to respond quickly to minor misbehavior without a major disruption in class time. This chapter will help you establish effective procedures for responding to most inappropriate behavior in your classroom.

GENTLE VERBAL REPRIMAND

Gentle verbal reprimands should be used the first several times a particular misbehavior occurs in class. This simply involves asking a group of students not to engage in an inappropriate behavior. The verbal reprimand tells students that the behavior is not acceptable in your classroom. If this strategy does not change student behavior, then a more formalized punishment system must be established.

Every teacher uses verbal reprimands. If used effectively, gentle verbal reprimands can frequently reduce the need to implement more formalized consequences. Gentle verbal reprimands should be unemotional or matter-of-fact statements that tell students why the behavior is inappropriate. Avoid sounding sarcastic, and if possible avoid issuing a direct command. For example, if the teacher says, "For heaven's sake, don't talk while I'm talking," she has almost issued a challenge. Below are examples of the types of statements that would be more effective.

> I would prefer if you didn't talk while I am lecturing. It makes it difficult for others to hear, and it makes it hard for me to give you the information you will need to pass your test.

> Class, I need your attention. It's gotten a little too noisy. You can talk quietly while working on your lab assignments, but too much noise will bother other classes. Go ahead and get back to work, but remember to talk quietly.

> (The following is an example of a private discussion.) Wendy, I am concerned about the way you spoke to me in class. Your comments about not liking the work in this class came across very rudely. I would appreciate it if you would come to me in private to discuss things that you do not like. It puts me in an awkward position when you make an announcement to the entire class.

If behavior improves following a gentle verbal reprimand, let the student know that you appreciate his cooperation. This gives the student recognition for appropriate classroom behavior and tells him that you are pleased with his efforts.

If the problem occurs a second time, try the gentle verbal reprimand again, but phrase it differently. Use the verbal reprimand at least three times, but no more than six times for any given problem during the term. If the student or students do not change their behavior with several reprimands, you will not change their behavior with five hundred reprimands. Effective verbal reprimands work quickly. If you tell your students the same thing over and over again, or if you feel as if you are nagging, you have fallen into the criticism trap. As discussed in Chapter 7, you are probably reinforcing students for exhibiting the behavior you dislike. It is important to change your strategy.

SELECTING CONSEQUENCES WHEN INAPPROPRIATE BEHAVIOR CONTINUES

If you have tried verbal reprimands three to six times and a problem persists, you will have to decide whether to ignore the misbehavior or to implement a more formalized consequence. Select the option that is the most effective. Ignoring will generally be appropriate when students misbehave to get attention. Select one of the following options.

Option 1: Ignoring

Ignoring is an active strategy for teaching a student to behave in a more mature and responsible manner. An effective teacher will never "tolerate" inappropriate behavior. When ignoring is selected as a consequence to misbehavior, the student is being told that some behaviors are so childish, they are not worthy of a response. Because gentle verbal reprimands precede ignoring, the student will know the teacher is not condoning misbehavior by ignoring it.

Step 1. Carefully evaluate whether ignoring might be an effective consequence to the misbehavior. Ignoring will be appropriate only if the student is trying to get attention. Remember, every student is an individual. Though the behavior of two students may be similar, their intents may be very different. Look at the following examples.

Mary Louise has developed the nervous habit of tapping her pencil when she is under pressure. During exams the loud tapping is sometimes very disturbing to other students, but Mary Louise is completely unaware of her pencil tapping.

Cindy is a poor student and she gets bored during independent study periods. She has discovered that she can break the monotony momentarily by making annoying noises. She usually begins by tapping her pencil loudly on her desk. Other students usually begin staring at her, and eventually the teacher tells her to stop. It's really no big deal, but the disturbances give Cindy a little variety and a fleeting moment of control.

Both students have the same annoying habit; they tap their pencils loudly enough to disturb others. However, because the intent is different, the problems must be dealt with differently. Ignoring will have absolutely no effect on Mary Louise because she will continue tapping her pencil, oblivious of what she is doing. On the other hand, you might consider using ignoring as part of a management system for Cindy because she taps her pencil to get attention. When the attention is consistently ignored, the reinforcement is removed.

In trying to determine whether the goal of the misbehavior is attention getting, look carefully at the behavior of low performers. Some students will misbehave to cover up academic problems. "Act tough and it will look like you don't want to do the work. No one will know that you can't do it." If you ignore this type of misbehavior, it will continue. It is not being reinforced by attention; it is being reinforced by the student's perception that everyone will think he is a "tough guy" instead of a "dummy." Ignoring will not remove that reinforcement so the misbehavior will continue.

Keeping in mind the need to evaluate the goal of misbehavior, the following misbehaviors are often effectively reduced by ignoring:

- Complaining
- Annoying noises
- Rude comments
- Talking out

- Chronically ignoring instructions and then asking to have them repeated
- Calling out answers instead of raising hand

Step 2: Determine whether the attention-getting misbehavior is mild enough for you to consistently ignore. If you can ignore the behavior, you can also teach other students to ignore the behavior. However, if the behavior is so severe that it disrupts class, a more severe consequence will have to be used. It would obviously be absurd for the teacher to ignore such behaviors as screaming, overt defiance, and destruction of materials, even though the intent may be to get attention.

Step 3: Define the behavior that will be ignored. The easiest way to define a misbehavior is to think of situations that typically result in the misbehavior, and then list different ways the student might act. Next, categorize behaviors you will encourage, behaviors you will ignore, and behaviors that cross a borderline into something more severe. The following illustration shows how a teacher might define chronic complaining by use of examples.

Situation: Students are given a homework assignment.

Student Comment	Teacher Response
"Math is stupid!"	Ignore
"I hate homework."	Ignore
"More junk to do!"	Ignore
"What is the point of learning to do quadratic equations?"	Explain once, then ignore
(Student acts disgusted)	Ignore
"I hate this ——————!"	Implement consequence for swearing
"Are we going to have homework every night this week?"	Reinforce by answering

Don't feel that you have to list everything the student might say or do. This exercise is designed to help you explore the range of things the student might say or do, increasing the likelihood that you can respond consistently to the student.

Step 4: Discuss the problem with the student or students. In most cases, it is useful to inform students of your plan to ignore a problem. In some cases this will eliminate unnecessary testing. If you begin ignoring a misbehavior you have previously responded to, students may wonder whether something is wrong with you. Students will assume you haven't heard or are preoccupied. This means that they need to try harder to get your attention. A sample discussion follows.

Class, I am very concerned about the number of students who jump into class discussions without raising their hands. This makes it difficult for some students to get a chance to take part. I've also noticed that some of you have been interrupted, and our discussions have become chaotic. When I ask a question, I often hear several different answers at once. I've asked you to remember to raise your hands several times. Since I know that you are intelligent enough to remember that you need to raise your hand, you will no longer be acknowledged when you fail to raise your hand and wait to be called on. We will all benefit from following the rule about raising hands.

Step 5: If the misbehavior is chronic, expect it to get worse before it gets better. If a student has spent years getting attention through misbehavior, she is unlikely to abandon this strategy immediately. The student still needs attention, and it will take some time to teach her that it is easier to get your attention through appropriate behavior.

Be persistent. If the behavior does get worse before it gets better, you are on the right track. The student is telling you that she does misbehave to get your attention.

Step 6: When the student misbehaves, act as if he is not in the room. You cannot hear him and you cannot see him. Do not respond to the student's misbehavior with body language, the tone of your voice, or with eye contact or facial expressions. Avoid making references to the student in any way.

Step 7: While the student is engaged in unacceptable behavior, interact with students who are behaving acceptably. This emphasizes your interest in students who are working hard.

Most teachers have heard that they should praise a student who is working appropriately when someone misbehaves. Though the intent is the same as working to "interact" with students who behave appropriately, this type of praise can backfire. The student who is praised is set up as a "goody-goody." Students may begin misbehaving just to avoid being singled out. This does not imply that positive feedback has no place in the secondary school. It simply should not be used in response to another student's misbehavior. It doesn't take long for secondary students to recognize that the praise is really in response to the misbehaving student. Therefore, the misbehavior has not been ignored.

Step 8: When the misbehaving student behaves acceptably, interact with him. Demonstrate that you will ignore the student only when he acts immaturely. As soon as the student behaves as expected, he is a contributing member of your classroom.

As a general rule, try to interact positively with the student at least three times for every time you have to ignore him.

> Peter has a long history of difficulties with his teachers. He is frequently in an adversarial relationship with adults because he is continually making rude comments. Mr. Carney has talked with Peter about his problem and informed him that he will ignore comments he finds offensive, but that he will always be happy to see Peter at all other times.
>
> In the hall the next day, Mr. Carney stops to chat with Peter about Friday's basketball game. When Peter enters class, Mr. Carney makes it a point to nod hello to him. During Mr. Carney's class discussion, Peter joins in by saying "Real exciting stuff! It's enough to put an insomniac to sleep." Mr. Carney immediately turns to the map and shows students locations of Indonesian refugee camps and asks another student to name some of the countries people have fled from. A few minutes later Mr. Carney notices that Peter is paying attention to him describing the effects of malnutrition. Mr. Carney immediately looks at Peter and says, "Peter, what is one of the more tragic results of these wars?"
>
> While the students are working on independent work assignments, Mr. Carney sees that Peter is reading his text. As he moves through the room, Mr. Carney stops and checks to see how Peter is doing on his assignment. When students exchange papers, Mr. Carney sees that Peter is continuing to cooperate. Peter is asked to read the first question.

The goal of this procedure is to teach the student that you are truly interested in him. The attention given to the student when he is behaving well increases the power of ignoring.

Step 9: If other students give the student attention for inappropriate behavior, teach your class to ignore the inappropriate behavior. Peer attention is extremely important to secondary students and is often more powerful than anything a teacher does. If peer attention is reinforcing inappropriate behavior, you will need to teach your class to cooperate in your efforts.

The first way to achieve this is through modeling and gentle verbal reprimands. When the misbehavior begins, demonstrate the ignoring strategy by remaining calm and keeping your attention focused on students who are engaged in positive behavior. If students give the misbehaving student attention, ask them to focus their attention on their own work. You may use a comment similar to those below.

> I would appreciate it if you would focus on our discussion. I know that you are mature enough to let others figure out how to function as members of this class.

> It is important for all of us to mind our own business and give our attention only to things that have to do with this course.

If students continue giving attention to inappropriate behavior, implement a more structured approach. The easiest strategy is to have students lose points for participation and effort grades when they give attention to misbehavior. For more information on setting up participation and effort grades, see Chapter 2.

Step 10: Evaluate the effectiveness of the procedure. The problem should show improvement by the end of a week. If you are not seeing improvement, go through the following questions:

- Can the student experience success on academic tasks?
- Have you been effective at giving NO attention to the inappropriate behavior?
- Have you effectively removed the attention of other students from the misbehavior?
- Have you been effective at interacting positively with the student when behavior has been appropriate?

If the answer to any of these questions is "no," fine tune the procedures. If the answer to all these questions is "yes" set up a mild punishment for future incidents of misbehavior and set up a structured reinforcement system for appropriate behavior. Chapters 3 and 4 will help you motivate the student to meet positive expectations, and the following options will give you suggestions for setting up a mild consequence.

Option 2: Filling Out a Behavior Improvement Form

A mild but sometimes useful consequence involves having students who engage in a misbehavior fill out a form like the sample shown in Figure 8-1.

This form is useful when a misbehavior occurs that the teacher has not anticipated and when a gentle verbal reprimand is not sufficient given the severity of the misbehavior. The form requires the student to tell in writing what has happened. This allows her to tell her side of an incident without setting up the possibility of a verbal argument with the teacher or other students. The form requires the student to think of ways to handle a similar circumstance in the future. It also forces the student to evaluate the inappropriate behavior by determining whether there should be a consequence. Finally, the Behavior Improvement Form allows the teacher to respond immediately to inappro-

Figure 8–1   Behavior Improvement Form

Behavior Improvement Form

Name_____   Date_____

What were you doing that was inappropriate in the classroom?

What happened right before the incident?

Should there be a consequence for your actions?   yes   no

If yes, what consequence would be fair?

What could you do differently in the future to avoid this problem?

---

priate behavior without having to set up consequences on the spur of the moment. This consequence is especially useful for behaviors that have not actually been discussed as being unacceptable. Rather than immediately implementing a formal consequence, the form demonstrates to the student that even though the behavior is unacceptable, the teacher is willing to listen to the student's side of the story.

Step 1: Keep a supply of Behavior Improvement Forms readily available.

Step 2: Give each student involved in an appropriate behavior a Behavior Improvement Form to complete before the end of the period. Collect the forms at the end of the period. Tell students that you will look the forms over and discuss the problem with them the next day.

Step 3: Discuss the forms and inappropriate behavior with students. When you discuss the forms and inappropriate behavior with students, share any differences in how students perceived the situation. Many problems arise out of a misunderstanding. Focus on ways a similar problem could be handled more maturely.

If students have identified reasonable consequences, select one that you will implement if the inappropriate behavior occurs again. Students frequently suggest consequences that are far too severe. If this is the case, modify the consequence to fit the misbehavior. Tell students that the specified consequence will be implemented if the behavior occurs in the future.

End your discussion by emphasizing alternative behaviors students can choose from. Try to emphasize that you have a positive expectation for their behavior and that you expect them to be mature and responsible.

Step 4: Reinforce students for appropriate behavior. If students improve their behavior, or if you notice them handling similar situations in appropriate ways, let them know that you are aware of their increasing maturity.

Step 5: If the misbehavior occurs again, implement the consequence specified on the previously filled out form. It is a good idea to keep a file of any completed Behavior Improvement Forms for each class. This allows you to quickly look up what the consequence should be for a future offense.

Step 6: If the misbehavior is not eliminated by the simple use of the Behavior Improvement Form, implement a more structured reinforcement procedure to build appropriate behaviors.

Note: If a student does not fill out the Behavior Improvement Form, determine whether the student's academic abilities have made it difficult to complete the form. If the student is a low performer or lacks confidence in her writing ability, she may fail to complete the form because she doesn't know how. Meet with the student after class and help her complete the form. However, if the student has the academic skills to complete the form and fails to do so, require her to complete the form by the next class period. Let her know that she will have to stay after school until it is completed if it is not ready at the beginning of the next class period.

Option 3: Discussions

Discussing behavioral problems with students can sometimes help to reduce inappropriate behavior. Discussions can help students recognize that they have control over their actions and that in any given situation there are different ways they could choose to respond.

Step 1: Wait to conduct the discussion until a neutral time. Plan to discuss the problem when you and the student involved are calm. This generally requires a cooling-off period. You may choose to discuss inappropriate behavior the next day. If you discuss the problem immediately after the misbehavior, some students may be reinforced for misbehaving because of the attention they receive and by the fact that they can get you to stop teaching and have a discussion. Delaying the discussion reduces the likelihood of this problem.

Step 2: Discuss the problem with those involved. If the problem is with one to three students, arrange to have your discussion only with those involved in the problem. However, if the problem occurs with several students, hold your discussion with the entire class. Even though the majority of the class is not involved, the problem becomes a class problem if several students are involved.

Step 3: Identify the problem. Begin the discussion by explaining to students how you perceive the problem. Give the students an opportunity to explain the problem as they see it. Do not allow the discussion to degenerate into a session of accusations and denials. Establish the basic events that led to the problem and what happened.

Step 4: Explore behavioral alternatives to similar situations. Help students explore other ways of dealing with a similar situation. Students frequently know only one way of responding to a situation. For example, when a student is called a name, he may think his only alternative is to fight with that person. The student may not realize that he has the option of turning away from someone who calls him a name.

Step 5: Assist the student in recognizing that he has the power to choose how he wishes to respond. Help the student understand that he can act in his own best interests. No one else has the power to make him behave in a way that he chooses not to.

Note: the suggested structure for these discussions is taken from work on Rational Behavior Therapy (RBT) formulated by M. C. Maultsby and his associates. For further reading on RBT, see the references.[1]

Option 4: Parental Contact

If parents are supportive and interested, parental contacts can be a useful strategy for eliminating inappropriate behavior in the classroom. Even if the parents are not supportive, the parental contacts may still be necessary as a matter of form, but do not expect the parents to have any positive impact on the student's behavior.

Step 1: Inform the student that you will contact his parents if he continues to engage in the misbehavior. Conduct this discussion at a neutral time, and let the student know that if a similar incident happens again you will inform his parents of the problem. End the discussion by communicating a positive expectation for his future performance.

Step 2: Ignore defiant responses. When hearing that parents will be contacted if misbehavior continues, students frequently respond with, "So what!" Plan to ignore this type of response. Student's verbal statements are frequently not a reliable indication of how they actually feel. The student may actually be quite concerned about the parental contact and may simply be trying to cover up her concern acting as if she does not care.

Step 3: If the misbehavior does not happen again, let the student know that you are pleased with his performance and that you would like to inform his parents of his appropriate behavior in class. Let the student know that you are pleased with his improvement, and if the student continues to behave well, tell him that you are going to write a note to his parents letting them know how much you enjoy having him in class. This note will serve several purposes. A note of praise to the home provides an opportunity for the student and parents to have a positive interaction because of appropriate behavior at school. It demonstrates to the student that you are aware of his efforts to cooperate. Finally, the note demonstrates that you feel the student is important enough to keep his parents informed. A sample note is provided here:

Dear _____ ,   (parents)

Your son, Joe, is in my sixth-period English class. Over the first few weeks of school, I have seen him demonstrate an increased sense of maturity and growth. I thought you might want to share in our pride over his accomplishments.

I am really enjoying working with your son and look forward to seeing his continued growth.

Sincerely,

If the student says that he does not want you to contact his parents regarding his cooperation, respect his wishes. Let the student know that you would like to let his parents know how well he is doing, but that you will do as he chooses.

---

[1]Maultsby, M. C., *Handbook for rational self-counseling.* Lexington, Kentucky: University of Kentucky Medical Center, 1971.

Maultsby, M. C., and A. Ellis, *Techniques for using rational-emotive imagery (REI).* New York: Institute for Rational Living, 1974.

Maultsby, M. C., P. Knipping, and L. Carpenter, "Teaching self-help in the classroom with rational self-counseling" *Journal of School Health,* 1974, 44, 445–448.

Step 4: If the student continues to misbehave after your initial discussions, contact the student's parents to inform them of their child's failure to cooperate. Call the parents and maintain a matter-of-fact tone. Explain the problem, and let the parents know that you have informed the student that they would be contacted. Tell the parents that you feel the problem may be eliminated if they will communicate their support of your policies to the student. Request that the parents speak with their child, but ask that they avoid setting up any punishments for the behavior. If the parents try to punish the student, more misbehavior will sometimes occur as the student seeks to get additional attention from his parents by misbehaving at school.

If the parents seem to be interested and supportive, let them know that you will be back in touch with them in the next several days. If behavior improves, thank the parents for their support. If there is no improvement, contact the parents again and try to work together on a future plan of action for the problem.

Step 5: If parental contacts do not result in improved behavior, set up a home-based reinforcement system. If the behavior does not improve with simple home contacts, ask the parents if they would like to arrange for a conference to set up a behavior improvement plan. If they are interested, see Chapter 6 for details on setting up a home-based reinforcement system.

Step 6: If working with parents fails, or if parents do not seem receptive, set up alternative procedures. If at any point the parents become uncooperative or seem to resent your contacts, back off. It is very difficult to change the attitudes of parents who are not interested in working with teachers. You will need to establish a different consequence for inappropriate behavior.

Option 5: Isolation within the Classroom

When students seem unable to control their behavior, isolation within the classroom can frequently be an effective consequence. Behavior problems that are related to lack of control include angry outbursts, chronic swearing, chronic talking, and chronic crying.

Step 1: Set up a place to isolate a student within the classroom. Isolation within the classroom requires enough space in the classroom to have a chair and desk that are somewhat separated from other students. A few feet of separation is sufficient; however, the space needs to be kept clear of all other activities. When isolation is necessary, it will be important to use this space without shifting furniture and material.

Step 2: Specify any behavior that will result in classroom isolation. Students must understand what behaviors are unacceptable and why they will be isolated from the rest of the class when they choose to engage in those behaviors.

Step 3: Determine a length of time the student will stay in isolation once she is in control. The amount of time the student should stay in the isolation area should be consistent. It should not vary according to the severity of the misbehavior. The amount of time can be as short as five minutes or as long as the remainder of the class period.

The amount of time established does not begin until the student is in the isolation area and quiet and under control. When the student is in the isolation area and under control, inform her that she will be allowed to join the class in X number of minutes.

Step 4: Establish procedures to follow if the student refuses to go to the isolation area. One procedure is to let the student know you will keep track of the amount of time that passes before he gets to the isolation area. This time will be owed after school or during a lunch period. A second procedure is to let the student know that if he refuses to go to the isolation area, he will be defying a specific instruction. This will result in referral to the office. See "Owing Time" (Option 6) in this chapter and Chapter 9, *School-Wide Discipline Policies.*

Step 5: Discuss the procedures with the student prior to implementation. Once you have set up your procedures, privately discuss the behavior problem and the procedures you will follow with the student. Your discussion should take place at a neutral time. Make certain the student understands exactly what behaviors are unacceptable. Tell her where you will ask her to go, how she will need to behave once in isolation, how long she will stay, and what will happen if she refuses to go. Keep the tone of the discussion businesslike and nonaccusatory. If possible, imply a positive expectation. End the discussion by presenting things the student can do to be successful in your class.

Step 6: Reinforce the student for appropriate behavior. If the student begins to behave more maturely for longer periods of time, privately let him know that you recognize his efforts. If misbehavior is a severe problem, you may need to set up a more structured reinforcement system. (See Chapter 6.)

Step 7: Evaluate the effectiveness of your consequences and reinforcement procedures. If the misbehavior does not decrease significantly within two weeks, you will need to explore other options. Consider implementing one of the other consequences discussed in this chapter or in Chapter 9, and examine the effectiveness of your interactions with the student, your grading system, and your structured reinforcement systems.

Option 6: Owing Time

Many misbehaviors are a waste of classroom time; therefore, owing time is a consequence that tells students they must pay back any time they've wasted. If a student wastes class time, he will need to pay back time from a time he values. This may be during a lunch period, a break, before school, or after school.

Step 1: Define the misbehavior and identify borderlines between acceptable and unacceptable behavior. Specify exactly what the misbehavior is and when you will implement the consequence of owing time. You must be specific enough to eliminate the need for students to test to see if you will be consistent.

Step 2: Determine the amount of time that will be owed for the misbehavior. If the misbehavior occurs frequently but lasts for only a short period of time, the student should owe a set period of time for each infraction. For example, if the student has problems with swearing or name calling, he should owe a predetermined period of time for each incidence of swearing or name calling, usually something like five minutes.

If the misbehavior lasts for a period of time, the student should owe the actual amount of class time wasted. For example, if the student refuses to follow directions, the student should owe the actual amount of time that passes until she follows the instruction. If the student has problems being out of her seat inappropriately, the student should owe the amount of time she spends out of her seat.

Step 3: Determine when students will pay back time. Students may be able to pay back time after school. However, this alternative is sometimes difficult to enforce as it may create problems with buses and after-school activities. If staying after school is a problem, it may be important to set up a school-wide policy for keeping students after school. This procedure is discussed in Chapter 9.

Having students come in before school is sometimes easier to arrange; however, it may involve contacting parents to make sure the student arrives early enough. Again, bus schedules may make this option difficult to enforce.

Another option is having the student owe time from his lunch period. You cannot deprive the student of his lunch, but you can take some of the social time from his lunch period. In some cases, owing just a minute or two of time can be very effective because the student will end up at the end of the lunch line.

Finally, it may be possible for the student to owe time right after your class. This again will require a school-wide policy. Owing time after your class may result in the student being tardy for another class. This will be effective only if there is a stringent consequence for tardiness. In using this procedure, it is important to inform students that they will not be given a pass into their next class. If they are tardy due to owing time, they must face the consequences for being tardy.

Step 4: Have the student do nothing during time that is owed. Requiring the student to do nothing during owed time is actually more aversive than having the student do academic work. If the student is given work, the time goes very quickly. Doing nothing demonstrates that time is valuable.

Step 5: Establish procedures for students who fail to pay owed time. It will be important to let students know they must pay their time. Let students know that their time will be doubled if they fail to show up. If a student fails to put in owed time a second time, refer the student to the office for further disciplinary action.

Step 6: Discuss the misbehavior and owing time with students. If the problem is with an individual student or a few students, have a private discussion. If the problem involves several students in your class, carry on a class discussion. Clearly specify what behavior will lead to owed time. When it is appropriate, identify the borderline between acceptable and unacceptable behavior. Explain the consequence of owed time and how you will record the amount of time they might owe if they choose to engage in the behavior in the future. Make sure students understand. This should eliminate any reason to explain, rationalize, or justify your actions when you tell a student that he owes time.

Step 7: Provide students with reinforcement for improved behavior. If the misbehavior ceases or happens less frequently, let students know that you are impressed with their efforts. If the problem is severe, you may need to include a more structured reinforcer as discussed in Chapter 6.

Step 8: Implement the consequence calmly. Any time the specified misbehavior occurs, implement your plan consistently and without emotion. You will need to demonstrate that the student cannot upset you by her actions. She simply must pay the consequences.

Step 9: Evaluate the effectiveness of owing time. If the misbehavior does not cease or decrease, seek an alternative discussed in this chapter or in Chapter 9. Also examine the effectiveness of your interactions, grading systems, and other reinforcement systems.

Option 7: Loss of Points

Taking points away from students frequently results in more damage than good. The major risk is in destroying the motivation of a student who is barely making it. If the student is working hard to maintain a *C,* a loss of points may make him feel as if his efforts are not worth the trouble. If a student loses points for tardiness one day, he may decide that it isn't worth working that day; he has already lost the points he might have earned. Because the student fails to work that day, he may lose not only points but fail to learn important concepts. The next day the student may have difficulty with a lesson because he has missed out on information that was needed to understand the new lesson. Or, the student might do poorly because he missed out on needed skill practice. In any event, it will be very easy for the student to go into a downhill slide. Once the student realizes he has no hope of catching up, the student is lost. What may begin as an attempt to teach students appropriate classroom behavior may result in turning off students.

Taking points away from students for poor behavior may not only have a negative academic impact on some students, but it may also be ineffective with students who have the greatest behavior problems. The threat of losing points will be most effective with students who are motivated to earn good grades. Unfortunately, students with the poorest classroom behavior usually care the least about grades. They are already doing poorly so a loss of points is meaningless. If your students follow this general pattern, do not consider using a loss of points as a consequence.

Note: If your students do not seem to be sufficiently motivated by grades, study Chapter 2, *Effective Grading Systems*. This chapter will help you establish a more motivating grading system. The grading system does suggest that a portion of the grade be based upon student behavior. However, instead of losing hard-earned academic points due to misbehavior, students earn points for engaging in appropriate classroom behavior.

Option 8: Assigning Extra Work

Assigning additional work for misbehavior is one of the weaker consequences for poor behavior. It will generally work only if the misbehaving students are highly motivated. However, if poorly motivated students are required to do more work for a misbehavior, you may end up primarily reinforcing the attitude that school work is punishing. If this attitude continues, you may end up with a student who will not even do her regular work.

If the student is not currently turning her work in anyway, adding more work can also compound the student's academic difficulties. The additional work may result in destroying any motivation the student may have had. Her thinking will be, "Additional work will certainly make it impossible to catch up, so why try?" In most classrooms, this is a consequence to avoid.

Option 9: Sending Students Out into the Hall

This traditional consequence is actually far less effective than many of the other consequences discussed. Owing time and isolation within the classroom will be far more effective in discouraging inappropriate behavior in the classroom. The biggest difficulty with sending students into the hall is that they are left unsupervised. The student is therefore free to do as he wishes. This is actually a risky consequence. You must trust the student to do as he was told. What happens if the student leaves the grounds? What happens if the student bothers another class? What happens if the student becomes injured while unsupervised? Because these questions are difficult to answer, it may be best to avoid sending students into the hall.

In addition to the risk involved, sending students into the hall is frequently ineffective because the hall can be fun for the student who misbehaves. The student is free to interact with anyone who happens to be around. She is on exhibit as a troublemaker, and this may be a positive image for the student. Being sent to the hall may actually reinforce some students for inappropriate behavior. This means that they will misbehave in the future so they can be sent out again.

Option 10: Sending Students to the Office

Sending students to the office will be a necessary consequence for severe misbehavior. However, for minor misbehavior, it is essential for the classroom teacher to handle consequences. When a student is sent to the office for a minor offense, the student's perception may be, "The teacher doesn't know what to do with me, so he is sending me to the office."

Sending students to the office is a consequence that must be reserved for major offenses because teachers who send large numbers of students to the office may not be taken seriously by office personnel. It will be difficult for the office to take problems seriously if they are asked to deal with your problems on a regular basis. However, if you rarely send a student to the office, it will be obvious that the student has a severe problem.

Use of the office for severe discipline problems must involve a school-wide discipline policy. Procedures for setting up a consistent policy for the entire school are discussed in the next chapter.

Option 11: Corporal Punishment

Corporal punishment has severe drawbacks as a consequence for misbehavior. The potential for legal complications outweighs any effectiveness that might be gained by a classroom teacher. While it may seem that educators are being denied use of their most effective consequence to misbehavior, corporal punishment in itself has many disadvantages.

First of all, corporal punishment is rarely punishing to those students who have the most inappropriate behavior. To many secondary students, a mild form of corporal punishment is more of a joke than a punishment. In order for corporal punishment to be effective to some secondary students, it would have to be so severe that the risk of injury would be very real. Implementing this type of punishment can rarely be done without emotion. Applying corporal punishment can frequently be more punishing to the person who is implementing the consequence than it is to the student who has misbehaved.

Where corporal punishment is used, you will also find that a paddling may have become a status symbol to some groups of students. This occurs particularly when paddling has become an everyday occurrence. Once a school begins using corporal punishment, it is easy to fall into the trap of using corporal punishment for minor as well as major offenses. As corporal punishment is used more and more, there may develop an adversarial relationship between adults and students. In this atmosphere, it is difficult to encourage students to grow and mature.

The final compelling drawback to the use of corporal punishment is that it provides students with a model of aggression. The school demonstrates to students that you use physical violence whenever you want someone to behave differently. This implies that the person with the most power is the person who is right. Schools must provide a model that teaches students to work disagreements out intelligently rather than physically. When students behave inappropriately, it will be necessary to teach them to be self-disciplined and motivated by always dealing with any behavior fairly, calmly, and objectively.

Chapter 9

SCHOOL-WIDE DISCIPLINE POLICIES

Every secondary school should have a comprehensive discipline policy. Without a school-wide discipline policy, it is difficult for students to know what is expected, and it is difficult for teachers to know how to handle problems. While effective discipline occurs within each classroom, an effective school-wide discipline policy provides the entire school with common expectations for student behavior and consistent guidelines for dealing with misbehavior.

The basic structure of the secondary school dictates the need for a comprehensive school-wide plan. In the elementary grades, students learned that they were accountable to one person—their classroom teacher—for five to six hours each day. When students reach the secondary school, there is no single adult in charge. Five to seven teachers work with each student, and students are accountable to no specific adult during breaks, between classes, and before and after school. Limited contact with each adult results in a limited amount of adult influence. A school-wide discipline plan can help overcome some of the inevitable problems associated with the organization of secondary schools. A comprehensive plan will help students learn that the staff shares basic expectations for student behavior whether they are in the classroom, halls, cafeteria, or restrooms.

Since this book is geared to the classroom teacher, it isn't possible to go into full detail on how to set up school-wide discipline policies. However, the remainder of this chapter will study the features of an effective policy and examine school-wide consequences for misbehavior. If your school is interested in designing or revising building policies, this chapter can serve as a starting place. However, administrators and teachers need to work closely together to establish policies and procedures that will work for your school.

RECOMMENDATIONS FOR DEVELOPING AN EFFECTIVE SCHOOL-WIDE DISCIPLINE POLICY

Step 1. Include an overall statement of positive expectations for student behavior.

A school-wide discipline plan typically identifies what will happen in the event of misbehavior. While the disicpline plan must inform students of consequences for misbehavior, this alone sets up a negative expectation for student conduct. An overall statement of positive expectations will tell students that they are expected to work cooperatively toward academic excellence. Here is an example of a positive statement:

> Your parents, our community, and the school district have worked together to provide you with a staff, building, and equipment to help prepare you for a future of success. We are committed to giving you the best education we can and know you will take special pride in keeping our school "First Class."
>
> Through the year you be will expected to assume the responsibilities listed below.
> 1. Attend class regularly.
> 2. Be in your assigned seat with all necessary materials when the final bell rings.
> 3. Give every assignment your best effort.
> 4. Treat every student and teacher with respect.
> 5. Follow the specific rules in each class.
> 6. Help maintain the building and all school equipment and materials.

Step 2. Require each teacher to establish a set of relevant classroom rules.

Rules must vary from classroom to classroom as the subject area, course organization, and varying teaching styles dictate different needs. Students will have no difficulty working within a variety of rules as long as teachers have outlined clear expectations for behavior.

Step 3. Establish a set of consequences that can be used by teachers within the classroom.

The discipline policy must emphasize that the majority of inappropriate behavior will be handled in the classroom. Teachers should document their attempts to resolve minor misbehavior within the classroom prior to any referral to the office. Classroom consequences for misbehavior might include parental contacts, use of Behavior Improvement Forms, isolation within the classroom, time owed, and the effective use of a grading system. These consequences are covered in detail in Chapter 8. Each teacher should decide which consequences would be most appropriate for her class structure.

Step 4. Make a list of unacceptable student behaviors and determine which behaviors should be referred to the administration.

A small set of severe misbehaviors cannot be handled in the classroom. This includes behaviors that completely disrupt the learning environment, possibly threaten the well being of the teacher or other students, demonstrate direct defiance, or break the law. Another set of misbehaviors must be handled by the office because they occur in the halls, buses, and other settings not directly supervised by classroom teachers.

Misbehaviors should be discussed with the staff, and members should jointly determine what constitutes a misbehavior and who will deal with the misbehavior. For example, it will be important for staff members to agree on how to handle "making out" in the halls; first the faculty will need to define it by identifying touching that is acceptable and touching that is not acceptable. Next, there must be agreement as to how the problem will be handled.

A partial list of misbehaviors is shown here, identifying the kinds of behaviors that might best be handled through the office and the kinds of behaviors that should be dealt with in the classroom.

Use of drugs—referral

Fighting—referral

Throwing furniture—referral

Refusal to comply with a direct teacher command—referral

Talking back in class—classroom consequence

Possession of a dangerous weapon—referral

Student loud and disruptive in class—classroom consequence

Verbal argument between students in class—classroom consequence

Truancy—referral

Tardiness—referral

Swearing in class—classroom consequence

Step 5. Develop an office referral form.

When a teacher needs to refer a student to the office for misbehavior, there should be a standard form that she is required to fill out and send with the student. The form should require the teacher to specify what the problem was and what she has previously done to solve the problem. A form of this type has two distinct advantages. First, it requires the teacher to state her perspective of the incident. This provides important information to the administrator who must deal with the referral. It can help the administrator find out if the teacher's view of what happened is significantly different from the student's view. A second advantage of the form is that it requires that the teacher will have tried some alternative strategies prior to the time she refers the student to the office. This will help reduce the number of referrals for minor misbehavior.

Figure 9–1 is a sample referral form.

Figure 9–1   Office Referral Form

OFFICE REFERRAL FORM

Student name _____

Date of referral _____

Class period _____

Teacher _____

Reason for referral: _____

_____

_____

Description of measures taken to resolve the problem prior to referral: _____

_____

_____

_____

Parents contacted? _____ Date of contact: _____

Comments: _____

_____

Step 6. Establish consequences to be used for referrals.

The next section of this chapter identifies possible consequences for misbehaviors that have been referred to the office. From the list of misbehaviors, identify reasonable consequences. These will be written into the discipline policy.

Step 7. Specify what actions will be taken in the event a student breaks a law.

A portion of the policy should be worked out in conjunction with local officials. Ask the police, juvenile authorities, and perhaps a local judge for recommendations on when the school should involve authorities for such offenses as vandalism, use of alcohol or other controlled substances, truancy, possession of weapons, and physical violence. The policy should state at what point behaviors in school will be turned over to civil authorities.

Step 8. Establish procedures for implementing consequences when referrals have been made.

The most important feature of the plan will be the immediate processing of behavioral referrals and a consistent implementation of consequences. Many schools have a fine policy in writing, but get ineffective results because referred students end up sitting in the front office for long periods of time waiting for the assistant principal. While students wait in the office they are often reinforced for their misbehavior. They have gotten out of class. They may get to interact with people passing through the office, and they may enjoy being on display as troublemakers.

Step 9. Establish record-keeping procedures.

An effective school-wide discipline plan must include systematic record keeping. Adequate records allow staff members to determine whether the current discipline policies are working for individual students, teachers, and for the student body as a whole. Without adequate records, discipline decisions are a matter of personal opinion and uninformed guesswork.

There are many different record-keeping models that can be implemented. Since it is beyond the scope of this book to explore school-wide discipline plans in detail, the following list of questions will assist you in developing a record system that provides needed information. The questions should be answered by the record-keeping system. Two sample forms (Figures 9–2 and 9–3) follow, showing examples of ways a secondary-school administrator might keep records on individual students and teacher referrals.

1. How many referrals were made by an individual teacher?
2. What grade level had the most referrals?
3. What period of the day had the most referrals?
4. What percentage of referrals was for problems outside the classroom?
5. What category of misbehavior led to the most referrals? (for example, fighting, class disruptions, vandalism)
6. How many students had more than five referrals? How many students had more than two referrals?
7. Given an individual student who had several referrals:
   a. What consequences were implemented?
   b. Who referred the student?
   c. What procedures were implemented to get the student more motivated?
   d. What was done to get parents involved?

Figure 9–2   Student Referral Record

STUDENT REFERRAL RECORD

Student: _____   Date of referral: _____

Teacher who made referral: _____

Reason for referral: _____

_____

Student's explanation of what happened: _____

_____

Action taken: _____

_____

Parents contacted? _____   Date of contact: _____

Action to be taken if problem occurs again? _____

_____

Is this the first referral for this problem? _____

If not, how many other referrals have there been? _____

Total number of office referrals for this student: _____

For repeated referrals, check the following:

Academic placement _____

Ratio of interactions between teacher and student _____

_____

Grading systems in the classes where problems occur _____

_____

Need for an individualized reinforcement system _____

_____

Need for counseling or other professional help _____

Figure 9–3   Record of Teacher Referrals

RECORD OF TEACHER REFERRALS				
Teacher who made referral	Name of student referred	Class period	Date	Type of offense

Step 10. Write up the school discipline plan.

Include the description of positive expectations. Identify any misbehaviors that will lead to immediate referral and outline the consequences that have been predetermined.

Step 11. Discuss the school discipline plan with all students.

The discipline plan should be distributed to and discussed with all students. This can be handled during homeroom or during all first-period classes. The plan should be presented to students on the first day of school or sometime prior to the time the plan is implemented.

Step 12. Design procedures for follow-up on repeated referrals on individual students, by individual teachers, and on specific problem areas.

Information gained from the record-keeping system should help a school administrator identify students who need an additional support system. Any individual student who has had four or more office referrals is obviously having trouble adjusting to the rules and expectations of the school. Chapter 6 explores systems for salvaging a student in this sort of trouble.

If an individual teacher has referred large numbers of students for problems in the classroom, this teacher may need help with classroom management and discipline. Have that teacher read Chapters 1, 2, 3, and 8. These chapters may be useful as resources for improving student-teacher interactions, clarifying rules, designing a more effective grading system, and providing effective consequences for misbehavior within the classroom.

If many of the office referrals seem to arise in a particular place such as the cafeteria or halls, the staff can work to design monitoring and discipline procedures for those specific areas. In Section IV, Problem 41, "Misbehaving in Hallways and Other School-Wide Areas," can be used as a resource if problems seem to be concentrated outside the classroom.

CONSEQUENCES FOR OFFICE REFERRALS

This section discusses school-wide consequences for student referrals. An effective school-wide plan may incorporate a combination of these options laid out in a series of consequences.

In designing school-wide consequences, keep in mind the recommendations listed earlier. Whether using discussions with the discipline officer, suspension, in-school suspension, after-school detention, or Saturday school, referrals should be made only when the misbehavior cannot be handled within the classroom, or if the misbehavior is severe enough to warrant an immediate referral. Severe misbehaviors should be specifically identified as part of the school policy, and there should be no question as to whether a behavior should be referred or not. All referrals should be accompanied by completed referral forms and parent contacts. This will help safeguard the procedures and ensure that the referral system is not abused or overused.

Suspension

Suspension from school is one of the most commonly used consequences for students who have been referred to the office. At one time, it was a reasonable discipline tool. No one expected schools to succeed with all students. Therefore, if a student was suspended several times and eventually dropped out, it was not perceived as a problem.

Schools could also count on many parents to ensure that time at home was not enjoyable for a student who had been suspended.

Times have obviously changed. The schools are now expected to educate everyone. With highly skilled teachers and adequate instructional methods, there is no reason why most students' can't be successful within the system. Though this change is certainly for the better, unfortunately, other changes have not been for the better. When students are suspended, schools cannot assume that their action will be supported by parents. Many parents have developed an adversarial relationship with the schools, and suspension only heightens the problem. Other parents lack the time, skill, and sometimes the concern to make sure that suspension is anything more than a vacation from school.

Schools cannot assume that suspensions will be aversive. A consequence that is intended as a punishment may turn into a reward. Students who are suspended rarely like school in the first place. When the student is suspended, she may get to sleep in, watch TV, and socialize with friends who have dropped out of school. This is hardly a punishment.

Another limitation of suspension is that it tends to label the student as a trouble-maker. If the student feels comfortable with this label, suspension can reinforce the student for being so "tough" that the school can't handle him. Suspension can actually lend a kind of dignity to inappropriate behavior.

There may be times when suspension is absolutely necessary; however, this should only be after the school has tried several alternative consequences to misbehavior. It is the responsibility of the school staff to do everything possible prior to suspension to teach students the behaviors they need to succeed in school. Everyone must recognize that to a degree suspension tells the student, "We don't know what to do with you so we are going to kick you out of school in the hopes that you will figure out how to behave on your own."

Suspension must be the last resort when everything else has failed. In determining consequences for misbehavior, out-of-school suspension should be listed only as the final consequence in a series of predetermined consequences.

Discussions

It is common practice for students to discuss misbehavior with an administrator, counselor, or teacher in charge of discipline. This is a reasonable procedure; however, without proper implementation it can result in students enjoying the time spent in the office and the opportunity to have a one-to-one discussion with one of the "head honchos."

Implement procedures that will guard against the possibility of students sitting in the office waiting to see the person in charge of discipline. This can be handled by making sure that someone is always "on call" to handle discipline problems. If this is not possible, there should be a nonstimulating holding area where the student must wait until her problem can be dealt with. The student should not be visible to others. She should have no one to talk with and she should not be able to watch others.

Use discussions only for a first minor offense. If a discussion is going to teach the student to change his behavior, it will work the first time. Discussions should include identifying the problem, exploring alternative ways for the student to handle a similar problem in the future, and assisting the student in recognizing that he has the ability to choose his responses. The student must understand that some responses will serve him better than others. References for this type of discussion are listed in Chapter 8.

Use discussions to determine whether the student's misbehavior is in part caused by an inability to handle work in the classroom. Many students will misbehave to avoid looking like a "dummy." If the administrator suspects that misbehavior is an outgrowth of frustration with academic tasks, a preventative measure to future misbehavior would include a recommendation for academic testing and a staff meeting to ensure that the student has an opportunity to succeed when effort is given.

In-school Suspension

In-school suspension (ISS) programs have proven to be an effective alternative to out-of-school suspension. An ISS program removes students from the classroom, but keeps students within the school during the period of suspension. This reduces the possibility that suspension turns into a student holiday, and it demonstrates to students and parents that the school will deal with misbehavior. Whether these programs are called in-house suspension, in-school detention, or simply detention, they are generally met with parental support. Students are not turned out into the street, and ineffective parents are not left wondering how they should be able to handle discipline when the schools can't.

Designate a location for ISS. Severe problems may warrant complete isolation from other students. This presents problems in many buildings, as it requires the construction of small booths or rooms. Each isolation area needs to be approximately eight feet square with walls built from the floor to the ceiling. Two or three units can be built at the back of an unused classroom, an oversized health room, counselor's office, or attendance office.

If it isn't possible to provide a completely isolated setting it may be necessary to designate one classroom for detention. This room would need to be free throughout the day. If ISS students must move to different rooms throughout the day, their detention is more stimulating. Passing times provide a break in the monotony of in-school suspension. This significantly weakens the procedure.

Identify how long students will spend in in-school suspension and how the time will be spent. The standard term of in-school suspension is three school days. This period of time was chosen because shorter time periods may not be aversive to students. During these suspensions, students must complete school work provided by the classroom teachers. This particular term of suspension has inherent problems.

1. Though the student may have difficulties in only one class, she will be removed from all classes for three days. This means that all teachers will be required to design independent assignments for the student. Teachers who handle behavior problems within the classroom may end up being required to do extra work when a few teachers make frequent referrals.

2. Monitoring academic work also becomes a problem. Who determines whether assignments have been completed satisfactorily? What happens if the students fails to complete work during the three days in ISS? What happens if the student lacks the academic ability to do the work independently?

An alternative ISS program puts students on a graduated schedule of consequences.

First referral—Fifteen minutes in ISS with the student doing nothing

Second referral—One hour in ISS with the student doing nothing

Third referral from the same class—Three days in ISS during the class period where problems occurred with class assignments optional from the teacher who has referred the student

Fourth referral—Three full days in ISS with assignments from all classes

Though the consequence for the first and second referral seems mild because of the short time periods involved, the majority of misbehaving students find this time aversive because they are not allowed to do anything. The time becomes boring. The mild consequence on the first and second referrals also serves as a buffer zone against the possibility that a particular teacher was having a difficult day and overreacted to a possible misunderstanding.

The graduated schedule of consequences also provides extra steps prior to the time the school must consider out-of-school suspension. In the first system, out-of-school suspension is usually recommended on the third offense. In the graduated system, there will generally be five or more referrals prior to the time out-of-school suspension is considered. During the intervening time, staff should have additional opportunities to salvage the student. This system can also specify that certain severe problems such as use of drugs results immediately in three days of in-school suspension.

Finally, in cases of relatively minor misbehavior, the graduated system forces the student and teacher to deal with each other in a short period of time. Students do not miss out on large amounts of class time. In the graduated system, students would miss only one hour and fifteen minutes of class with two referrals versus a loss of six full days with the three-day suspension pattern. The graduated ISS provides a consequence to inappropriate behavior, but gets the student back into the classroom. This reduces the likelihood that teachers inadvertently use ISS as a dumping ground.

The major disadvantage of this plan is that it almost necessitates the use of complete isolation. If students are only partially isolated, fifteen minutes of doing nothing becomes fifteen minutes of watching other students. The procedure is weakened because the time passes much more quickly. The procedure is effective only if the time is very boring.

Set up guidelines for behavior and handling misbehavior in ISS. Students, teachers, and parents must understand that ISS is the best alternative to out-of-school suspension. Any abuse of the procedure forces the school to resort to out-of-school suspension. This should be clear to the student and the student's parents whenever a student is assigned to ISS.

Rules must be clearly specified and communicated to the student. A sample set of rules is shown here.

1. Remain quiet.
2. Stay seated.
3. Use of restrooms will be allowed only during times listed on the board. If you need to use the restroom, quietly raise your hand.
4. If you have been assigned work, you may ask the supervisor for assistance two times each hour.

Determine who will supervise ISS and provide specific training and guidelines to follow. Classified personnel are frequently assigned to supervise ISS while they complete other clerical tasks. If noncertified personnel are assigned this duty, be sure to follow all the legal requirements of your district for supervision of students.

ISS may be supervised by a different staff member each class period. If this is the case, everyone involved should receive training in the specific procedures to follow. Supervisors should understand that their role is to be neutral. Misbehavior has resulted in the loss of privileges, one of which is interacting with others. The list of the following guidelines and the information in Chapters 7 and 8 may be used as resources for training supervisors of ISS.

1. Do not try to counsel ISS-assigned students.
2. Interact as little as possible with students.
3. When a student checks into ISS, tell the student the rules. Ask the student if he has questions. Assign a seat.
4. If the student talks or makes noises, let the student know that time owed in ISS has not started until the student is quiet. The student should know that he can be released from ISS only when he has sat quietly for the assigned time.
5. If the student becomes violent or defies a direct instruction, contact the front office. This will be dealt with by the principal or vice-principal.
6. If there is more than one student in the room, do not allow interactions. Place desks so that students cannot look at each other. If students turn to face each other, inform them that their time in ISS has to start over again.

Design the structure of your ISS program to fit the needs and situation of your school. Also, be prepared to make revisions and adaptations in the program as you notice weaknesses in the system. The best criterion for evaluating an ISS program is the percentage of repeated referrals. As long as there are relatively few "repeaters," the program is probably a good one.

After-school detention

One of the most common consequences to inappropriate behavior has been keeping students after school. However, due to the number of students now riding buses, this consequence is now more difficult to implement effectively.

Determine how often after-school detention will be available as a consequence to misbehavior and who will supervise. The easiest, but least effective, after-school detention (ASD) plan provides an after-school consequence to misbehavior once a week. Students who have received detentions any time during the preceding five days owe time in detention. One or two teachers supervise the detention room on a rotating basis. Any teacher may assign a student to detention by informing the student, contacting parents, and informing the office. While this system may be easy to use, the results are typically weak due to the following reasons:

• There may be a long delay between the misbehavior and consequence. Since the delay may be as much as seven days, immature students frequently look at an after-school detention with the attitude, "Who cares what happens next Thursday?"

• If large numbers of students end up reporting to ASD each week, it is impossible to eliminate all socialization. ASD can become a big social hour where all the problem students congregate each week.

• The consequence can be implemented only once a week. If a student misbehaves in one class, she may as well goof off in other classes. She already owes time in detention and further misbehavior will not change the consequence. The once-a-week consequence will not be effective for students with habitual misbehavior because they usually misbehave too often for the consequence to make an impact on their behavior.

A second ASD plan involves running an after-school detention room every day. Teachers would rotate duty for one week at a time. This allows for a more immediate implementation of consequences and more frequent use of the consequence when necessary. The major drawback in this procedure is transportation problems. This can be resolved by having the student report to detention the day after the student has been referred. The one-day delay weakens the procedure slightly, but it allows the parents to be notified that alternative transportation may need to be arranged. If this type of plan is incorporated, parents will need to provide phone numbers where they can be reached or where messages can be left. A sample parent letter is shown here.

Dear Parents,

In our continuing effort to provide an enriching learning atmosphere, the staff of _____ is implementing a new discipline procedure. We will be keeping students after school for any of the following infractions:

Wasting class time
Being disruptive or disrespectful in class
Not completing homework
Repeated tardiness
Truancy
Misbehavior in the cafeteria, halls, or on the bus

Each of these problems interferes with the process of learning. If a student exhibits any of these behaviors, a teacher may keep the student after school. We recognize that this may cause transportation problems; therefore, we will notify you one day in advance of the detention. If a problem occurs on Tuesday, we will notify you that the student will stay after school on Wednesday.

If your child has to stay after school, the teacher will try to reach you between 3:00 and 3:30 P.M. This will give you twenty-four hours to arrange transportation. Please return this form with three telephone numbers where the teacher can reach you or get a message to you.

These procedures have been discussed with all students. However, please go over them with your son or daughter. We appreciate your support in this matter.

Sincerely,
The Staff of _____

Phone number where I can usually be reached between 3:00 and 3:30 P.M. _____
Additional Message Numbers _____ _____

Parents' Signature _____

After-school detention may follow one of the patterns described above, or students may be required to report to teachers who have had difficulties with them. If individual teachers supervise their own after-school detention, you are actually working with a classroom consequence. This is a form of "time owed." This consequence is actually the most effective form of after-school detention and should not require the use of the formal referral procedure.

Saturday school

The final school-wide consequence to misbehavior is Saturday school. This consequence requires students to report to school for several hours on a Saturday. This procedure is typically aversive to misbehaving students, but difficult to implement effectively. Because of the severity of this consequence, there is no alternative but to give students an out-of-school suspension if they fail to show up. If used, the Saturday school should include the following guidelines.

Saturday school should be set up, monitored, and run by an administrator. This means that someone needs to be on call to handle any Saturday school detentions. No individual teacher should have the authority to assign a student to Saturday school. Because individual teachers will have varying degrees of tolerance to misbehavior and varying standards for judging misbehavior, you must guard very carefully against the possibility that Saturday school is used for behaviors that could be handled during school hours.

Written guidelines should dictate what types of behaviors will lead to a Saturday school consequence. For the majority of misbehaviors, there should be a series of consequences and procedures used to teach the student more appopriate behaviors prior to resorting to Saturday school. If the consequence is overused, Saturday school can also become a status symbol for students who take pride in misbehavior.

Procedures need to be clearly outlined for parents. Everyone must clearly understand that failure to comply with a Saturday school referral will result in out-of-school suspension.

CONCLUSION

Designing an effective school-wide discipline policy requires that a staff work together to hammer out guidelines and procedures for handling student behavior constructively and consistently. Once the policy is laid out, the entire staff must make a commitment to follow through with the procedures.

While a school-wide discipline policy is an important feature of school discipline, it will primarily be a tool for handling only the most severe behavior problems. Teachers must recognize that discipline within the classroom is primarily a teaching responsibility, and most misbehavior will be dealt with immediately within the classroom.

Section IV
TROUBLESHOOTING SPECIFIC PROBLEMS

1. Making excuses for everything
2. Swearing
3. Talking back
4. Talking during lectures
5. Failing to raise hands
6. Forgetting to bring textbooks to class
7. Taking too long to write answers
8. Cheating
9. Threatening to commit suicide
10. Feeling picked on by the teacher
11. Chewing gum
12. Tipping back in a chair
13. Hypochondria
14. Being off task during independent seatwork
15. Talking during class—one or two students
16. Talking during class—several students
17. Misbehaving during independent seatwork time
18. Making "wisecracks"; being a "smart aleck"
19. Misbehaving after being reinforced
20. Doing nothing—passive resistance and failure to be motivated by **anything**
21. Being embarrassed by praise or not liking praise
22. Acting violently or being out of control
23. Destroying property—vandalism
24. Name-calling
25. Fighting
26. Threatening violence or extortion
27. Poor test-taking skills or test anxiety
28. Poor listening skills; not following verbal directions
29. Handing in late or incomplete assignments
30. Failing to follow written directions
31. Turning in sloppy written work
32. Poor planning on long-term assignments
33. Failing to complete homework assignments—a class problem
34. Failing to complete homework assignments—an individual problem
35. Skipping class or absenteeism with no excuse
36. Excessive excused absences
37. Arriving late or tardy
38. Stealing
39. Using and abusing drugs
40. Smoking
41. Misbehaving in hallways and other school areas
42. Poor academic skills

Problem 1
MAKING EXCUSES FOR EVERYTHING

DESCRIPTION

By some quirk or fate, nothing ever seems to go right for Robin and it is always someone else's fault. Robin's gym teacher, Miss Cleese, has heard everything. Robin didn't turn in her tumbling report because her grandmother accidentally threw it away. Robin didn't have her gym clothes because her mother didn't do the laundry. Robin didn't have her exercise assignment because her locker partner took home the book she put it in. Robin talked out of turn because someone else asked her a question. Miss Cleese has listened to Robin's excuses time and time again. Occasionally, Robin's excuses do seem to be legitimate. However, Miss Cleese finds that she really does not trust Robin. It has become more and more difficult to believe anything that Robin says.

CONTRIBUTING FACTORS

A student who always has excuses feels that she can avoid being accountable for her own behavior. In the past, she has probably managed to get out of work and has avoided negative consequences for her actions. Since the strategy has been effective, making excuses has become a habit. This habit may have begun innocently, but has resulted in the student's becoming an unreliable person who may enjoy trying to con her teachers.

Students who constantly make up excuses may also be students who need attention. While making up excuses, they receive a lot of immediate and individual attention from the teacher. When a student makes excuses, the typical interaction will require thirty seconds to five minutes for negotiation and discussion. Over the course of the week, the student can manipulate a lot of adult time.

PROBLEM SOLVING

Step 1: List situations and excuses used by the student.

Think of as many situations as possible that resulted in the student making excuses. List the situation and the excuses used by the student.

This list will be used to show the student that she has a chronic problem. To demonstrate the severity of the problem, you will need eight to ten examples. If you cannot list eight to ten situations, keep anecdotal records for the next few weeks. If possible, get other teachers involved in the process. It will be important to list as many specific examples as possible from a number of settings.

Step 2: For each situation listed, specify acceptable ways for the student to handle the situation without blaming others.

Some suggested ways for acceptably handling different situations are listed below.

Situation: Assignment not ready to be handed in

Excuse: "My grandmother threw it away."

Acceptable Response: "My assignment was accidently thrown away so it will be a late paper. I need to put things in safe places."

Acceptable Response: "My assignment isn't ready. I understand the consequences and will try to get it in as soon as possible."

Situation: Reprimanded for talking in class

126

Excuse: Blame the other student.

Acceptable Response: "Sorry."

Acceptable Response: Simply quiet down.

Acceptable Response: Ignore the other student in the first place.

The completed list will be used as a tool for teaching the student the borderline between acceptable and unacceptable ways to handle the same situation.

Step 3: Decide how to respond to the student when excuses are made in the future.

Your response will vary depending upon the specific student you are working with. Though the responses may vary among students, you must be consistent in using the same response each time with an individual.

A mild verbal reprimand should be used with students who are unaware of their behavior. This should be used with students who are likely to improve if they can learn to identify when their responses are inappropriate. A mild verbal reprimand involves telling the student what she is doing and prompting her to try a more acceptable response. "That is an excuse. Think of another way to handle the problem." If the student cannot think of an alternative, provide her with a way to handle the situation. This procedure teaches a student to look at her behavior and to explore other more appropriate responses.

If the student seems to need attention, ignoring is the most effective strategy for responding to excuses. Any time the student begins making an excuse, plan to turn away and become involved in another activity. The student must learn that giving excuses will not earn your attention.

If the student is unlikely to improve with verbal reprimands or ignoring, establish a "time owed" consequence. Establish an amount of time owed each time the student makes an excuse. This can be as little as five minutes from a break, before school, after school, or from an enjoyable class activity. Even though the amount of time is small, it will cause the student an inconvenience to have to report back to your room. For more information on time owed, see Chapter 8.

Step 4: Discuss the problem with the student.

Select a neutral time to discuss the problem with the student. Ask the student to listen carefully to you for a moment so the discussion does not degenerate into accusations and more excuses. Explain to the student that you would really like to trust her, but you are having difficulty knowing when to believe her because of the number of excuses she has. Go over the list of situations you have prepared. Tell the student that many of her excuses may be real, but that she needs to learn to take responsibility for her assignments, papers, materials, and behavior without blaming others. Go over each situation that occurred and the other ways that she could have dealt with the situation. Ask the student to suggest more mature ways in which she might have responded to the different situations. Tell the student that you would like her to try dealing with these types of situations in the mature way you have been discussing. Let the student know how you will respond to excuses in the future. End the conversation by emphasizing that you know she can learn to accept responsibility.

Step 5: Reinforce the student as she learns to deal more maturely with difficult situations and shows that she is accepting responsibility.

When the student is able to cope with the responsibilities of class and takes responsibility for her own behavior, be sure to take the time to let her know privately that you have seen a lot of growth and maturity. When the student goes a solid week without making up excuses, provide a more substantial reinforcer. This might include giving her a class responsibility such as taking roll "because you can trust her." "Robin, you have certainly been showing me that you can accept responsibility. I need someone to take roll for me so that I can prepare the P.E. equipment. Would you be willing to assist me?" Other suggestions include writing a note or letter to the student, taking a moment or two to talk individually with the student, or providing improvement points if you are including class performance points in your grading system.

Problem 2
SWEARING

DESCRIPTION

Several students in Mr. Hilt's first-period class casually swear three or four times during the class period. Mr. Hilt is not terribly shocked or offended by the swearing as these students are otherwise cooperative in class. Mr. Hilt is concerned, however, because swearing is against the school rules. Mr. Hilt also wonders if he is doing students a disservice by not reacting to the swearing. This language will certainly be offensive to many people and is not acceptable in many settings. Mr. Hilt would like to teach his students that swearing is not acceptable, but doesn't want to make a big issue of it.

CONTRIBUTING FACTORS

Students frequently swear because swearing is a part of their language environment. If students have parents or peers who swear, swearing becomes a natural part of their language. It becomes a habit, much like saying "you know."

Other students begin swearing because they think it makes them appear more sophisticated, more mature, or more tough.

Finally, some students swear to antagonize adults. Their intent is to provoke an emotional response from an authority figure. In this case, swearing becomes an attention getter. For students who are hooked on emotional conflict, swearing may be an easy way to engage an adult in conflict and become the center of heated attention.

PROBLEM SOLVING

Step 1: Discuss the problem with your class.

At a neutral time, explain to your class that you are concerned about the amount of swearing you hear. Tell students that your feelings about swearing are irrelevant. Your primary concern is that swearing is not appropriate in a public setting, including in school and eventually on a job, as it is offensive to many people. Tell students that some people will judge them solely on the basis of their language. If a student chooses to swear, some people will conclude:

> This is a "bad" person.
> This person has no regard for others.
> This person is illiterate.

Students who swear may find they are not welcome in some homes. They may find they are not chosen to represent the school or a club because of their language. Many opportunities can be lost if people think the student will embarrass them. Most of all, as swearing becomes a habit, students may eventually lose job opportunities.

Ask students to refrain from using bad language while they are in your class. Tell students that you are discussing the problem with them so they can work on improving their language on their own. Let them know that you will need to set up a consequence for swearing if it continues.

Step 2. If the situation begins to improve, let students know that you are impressed with their maturity and restraint.

Tell students that you are pleased they were able to handle the problem on their own and are glad not to have to impose a consequence.

Step 3. If the situation does not improve within a week, set up a consequence for swearing.

The consequence should be relatively mild so the problem does not get blown out of proportion. For each incidence of swearing students could owe five minutes from their lunch period, break, after school, or from any enjoyable class activity. The amount of time needn't be excessive. Five minutes from lunch may mean that the student cannot eat with friends or it may mean that he will have to stand at the end of the lunch line.

If you have included participation and effort in your grading system, a failure to earn class performance points can also be a consequence to swearing. (See Chapter 2.) This will demonstrate that the students' swearing has affected their overall classroom performance, much like swearing could affect a job evaluation. The specific point fine will depend on the number of points students can earn during the week for participation and effort. The fine needs to be significant enough so that students feel they have lost something, but not so high that they feel there is no reason to keep working in class. The point fine for each incidence of swearing should be between five and ten percent of the possible weekly points.

Step 4. Discuss the problem and future consequence with students.

Let students know that they seem to need help in breaking their habit of swearing in class. Explain the consequence. If you decide to use owing time, specify the amount of time that will be owed for each incidence of swearing and when the time will be paid. If you decide to use a point fine, specify the number of points that will not be earned for each incidence of swearing.

It will also be important to provide students with examples of exclamations that will be acceptable. This can be accomplished by generating a list of responses you have heard students make that are acceptable, or you may wish to allow the students to generate possible examples of acceptable exclamations.

Finally, tell students that any questionable comments will be considered swearing. You might suggest that it would be best to avoid questionable terms, or terms that could be easily misinterpreted. End the discussion by making sure that students understand the consequences, and ask if there are any questions.

Step 5. Calmly and consistently implement consequences.

When you hear someone swear, calmly and unemotionally implement the preestablished consequences. Do not negotiate with the student. If the student wishes to talk about the incident inform him that he can talk to you after class. Do not take class time to discuss the incident.

Step 6: If the amount of swearing is significantly reduced, let students know that you appreciate the improvement.

If this has been a problem with a large number of students, praise the class for their restraint. If swearing has been a problem with only a few students, let them know privately that you are impressed with their self-control and maturity.

Problem 3
TALKING BACK

DESCRIPTION

James is a ninth-grade student in Mrs. Meyen's English class. Whenever Mrs. Meyen asks him to do something, he always responds with a hostile comment. "Why should I?" "How stupid!" Any response from Mrs. Meyen results in an accelerating hostility. James is a very angry, unreachable student. He always has the last word in any confrontation. Mrs. Meyen is normally a very patient teacher, but even she is ready to give up on James. A positive interaction with James seems to be impossible.

CONTRIBUTING FACTORS

James has learned to talk back, to be angry, and to be explosive. His interactions at home are probably very similar to the ones at school. Typically, a student like James has grown up with confrontation—confrontation with parents, confrontation with teachers, and often confrontation between parents. The student has learned to interact with adults in only one way. It will not be easy to change this student's behavior. It may be necessary to actually teach the student alternative ways of responding to an adult.

A student like James may also have gotten hooked on the intensity of a hostile interaction. During a confrontation, the student experiences an emotional high. While this emotion is extremely negative, its sheer intensity can be reinforcing. The student may not be aware of it himself, but may actually thrive on the level of intensity and the one-to-one attention he receives when he provokes adults.

Finally, the student who talks back may think he can gain power and influence by challenging the teacher in front of his peers. Once a hostile interaction has begun, the student may feel compelled to get the last word in order to save face in front of the class.

PROBLEM SOLVING

Step 1: Define "talking back."

In doing so, your definition must leave no leeway for misunderstanding. A student like James may tone down his responses for a short while, but within a few days he will begin testing your definition by continually accelerating the degree of his hostility. You will feel as if you are walking on pins and needles with this student. Within a few days, the student will be right back to where he started, unless you can clearly identify what is talking back and what is not. You must try to anticipate the types of comments the student is likely to make. Think about the particular student's voice inflection, volume, facial expressions, gestures, and body language. All these variables have an impact on what you consider to be "talking back." Your definition might look like the following:

James is talking back when any of the following things are noticeable:

- Voice raised so other students can hear
- Voice raised so other students look up

- Derogatory comments regarding your personality, performance, or assignments
- Uses loaded terminology such as "crap," "screw you," "shove it"

Step 2: Carefully identify the borderline between acceptable and unacceptable responses.

As noted before, this student will test the borderline between acceptable and unacceptable responses. You must be prepared to clarify what is acceptable and what is not. You must also be prepared to respond to what is acceptable and what is not. To help you draw a distinct line between acceptable and unacceptable responses, think of at least five situations where you and the student may have a conflict. Then for each of these situations, think of three ways the student could respond unacceptably and three ways that would be acceptable. Your acceptable responses should be examples of comments the student could make without embarrassing himself in front of peers. An example is provided below.

Situation: James is sitting and staring out the window. "James, please get started with your writing assignment."

Unacceptable Responses: Says, "Screw you"; shouts, "All right!" says, "I hate this crap."

Acceptable Responses: Says, "Okay"; says nothing, but gets started; asks, "Does this need to be done by the end of the period?"

Step 3: Identify a consequence for talking back.

When the student has engaged in a "talk back," follow these procedures:

- Tell the student he owes five minutes. (For details on times owed see Chapter 8.)
- Before the student has a chance to respond, give the student a matter-of-fact command that requires some physically visible action. You need to be able to see that the student is following your direction. Your command could be something like, "You need to get in your seat and begin writing." Avoid giving an instruction like, "You need to cooperate."
- If the student carries out your instruction, there is no further consequence.
- If the student does not comply with your instruction, immediately send him to the office. This should result in a phone call home.

There are several advantages to this sequence. The first infraction results only in a mild consequence. This allows the student to save face if he does not continue to talk back. A severe consequence on the first offense increases the likelihood that the student will continue his confrontational stance. If the first consequence is severe, the student has very little to lose by continuing. Another advantage to this procedure is that the teacher will stay calm during the whole interaction. This is imperative as the student's out-of-control behavior is triggered by an intense interaction with someone else. A final advantage to this sequential procedure is that once the teacher has given the instruction, she can withdraw from the situation. It becomes the student's responsibility either to follow the instruction or be removed from class.

Note: It is recommended that your school have a preestablished policy for handling situations that involve the direct defiance of a teacher. If your school does not have preestablished consequences, see Chapter 9 for ideas on how to begin setting up standard discipline procedures.

Step 4: Examine the relationship between the student's academic abilities and the academic expectations in your classroom.

If the student's basic skills are far below classroom expectations, hostile behavior may be partially the result of frustration and partially the result of trying to hide his inabilities. Make adjustments in your class structure by establishing a peer tutor, providing more directed instruction, or by making adjustments in assignments. Until the student sees that he has some chance of being successful, you cannot expect to reduce the level of hostility. For more information on diagnosing and remediating academic deficits, see Problem 42, "Poor Academic Skills."

Step 5: Provide delayed positive feedback when the student is able to restrain himself.

When the student restrains himself in a situation where he would normally talk back, provide delayed positive feedback. This means you need to wait until a later time when you can privately let the student know that you are aware and appreciative of his efforts to be in control. Your feedback needs to be very nonchalant. You do not want to make this a big deal and embarrass the student. You simply want the student to be aware that you have observed his efforts.

Step 6: Discuss the problem and the plan with the student.

At a neutral time, not immediately after a problem, ask to speak to the student privately. Inform the student about the problem and your plan for solving the problem. Be especially careful to make sure the student understands the definition of talking back and the borderlines between talking back and acceptable interactions. Inform the student about the consequence for talking back and about your goal to give him positive feedback when you see improvement. If the student can suggest reasonable revisions or adjustments in the plan, incorporate the suggestions.

Step 7: During the first several weeks the plan is in operation, increase positive interactions with the student.

Demonstrate to the student that you are interested in him as a worthwhile individual. This can be done through some of the following suggestions:

- Say hello to the student in the hall.
- Greet the student as he comes into class.
- Comment favorably on the student's clothing or appearance.
- Inquire about one of the student's interests.
- Comment on the student's academic efforts.
- Make an effort to include the student in discussions.

Chapter 3 provides additional information on increasing positive interactions.

Step 8: When the student has been successful for a week in avoiding hostile interactions, provide a structured reinforcer.

A structured reinforcer should be something that continues to demonstrate your respect for the student. Some reinforcers to consider might include a phone call to parents, a letter of commendation, a conference with the principal to congratulate the student on his improvement, or perhaps the honor of taking on a classroom responsibility. The structured reinforcer should help the student to feel pride in his ability to demonstrate maturity and success.

Problem 4
TALKING DURING LECTURES

DESCRIPTION

Ms. Jessey is a science teacher who has problems with her seventh-period class's continual talking during lectures. Ms. Jessey is a conscientious teacher who teaches life science because she loves the subject and really enjoys high school students. However, during seventh period, Ms. Jessey is finding that she neither enjoys her students nor her subject.

In first confronting this problem, Ms. Jessey has considered whether her lectures are boring to her students. However, Ms. Jessey knows that she gives the same basic lectures to two other classes during the day, and does not have the same difficulties. Ms. Jessey has also noted that the problem in seventh period is not just with a few problem students. Different members of the entire class talk at different times.

Ms. Jessey has tried telling students to be quiet. Within a couple of minutes someone else is talking. This pattern has continued day after day, and Ms. Jessey feels that something has to be done. Her lectures have lost their effectiveness, and her seventh-period students are not learning.

CONTRIBUTING FACTORS

Social interaction with peers is a very important part of life for secondary students. Some classes will be composed of a number of students who really enjoy interacting with each other, at the expense of learning. In addition, a subject may be fascinating to a teacher, but uninteresting to a number of students. Daily, teachers are faced with the difficult job of teaching students to be interested. If a group of students enjoy talking together, this job becomes doubly difficult as the talking interferes with the teacher's efforts to make a subject interesting for students.

Another contributing factor is that the students may find that in many classes there is no accountability for talking. In Ms. Jessey's class, students have found that they get attention from the teacher when they talk. They disrupt the lesson and they get to interact with their peers in the process. There is no compelling reason for students to take responsibility for their own actions.

PROBLEM SOLVING

Step 1: Establish clear guidelines for student behavior during lectures.

Require students to raise their hands and wait to be called on when they have questions or comments. This eliminates confusion. Recognition from you will give students a clear understanding that they have been given permission to talk. All other talking will be unacceptable. This will also encourage students to talk only when they have something to contribute to the class activity.

Step 2: Establish a consequence for unacceptable talking.

Verbal reprimands should be used initially so that students clearly understand what is unacceptable. However, verbal reprimands should be used only on the first day that you have presented the rule that students will talk during lectures only when they have raised their hands and been acknowledged by the teacher. Beyond the first day, it will be important to establish a more formalized consequence.

The consequence for talking during lectures should be something that is moderately aversive to students. Avoid establishing a severe consequence for the relatively minor misbehavior of talking. If a severe consequence is used, it will be difficult to implement consistently. Understandably, teachers avoid imposing severe consequences and thus wait to do anything about the problem until the misbehavior has gone on for some time. This results in inconsistent reponses to student talking and students testing to see how much they can get away with. If you wish to eliminate inappropriate talking and avoid nagging students, it will be important to consistently implement a reasonable consequence.

Here are three reasonable consequences for talking during lectures:

• In-class time out: Students who engage in inappropriate talking during a lecture are isolated within the classroom setting for a predetermined period of time. Five minutes for each infraction is a reasonable period. This procedure demonstrates to students that their inappropriate behavior has resulted in their not being allowed to be a part of your class. The major disadvantage to this procedure is that it may be difficult to physically separate more than one student at a time. Since talking will usually involve more than one student, this consequence may not be a realistic option in your classroom.

• Reduction of daily participation points: If you have built participation points into your grading system, a loss of points for talking inappropriately can be an effective consequence. The number of lost points must be predetermined. If the weekly grade for participation and effort allowed a student to earn up to thirty points, each talking incident might result in reducing the amount earned by one point. This would be enough so the student would notice a difference, but not so much as to discourage the student to the point of giving up. As a general rule, never reduce a student's daily grade for participation by more than 25 percent for any one incident.

• Time owed: If students talk during lecture time, they have wasted their time, your time, and the time of other students. A logical consequence is for them to pay for this loss with time they value. Students can owe you time from before school, after school, during a break, and so forth. Establish how much time the student will owe for each incident of talking. The amount of time should be relatively brief. Five minutes may be sufficient, as students will learn quickly that even five minutes is aversive when it comes off time they value. During owed time, students should not be allowed to do anything. They may not study or talk with you. This time should not be productive to the students in any way.

Step 3: Discuss the problem, guidelines, and consequences with students.

Tell students that talking during lectures is making it difficult for you to give them the information they need to learn in order to pass the class. The new rule will be that talking during lectures will be allowed only when they raise their hands and are called on. All other talking will be unacceptable.

Tell students of the new consequences for unacceptable talking.

Ask for input from the students. Accept any reasonable concerns and make any needed adjustments in your plan.

Step 4: Calmly and consistently implement your consequence when *any* student engages in unacceptable talking during lectures.

Consistency in implementing the predetermined consequence is very important. If you fail to be consistent, students will begin testing to see how much inappropriate talking they can get away with.

Step 5: Provide positive feedback to the class and to individuals as improvement is noted.

Students should learn to take pride in the maturity and consideration their class demonstrates. Occasionally, tell students that you appreciate their cooperation. Praise should be brief and matter of fact. "We have covered a lot of ground today. Your cooperation and maturity are appreciated."

If certain individuals have been chronic talkers, privately inform them that you are aware of their efforts. Let them know that you are now enjoying having them in class and that their improved behavior can help them succeed in their other classes as well. If the improved behavior is a significant change, you may want to provide a more structured reinforcer such as a letter of commendation or a letter to parents, or you may have the principal make a special effort to let the student know that he has heard of the student's growth and demonstration of maturity.

Step 6: If the foregoing steps do not significantly improve behavior during lectures, set up a structured reinforcement system with the class.

For information on these types of systems, see Chapter 5. Also see Problem 5, "Failing to Raise Hands."

Problem 5
FAILING TO RAISE HANDS

DESCRIPTION

Mrs. Schutz is a high school English teacher. During her college training, it was suggested that making students raise their hands before contributing to a discussion sometimes stifled student spontaneity, and discouraged students from participating. However, after teaching Junior English for two years, Mrs. Schutz has realized that a few students always end up dominating discussions. Mrs. Schutz has decided to ask students to raise their hands if they have questions or comments. Mrs. Schutz has also decided to have students raise their hands if they have questions or need help during independent work times. With a class of thirty-eight students, Mrs. Schutz doesn't want to end up helping only those who are the most insistent and aggressive about getting her attention.

By the end of the first week, Mrs. Schutz is feeling very exasperated. During a typical lecture or class discussion, she finds herself constantly reminding students that they should raise their hands. During independent work times, Mrs. Schutz still finds that students ask her questions without being called on. No matter how many times she tells students to raise their hands, students call out fifteen to twenty times during the period.

CONTRIBUTING FACTORS

Students will call out answers, comments, or questions to receive recognition from the teacher. The attention they desire is not necessarily negative attention. Some students will call out because they legitimately need help, and others will call out because they have something worthwhile to contribute.

Frequently, students will forget to raise their hands because calling out questions, comments, and answers has become a habit. If a class is very small and students are equally assertive and able, it may not be necessary to have students raise their hands. However, it will be necessary to teach students to follow the appropriate rules at the appropriate times.

Students will also "forget" to raise their hands when it is more expedient to get the teacher's attention by calling out. Imagine the following situation. Mrs. Schutz has a number of students raising their hands for hands for help during an independent work time. Several students are quietly and patiently waiting for their turn. As Mrs. Schutz leaves John, Peggy calls out, "Can I . . . .?" Since Mrs. Schutz is standing right next to Peggy and Peggy's question only requires a quick yes or no. Mrs. Schutz answers her question before responding to other students who have raised their hands. So much for waiting for your turn!

PROBLEM SOLVING

Step 1: Identify the typical activities that occur in your classroom and determine whether students should raise their hands during each activity or be allowed to speak spontaneously.

In determining whether students should be allowed to speak spontaneously or raise their hands, take into account the number of students involved in the activity, the type of activity, and the types of students you are working with.

If you are working with large numbers of students, it will be appropriate to require students to raise their hands during most activities. If you are working with small numbers of students, hand raising will be necessary only if you have a few students who tend to dominate the group. For example, if you are a drama teacher working with a small group responsible for set design, it would be appropriate to allow students to freely discuss their plans. However, if your entire class of twenty is planning the set design together, it would be more appropriate to have students raise their hands with their suggestions.

The type of activity you are conducting should also be considered. If you are having your class practice a Spanish dialogue, interruptions could disrupt the sequence of the dialogue. Therefore, having students raise their hands would be appropriate. However, if you are having students practice conversational Spanish, it would be appropriate to have students speak spontaneously.

Step 2. Clearly communicate your expectations to students.

At the beginning of a class period, discuss with students the reasons for requiring them to raise their hands during different types of activities. Explain that hand raising will result in everyone having a fair chance to participate or get assistance. If you have identified activities during which students may talk without raising their hands, explain why these activities are different.

Step 3. Consistently ignore all students who do not raise their hands at the appropriate times.

Students will not learn to raise their hands if they can get your attention faster by calling out. Initially, it may be difficult for you to ignore students who do not raise their hands. It is natural to respond to a student who has called out by reminding the student to raise his hand and then to answer the student's question. "Jim, remember. You need to raise your hand if you have a question. Don't forget next time. Now, what can I do for you?" Even though the student hasn't raised his hand, he gets the help he wants.

Consistency is also difficult to maintain when students fail to raise their hands but politely ask you a question at a convenient time. If you are walking by a student's desk and the student quietly asks, "Do we need to do both pages?" it is unnatural to ignore the student. However, if you expect students to raise their hands and wait for recognition, it is important for you to consistently ignore those who forget to follow the rule. You must demonstrate to students that the only efficient way to get your attention is to raise their hand.

Step 4. Reinforce hand raising by quickly calling on students who quietly raise their hands.

Try to call on students as quickly as possible. You need to demonstrate that hand raising really does get your attention. If you fail to respond with reasonable immediacy, students will tire of this procedure and resort to calling out. Asking students to raise their hand requires students to be patient and mature. In return, you must not require students to wait for inordinate periods of time.

Step 5. Provide direct feedback to individuals who seem to have difficulty remembering to raise their hands.

Students who have difficulty remembering to raise their hands may need more direct feedback than other students in the class. Continue to ignore any student who forgets to raise her hand. However, as soon as the student raises her hand, be sure to call on her and specify why she is being given recognition. "Sandy, your hand is up. What is the answer to number 14?"

CONCLUSION: The first couple of weeks will be the hardest. However, if you can be consistent for two weeks, students will learn to raise their hands. Your consistency can result in providing every student with more of an opportunity to participate and ask for help.

Note: If part of the problem relates to students waiting to get your help during independent work, see Problem 19, "The Student Who Will Not Wait for Help From the Teacher."

Problem 6
FORGETTING TO BRING TEXTBOOKS TO CLASS

DESCRIPTION

In Mr. Benson's second-period chemistry class, there are typically two or three students who forget to bring their textbook to class. Some days students don't need their books, but more often than not, the text is needed when the class works together on a chapter, or when students complete assignments in class. Each time a student forgets his book, Mr. Benson gives the same old lecture about being prepared for class and wasting class time. Then the student is allowed to read with another student or go to his locker to get his book.

CONTRIBUTING FACTORS

The major cause of students coming to class without textbooks is that they have found there is no significant accountability for their forgetful behavior. A few students may be reinforced for forgetting their books by the attention they receive. Others may actually get reinforced by the fact that they are allowed to go to their lockers and miss several minutes of class. However, in most cases, students do not consciously forget their books. They simply forget their books because there is no compelling reason to remember.

PROBLEM SOLVING

Step 1: Design your grading system to include points for coming to class with all basic materials.

If your grading system does not include a percentage of the grade for class performance, see Chapter 2. Students need to be taught that being unprepared for class affects their grade. If they are allowed to retrieve their book, they lose valuable class time. If they are allowed to share a book with another student, they are wasting everyone's time. The lost time must result in a failure to earn points, as the student has not taken maximum advantage of the opportunity to learn. Each time a student forgets his book, he should not earn 10 percent of his weekly performance grade.

Step 2: Send any students who have forgotten their books to get them at the beginning of the period.

Regardless of the nature of your first class activity, check to see that all students have their books at the beginning of class. You may wish to have students place their books on their desks as soon as they take their seats so that you can quickly scan the room. Or, you may have students show their books as you call roll. Students who do not have books should be sent immediately to their lockers to get them.

Step 3. Periodically schedule the most enjoyable classroom activities at the beginning of the class period.

Most teachers schedule activities that students enjoy most at the end of the period. This would include free time, films, and independent study time. If this is a consistent pattern, students learn that missing the first part of the period simply gets them out of the activities they least enjoy. By periodically scheduling the more enjoyable activities at the beginning of the period, students will miss out but still be present for other class activities at the end of the period.

Step 4. Periodically schedule brief assignments and quizzes that require the use of the text at the beginning of the class period.

The quizzes and assignments should require only five to ten minutes to complete. As the assignments and quizzes will be given at the beginning of the class period, students who are sent to get books will have missed the opportunity to complete this work. If a student has left her book at home, do not allow her to do the work. Do not allow any of the students who have forgotten books to take the assignment or quiz at a later time.

Students should be allowed to make up the work with extra work outside class time. However, the make-up work should take more time than the assignment or quiz took in class. This procedure should demonstrate that it is much easier to remember a book than it is to make up work missed. The consequence is not so severe that the student cannot redeem herself. It simply makes it clear that valuable time is lost when students have to get their books.

Because mini quizzes and assignments could result in increasing the amount of time you spend correcting papers, design these assignments so that they can be easily graded by student assistants, or by students' trading papers. Objective quizzes and assignments will be much easier to grade than subjective essay tasks.

Step 5. Discuss the new class organization with your students.

At a neutral time, explain to students that too much time is being lost to make provisions for students who have forgotten their books. Explain that you are going to help them learn to be more responsible. Your plan will include not earning a specified number of performance points when books are forgotten, and it will also involve restructuring class time. Explain that certain activities will be moved to the beginning of the period. Also tell students that you will begin giving mini assignments and quizzes at the beginning of the period that will require the use of their books. If students have forgotten books, they will miss the opportunity of completing these assignments. Inform students that these points may be made up, but the work will take more time than the classroom work and will need to be made up outside class time.

Step 6. Check for books at the beginning of the class period and implement your plan.

Initially, you will need to conduct a daily book check at the beginning of each period. As students demonstrate increasing responsibility, you can conduct these checks on a periodic basis.

Step 7. When students have demonstrated a responsibility for their books, provide an occasional reinforcing activity.

When students have demonstrated over several days that they have learned to take responsibility for their books, provide an occasional reinforcing activity. This can be as simple as giving the class five minutes of free time. Be sure to let students know that the time is being given to them because they have saved class time by learning to be responsible.

Step 8. If one or two students still forget their books, establish a mild consequence.

The procedures previously discussed should work for most of the students. However, there may be one or two students who still occasionally forget their books. Privately inform any of these students that they will owe you time after school or from a break if they forget their book in the future. When students learn that they will owe five minutes after school or five minutes off the beginning of their lunch period, they usually work harder at remembering their books. For more information about owing time see Chapter 8.

Problem 7
TAKING TOO LONG TO WRITE ANSWERS

DESCRIPTION

In Ms. Hanna's sixth-grade language arts class, Ben consistently causes problems during the weekly spelling test and during any other activity where the teacher must wait for students to complete writing before going on to the next task.

During spelling tests, Ms. Hanna presents the spelling word, provides a sentence with the word, and then waits for a reasonable period of time while students write. When she is ready to present the next word, Ben invariably calls out, "Wait! I'm not ready yet." The problem is chronic enough that the class becomes restless while waiting for Ben. In fact, Ms. Hanna finds herself getting impatient because exercises take five to ten minutes longer than they should. This plays havoc with Ms. Hanna's ability to provide as much instruction as she would like.

CONTRIBUTING FACTORS

This problem is generally the result of one or two factors. Occasionally a student will simply lack the motor skills to be able to write at a reasonable speed. This is generally a student who does everything slowly. He talks slowly. He walks slowly. He is slow to finish tests, and he is slow to get out of the door. When lack of motor skills is not the problem, it is usually caused by a student's desire to get attention and to control what is happening in class. Occasionally, students will learn that they can manipulate events by keeping everyone waiting. Eventually this student may begin to see himself as a "slow-poke." It is not uncommon for the two problems to become interwoven.

PROBLEM SOLVING

Step 1. Determine what is causing the problem.

This can usually be done by determining whether the student writes slowly only during group activities. Ask yourself whether the student's writing rate varies on different tasks. If the rate varies and the student completes independent writing tasks at a fairly reasonable rate, the problem is behavioral. If the student seems to write slowly on everything, conduct an additional test in private. Explain that your would like to help him get through his writing assignments faster. Tell him that you are going to give him a list of easy spelling words and ask him to write as rapidly as he can. Present the words and observe how the student behaves while he writes. Is he tense? Does he hold his pen tightly? Is it an effort for the student to write faster? If the answer to these questions is "yes," the student probably has a motor problem.

If you cannot ascertain whether the student has motor problems or not, assume that he does. The student may have convinced himself that he is slow.

Note: The remainder of this plan is divided into two approaches. If it appears that the student is not able to write at a reasonable speed, follow the first set of steps. If it is apparent that he writes slowly to gain attention, follow the second set of steps. You may decide that you need to combine the two plans.

For the Student Who Cannot Write at a Reasonable Speed:

Step 2: Set up a series of exercises to help the student learn to write at a reasonable speed.

Like anything else, the student will need practice to increase his writing rate. Exercises need to be designed so that the student isn't put under undue pressure. Speed can only be built over time.

a. Discuss the problem with the student. Tell the student that you are concerned about his writing rate because it makes it very difficult for him to complete assignments and keep up with the class. Explain that his rate is not going to magically increase on its own, and like anything else, improvement requires practice.

b. Give the student a list of twenty spelling words that will be easy for him to spell. Tell the student that you are going to see how many of the words the student can spell neatly and correctly within two minutes. Present one of the spelling words to the student. As soon as the student has completed writing, present the next word. Continue this pattern for the full two minutes. Correct the words by counting all words that are spelled neatly and correctly. The student will repeat this exercise daily until he is able to complete the list of twenty words neatly and correctly in two minutes or less.

When the student has mastered the list, construct a second list and repeat the same process. Continue these exercises on a daily basis until the student can take a spelling test and keep up with the class. Once the process has been set up, a peer tutor can help the student. You may also be able to enlist the help of the student's parents. Keep in mind, the more often the student practices, the faster the problem will be remediated.

c. Until the student has learned to keep up with the class, explain that you will allow him to write every second or third spelling word during the regular test. Also have the student set up his test papers in advance so he is ready to begin immediately. Tell the student he should no longer ask you to wait for him because you will allow him to take the remainder of the test later in the period.

Step 3. If the student obviously struggles slowly through all assignments that require writing, consult the learning specialist in the building to see if writing rate exercises can be set up for the student.

For the Student Who Writes Slowly to Get Attention:

Step 2: Meet with the student privately to discuss the problem.

Tell the student that you are concerned about her behavior during spelling tests because it is disruptive to you and other students. Let the student know that you are also concerned because you know that this behavior will interfere with success in other classes. Tell the student that you recognize that she is able to write faster because you have seen her complete written work at a normal rate.

Tell the student that you will ignore her if she asks you to wait. Explain that you will watch other students and present the spelling words at a reasonable rate. If you are going too fast, explain that you will have to trust another student, who does not have this chronic problem, to inform you.

Step 3: (optional) If you suspect that part of the problem may be that the student also does not study his spelling words sufficiently, you may want to provide him with a method for studying similar to the sequence below. (This type of suggestion can be given to the whole class if you have other students who are having difficulty passing their spelling tests.)

Monday:	1. Have your parents or a friend give you a pretest.
	2. Write any misspelled word three times, saying the letters to yourself.
	3. Have someone give you another complete test.
Tuesday:	Fold a piece of notebook paper into four columns.
	1. Copy any words that were misspelled on either of Monday's pretests in the first column.
	2. Look at the first word. Say the letters to yourself. Then turn the paper to a blank column and write the word. Check to see that you have gotten it right. Repeat this process with each word.
	3. In the third column, write three spelling words at a time. Then check to see that they are correct.
	4. Repeat the same process in the fourth column.
Wednesday:	1. Have your parents or a friend give you another pretest.
	2. Write any misspelled words three times, saying the letters to yourself.

Thursday: 1. Repeat the process from Tuesday, only include any words that were misspelled on the Monday or Wednesday pretests
                 2. Take a final pretest.
                 3. Practice any words that are still difficult.

Lead the student through this type of practice procedure or one that you have designed.

Step 4: Have the student take a mini spelling test on relatively easy words so you can demonstrate the rate that you will expect him to write.

If the student actually keeps up, congratulate him. Let him know that you have confidence that he will be able to keep up with the regular spelling tests. Make sure the student understands that this can be done only if he practices and emphasize that you will count any words he does not have written down as incorrect.

Step 5: If the student falls behind during a spelling test and asks you to slow down or repeat a word, ignore him.

Do not look at the student. Act as if you did not hear him. Continue presenting the spelling test as if the student had never spoken.

Step 6: Any time the student keeps up with the group, let her know you are aware of her efforts.

This can be done by establishing eye contact, or by giving the student some non-verbal signal. You may also want to walk amongst all the students, stopping to see how various students are doing, and let the student know you recognize her efforts by putting your hand on her shoulder. Also plan to speak privately with the student. You are asking the student to give up attention she got when she kept everyone waiting. Replace this with attention for appropriate behavior.

Problem 8
CHEATING

DESCRIPTION

While administering a test in her tenth-grade history class, Mrs. Johansen notices that Vicki has been looking at her neighbor's paper. At first Mrs. Johansen isn't sure whether Vicki is cheating, but as time goes on, it becomes apparent that Vicki is attempting to copy answers. Mrs. Johansen has never before been aware of Vicki cheating in her history class. Mrs. Johansen does not want to allow Vicki to get away with cheating and is not quite sure how to handle the situation.

CONTRIBUTING FACTORS

Cheating has a variety of different causes, but the primary motivation is that all students want to succeed. Some students cheat because they do not have the academic skills to succeed. Some students cheat because they are not prepared for a test and run the risk of failure if they do not cheat. Others cheat because they have found they can succeed without doing the required work, while still others cheat because they are under too much pressure to excel. Their best efforts are never good enough.

Finally, there are a few students who cheat in a desire to get caught. These are students who desperately need attention and any attention is better than no attention at all.

PROBLEM SOLVING

Step 1: Avoid making a public accusation of cheating.

It will be important to handle the incident of cheating in private. If the class becomes aware of the accusation, it forces the student into denial and creates a teacher versus student confrontation. No one wins in this situation. Your ultimate goal with this student is to motivate her to do the required work on her own. The student needs to learn that she can be successful without cheating. If the student is humiliated in front of her peers, there is very little hope of building skills that will eliminate the perceived need for cheating.

Step 2: Make eye contact with the student to communicate that you are observing her behavior during the test.

Usually, a student who is cheating will frequently look at the teacher to see if she is being watched. When the student looks in your direction, make eye contact. Sustain that eye contact so the student knows you are concerned about her behavior.

Step 3: Discuss the problem privately with the student after class.

When the test is completed, quietly let the student know that you would like to talk with her after class. Describe to the student exactly what you saw. You should be calm, but firm. Avoid sounding angry or hostile. If the student sees that you are upset, it tends to imply that you have a problem instead of the student having a problem. Once you have provided all the details, allow the student to respond.

If the student denies having cheated, reiterate what you saw. Let the student know that any of these behaviors are not acceptable test-taking behaviors. Whether she was cheating is actually irrelevant. You cannot give her credit for the test under those conditions. Avoid engaging in an interaction that becomes a series of accusations and denials.

If the student admits she has cheated, continue with the following steps.

Step 4: On the first offense, provide the student with an alternative method for earning credit.

On the first incident of cheating, you cannot give credit for the test. Provide the student with an alternative for demonstrating how well she has mastered the material. This might include a make-up test after school or requiring the student to write a report. This relatively mild consequence is designed to avoid branding the student with a label she does not feel she can get rid of.

If the student refuses to make up the test, tell the student that she can either make up the test, or you will simply fail her on the original test. If she chooses the second option, let her know that you will also need to call her parents to explain the test grade.

Step 5: Contact parents if the student refuses to comply with the alternative method for earning the test credit.

If the parents are called, unemotionally describe what took place during the test. Let the parents know that the student does have the option of making up the credit.

Step 6: Discuss consequences for any further incidences of cheating.

Tell the student that any other incidences of cheating will result in failing the test. Her parents will be contacted, and she will be referred to the office. (See *School-Wide*

Discipline Policies.) Present this information as if you do not expect any similar incidences, but that you simply want her to know of your actions in the unlikely event of a second occurrence.

Step 7: Try to determine why the student felt she needed to cheat.

The foregoing measures are designed to demonstrate to students that cheating is not acceptable. However, these procedures will not alleviate the underlying cause of the problem.

Step 8: Take steps to help the student overcome the problems that have led to cheating.

Until the student is able to resolve the underlying cause of cheating, she may attempt to cheat whenever she does not feel that she is being strictly policed by teachers. This problem will be truly resolved only when the student has learned to take pride in her own success. This means that success must be possible without cheating. Below are possible directions in which to go given different possible motivations for cheating.

a. Lack of basic skills: If the student seems to be cheating because she lacks the basic skills to be successful, wait a few days, and then arrange to provide the student with extra help. You may wish to make structural changes in the organization of your class. For example, during independent study periods, you may want to meet with students who have difficulty. The study sessions can help students with materials they may not be able to read. They might help students learn to take notes, highlight important information and concepts, and rehearse information that needs to be mastered.

In addition, you may want to arrange for a peer tutor. Peer tutors generally benefit from the experience as much as the student who needs help. Peer tutors might be selected from students who are currently earning *B*s. These students could earn extra credit for the additional time spent tutoring. The extra credit plus the additional time spent on the subject should make it very likely for the tutor to earn an *A* in the course.

If the student's basic skills are obviously very low, she should also be referred to special services for further assessment of skill abilities and remedial programs.

b. Not prepared for the test: If the student is an able student, but obviously not prepared to take the test, she may need to learn how to manage her time better. If this is the case, refer to Problem 32. This problem deals with students having difficulty pacing themselves through a long-term paper or project, but the guidelines could easily be applied to teaching students how to keep pace with mastering information that will be tested.

c. Accustomed to getting away with cheating: If the student seems to be cheating because that is the easiest way to get a decent grade, she has probably succeeded with cheating in the past. In this instance, it will be necessary to be consistent with your consequences. You may wish to talk with all of this student's teachers and work together to consistently implement consequences for cheating.

d. Under undue pressure to excel: Students who cheat because of undue pressure to excel are generally very conscientious students. An incident of cheating will be fairly surprising as the student will otherwise turn in carefully completed work and earn reasonably decent grades. If you suspect that the student has cheated because of a need to excel, work on increasing positive interactions with the student. You will hope to build self-confidence in the student's achievements. You may wish to talk with the parents. Describe the amount of time that the student should reasonably spend studying and then suggest that the student's accomplishments within that time period should be commended. Stress the need to give the student attention for best efforts as opposed to excellence. Finally, if the student seems to be excessively nervous and anxious about grades and schoolwork, you may wish to refer the student to the school counselor, and implement the suggestions presented in Problem 27, which addresses test anxiety.

e. Needs attention: If the student was obviously cheating, you have probably seen a desperate cry for attention. If this is the case, work on increasing positive interactions with the student. (See Chapter 3.) In addition, you may want to refer the student to the school counselor.

Problem 9
THREATENING TO COMMIT SUICIDE

DESCRIPTION

Mrs. Kelly averages grades every two weeks and gives the students a current grade report. While completing the reports, Mrs. Kelley notices again that Adam Burke has not turned in any assignments for the last two weeks. Mrs. Kelley decides she must make it a point to talk with Adam.

As students are leaving class, Mrs. Kelley quietly asks Adam to stay for a moment. She tells Adam that she is very concerned about his failure to turn in work and is afraid that he won't pass the class unless he gets his papers in. Adam responds by saying, "I don't care about passing this stupid class! Maybe I'll just kill myself, and then I won't have to mess with this kind of crap anymore!" Before Mrs. Kelley can respond, Adam is gone. Mrs. Kelley is even more concerned about Adam and wonders what to do. Was Adam's outburst a serious threat?

CONTRIBUTING FACTORS

Suicide threats are very difficult to evaluate. They may be a sophisticated method for getting attention or sidetracking a teacher, or they may be a very desperate cry for help. Because there is no valid way for a teacher to assess the seriousness of the threat, the only responsible course of action is to assume that the student needs help. Four out of five teenagers who actually commit suicide have talked about suicide, or have threatened to commit suicide, before actually taking their lives.

PROBLEM SOLVING

Step 1: Be aware of potential danger signs.

Recently, a fair amount of media attention has been given to teenage suicides. A very common response to these tragedies is that no one close to the student has suspected the student was having the kinds of difficulties that might lead to suicide. There is no particular personality type that is more likely to be a suicide. One parent said, "If it could happen in our family, it could happen in anyone's family."

Some of the following behaviors may indicate that a student is in trouble. Though suicide may not be imminent, these signs may indicate that the student needs some kind of emotional support and assistance.

Any sudden change in behavior:
- passiveness or apathy
- lack of energy

- uncharacteristically aggressive behavior
- uncharacteristically emotional behavior
- uncharacteristically withdrawn behavior
- intolerance to frustration
- obvious displays of promiscuity

Problems with school:
- not turning in work
- truancy
- reduced participation in class activities

Changes in eating patterns

Changes in sleeping patterns

A general apathy

Obsession with death and dying

Talking about or threatening suicide

If a student talks about suicide or threatens suicide, act immediately.

Step 2: Meet privately with the student as soon as possible.

This step may put you in a very uncomfortable position because you will feel that the problem is beyond the scope of your training. However, if the student has indicated to you that he is in trouble, he probably trusts you. Do not wait. The student may need you now.

Begin the discussion by telling the student that you just wanted to have a conference with him because he seems to be having a difficult time. Try to avoid sounding accusatory. Simply describe some of the things that you have noticed. Ask the student if there is anything with which you can help. If the student is not responsive, do not force him to share with you. Just let him know that you are always available if he ever needs help.

If the student again expresses the idea that he is considering suicide, tell the student that you want to get him in touch with some people who might be able to help.

Regardless of the direction your discussion takes, calmly let the student know that you would also like to call his parents, just to let them know that you are concerned about him. If at this point the student indicates that problems originate from the home, use your own discretion. It may be best to handle the situation without contacting the parents.

Step 3: Contact the student's parents.

In most cases, parents deserve to know when someone suspects that their child may be having serious difficulties. Because you are not a mental health expert, you cannot evaluate how seriously troubled a student is. However, you can explain to parents that their child seems to be acting differently. If the student has mentioned suicide, you can tell the parents what was said. If the student seems to be obsessed with death, you can tell the parent how the student is acting.

If you only suspect serious problems, talk with the student's other teachers. Then call the parents. Let the parents know that you are calling primarily because you are concerned and thought they should know. Tell the parent what everyone has observed. The parent may also be aware of the student's depression. There may have been a family death or a divorce. Any number of things can trigger a teenage depression. The parent may be able to evaluate the situation well enough to know whether the student needs help. If the parent seems anxious, you may be able to suggest having the counselor call to determine whether additional help can be given.

Step 4: Discuss the problem with a counselor or school psychologist.

As soon as possible, meet with the counselor or school psychologist. This person may have additional suggestions and may want to become involved. If the problem seems to be very serious, you may need to contact your local mental health agency for additional help or referral.

Step 5: Work on increasing positive interactions with the student during your class period.

Regardless of the outcome of the steps above, make a conscious effort to increase your positive interactions with the student. Be natural, but show the student that you care about him. Greet all your students at the door and make it a point to include the troubled student. During independent work times, check to see how several students are doing and include this student. Provide the student with academic assistance if he is having difficulty in class. If the student typically does poor academic work, see Problem 42 for additional suggestions.

Note: Be what you are, a teacher who is concerned and interested. Recognize the limitations of your training and the amount of time you have available. Help the student by being there and by getting him in touch with others who are trained to work with this type of problem.

Problem 10
FEELING PICKED ON BY THE TEACHER

DESCRIPTION

In sophomore biology, Mr. Fadenrecht tells Leroy that he needs to stop talking during the class lecture or he will have to come in for after-school detention. Leroy responds, "Why are you always after me? Other people in the class talk, and you don't say anything about it. Whenever I do the least little thing, you jump down my throat!"

This of type of interaction occurs with Leroy several times a week. Mr. Fadenrecht does not want to treat Leroy any differently from the rest of the students in the class. Yet, several times each week, Leroy accuses Mr. Fadenrecht of treating him unfairly. Leroy's offenses are generally mild and Mr. Fadenrecht does not feel they warrant severe consequences. On the other hand, Mr. Fadenrecht is getting tired of hearing Leroy's accusations. To a teacher who tries to be fair, the accusations are upsetting and time consuming.

CONTRIBUTING FACTORS

When students accuse teachers of unfair treatment, there are several possible causes. The first consideration must be whether the teacher is actually treating the student unfairly. Every teacher has the potential of unconsciously treating one student more harshly than other students. If most of the interactions between a teacher and student are negative, it will be important to determine whether factors other than the student's actions are influencing the way the student is being treated.

Assuming that the student is being treated like everyone else in class, the student may accuse the teacher of unfair treatment because he has found he can change an established consequence. If a student like Leroy can sidetrack a teacher from implementing a consequence, or even get the teacher to overlook his behavior, the student will be reinforced for his accusatory behavior by getting away with minor misbehavior.

Accusing adults of unfair treatment may also be an ingrained habit because of the type of interaction the student has with his parents. Some parents reinforce their children's complaints by backing down any time the child claims he is being picked on. If the student has this type of interaction with his parents, it is inevitable that he will try this behavior on teachers as well.

Finally, some students will habitually accuse teachers of treating them unfairly because this frequently makes them the center of class attention and almost always gives them the teacher's undivided attention.

PROBLEM SOLVING

Step 1: Try to objectively evaluate whether the student has been treated fairly.

Identify several of the student's behaviors that you felt were inappropriate. Now visualize one of your best and most cooperative students engaging in the same behavior. Would you respond differently to this student? If the answer is yes, the student may be justified in feeling that he has been picked on.

You can also check out the student's accusations by asking other teachers whether the student makes the same claims in their classes. If he does accuse other teachers of treating him unfairly, it is fairly safe to assume that the problem lies with the student. It is very unlikely that three or four teachers will all treat the same student unjustly. However, if the student only makes claims against you, the problem probably lies in your relationship with the student. If the student does not follow the same pattern of behavior in most of his classes, it is probably not an ingrained part of his behavior.

The remaining steps in this plan should be followed whether you have been objective in your treatment of the student or not. If you have treated the student unfairly, implement the following steps and also strive to increase your objectivity. When interacting with the student, try to imagine that he is one of your more cooperative students.

Step 2: Make a list of situations that have resulted in the student accusing you of picking on him.

List what the student did, your response, and what the student said following your response. Try to identify at least five different situations.

Step 3: Identify procedures the student can follow when he feels that he is being treated unfairly.

Identify a time and place that the student can make an appointment with you to discuss any unfair treatment. Decide when these discussions might take place. They should occur at a neutral time—after school, before school, before the next class period, or during any break. Make yourself available for discussions after there has been a delay in time. You should not discuss the problem immediately after it has occurred.

Requiring the student to make an appointment to discuss an accusation of unfair treatment means that the discussion is delayed. The time delay will help you remain calm and objective. It also means that the student must feel strongly enough about the incident to go the the trouble of making an appointment with you. Finally, you can make sure the student is not the center of class attention by having a private discussion.

Step 4: Privately discuss the problem and plan with the student.

Go over the list of problem situations that you outlined in Step 1. Point out the inappropriate way the student has been voicing his concerns. Explain how his comments have disrupted class and tell the student that you would like to work out a more appropriate way to deal with his concerns.

Identify the times when you will be willing to talk with the student. Tell the student he will need to make an appointment to talk with you during one of these times if he feels he is being treated unfairly.

Specify that the student will also need to make the actual appointment in private—either before or after class—and that he will need to remain calm while arranging for the appointment. Inform the student that if he tries to make the appointment in an angry way, you will not listen. The way to make the appointment is to calmly say something like, "I would like to talk to you after school today if you have time." Demonstrating how to make the appointment will reduce the probability that the student will misbehave while making the appointment.

Finally, explain to the student that talking with you during an appointment will be the only appropriate way to voice concerns over unfair treatment. Tell the student you will not respond to complaints at any other time. Stress the fact that you will always attempt to treat the student fairly, but that you are willing to discuss any conflict only during an appointment.

Step 5: Consistently ignore the student if he claims he is being picked on.

Any time the student accuses you of treating him unfairly, you will need to ignore the student. If the student tries to involve you in an argument during class, it will be important to demonstrate that he will no longer receive attention for voicing his concerns in this way. Chapter 8 provides detailed information on how to effectively use ignoring.

Step 6: Praise the student for maturity if he chooses to set up an appointment time.

If the student makes an appointment to discuss unfair treatment with you, praise the student for his maturity in waiting to discuss the problem at an appropriate time. Listen calmly and objectively to the student. If his concerns are well founded, apologize and make adjustments to remedy the situation. If the concerns are not well founded, tell the student why you feel he is being treated fairly. Ask the student to imagine other students in the same situation. Explain that you would treat every student the same way. If the student is not satisfied with your response, let him know he is welcome to discuss the matter with the school counselor. Do not allow your discussion to degenerate into an argument.

Step 7: If the student does not make an appointment to speak with you and stops complaining about unfair practices, privately let the student know you are pleased with his mature behavior.

If the student changes his behavior dramatically, let the student know you are impressed with the way he has been handling himself in class. Keep communication lines open by checking with the student periodically to see how things are going.

Problem 11
CHEWING GUM

DESCRIPTION

Mr. Muir is annoyed with students who chew gum in his Spanish classes. The school has a rule against gum chewing, and it is particularly inappropriate in a foreign language class where students need to work on articulation. Mr. Muir has told students that gum chewing is not acceptable in his class. Nonetheless, Mr. Muir feels he still has to spend a lot of class time telling students to dispose of their gum.

CONTRIBUTING FACTORS

Students chew gum because they enjoy chewing gum. It seems to become even more enjoyable if they aren't supposed to do it. Because the activity is reinforcing in itself, some students will continue to engage in gum chewing unless there is a clear and consistent consequence.

Some students will also chew gum when they realize they can annoy the teacher, become the center of attention, and manipulate class time. This minor misbehavior can give the student center stage while he makes a big production of putting his gum in the wastebasket.

Finally, some students will chew gum just to see if they can get away with it. Gum chewing can be a very mild way of rebelling against the system. It is a minor misbehavior that even compliant students may feel comfortable experimenting with.

Note: Gum chewing is a problem when the custodial staff has to clean it off the furniture and floors. It is a problem when there is a school policy against gum chewing, and it is a problem if you do not want students to chew gum in your class. If none of these problems exist, it may be perfectly acceptable to allow your students to chew gum.

Step 1: Select a mild consequence for chewing gum in your class.

Students will need to learn that there is a consistent consequence in your classroom for chewing gum. This means that you should select a consequence mild enough that you will not be reticent about following through.

However, the consequence must be more than a verbal admonishment. It must be significant enough that the student would rather avoid the consequence than chew the gum. Owing time is one of the most effective consequences for gum chewing. It is easy to implement and not overly severe for the misbehavior. Any time a student is caught chewing gum, the student owes the teacher five minutes. Time is paid back before school, after school, during the student's lunch period, or from a break. During this time, the student must sit and do nothing. He has wasted class time, therefore he owes five minutes of his valued time.

Step 2: Discuss the problem and future consequences with students.

Explain to students that you do not want to waste any more time dealing with gum chewing. If you are enforcing this rule because it is a school rule, tell students you must all work to cooperate within the rules of the entire school. Inform students that this rule makes building maintenance more efficient and may save them from sitting or stepping on someone's discarded gum. If the rule against gum chewing is your own rule, explain why it is easier to run the class without dealing with gum chewing.

Explain the consequences you have set up for gum chewing. If the rule against gum chewing is not a school rule, you may want to remind students as they enter the room that they are not to chew gum. However, after the first few days, students should be responsible for remembering to get rid of their gum before class. If you have to take class time to have a student dispose of gum, the student will automatically owe you five minutes.

Step 3: When students are caught chewing gum, calmly and consistently implement the consequences.

Do not negotiate. If the student objects to your procedures, tell the student he may talk with you after class. Otherwise, ignore any protests by simply walking away or going on to another task.

Problem 12
TIPPING BACK IN A CHAIR

DESCRIPTION

Miss Reuter is concerned about students tipping back in their chairs. Two freshman boys in one of her math classes consistently tip their chairs, sitting way back with only two of the legs touching the ground. Miss Reuter has told the boys over and over again that all four legs should touch the ground. Grumbling, the boys put their chairs back into an upright position, but within a few minutes they are right back to tipping their chairs. Miss Reuter doesn't want to make a big deal of this problem. She doesn't want to be overly picky and doesn't want to appear to be an elementary teacher instead of a secondary teacher.

CONTRIBUTING FACTORS

Tipping back in a chair is primarily the result of habit. For some people, it is a comfortable position to sit in. The more students are allowed to sit in a tipping position, the more they will have a tendency to tip back in their chairs.

If a student is in need of attention, he may also find that tipping back in his chair increases his interactions with teachers. By tipping in his chair, the student finds that he can momentarily be the center of attention. If this is the only attention the student gets from adults, it will reinforce the habit of tipping back.

Note: Though this problem may not seem worth bothering with at the secondary level, it is a concern because of the potential for student injury. If the student is allowed to tip back in his chair, the habit becomes more deeply ingrained. If the student is injured at school, there is the potential for legal action against the school or teacher. Tipping back in a chair is basically inappropriate in a public setting. The student should learn to use the furniture as it was designed to be used.

PROBLEM SOLVING

Step 1: Try using gentle verbal reprimands several times.

Tell students that tipping back in their chairs is a dangerous habit, and then follow through with consistent reminders. Students may abandon their habit of sitting in a tipped-back position just by knowing that you will never allow them to remain in that position. However, if you have tried using verbal reprimands for two to three days and students are still tipping back, verbal reprimands will not improve the situation. Discontinue this procedure as students may be getting reinforced for tipping back through the attention they are receiving.

Step 2: Establish a consequence for tipping back in a chair.

The most logical consequence for tipping back in a chair is losing the privilege of using the chair. If the student can't sit in the chair correctly, he won't be allowed to use the chair for the remainder of the period.

Step 3: Discuss the problem with students and explain the consequence.

Explain to students why you cannot allow them to tip back in their chairs and inform them of the future consequence for tipping back in their chairs. Your discussion might be similar to the following:

> I'm still very concerned about people tipping back in their chairs. It seems like a picky thing to be concerned about but it is hard on the furniture, and it could be hard on you. Since reminders haven't worked, and I do not want anyone to get injured, you will simply lose the privilege of using a chair any time you tip back in it. Your chair will be removed, and you will need to stand for the remainder of the period. You will not be allowed to sit on your desk or on the floor. Does anyone have any questions?

Step 4: Consistently implement the consequences.

If a student tips back in his chair, quietly tell the student that he may not use his chair for the rest of the period. Remind the student that he may not sit on his desk or on the floor. If the student chooses to kneel, allow him to do so without comment. Implement this procedure in a matter of fact manner. The student should not feel that you are trying to humiliate him.

Step 5: Ignore any objections from the student.

Plan to ignore any comments from the student. You may hear statements like, "Boy, this is really stupid. Treating us like babies!" Resist the temptation to tell the student, "If you didn't act like a baby, I wouldn't need to treat you like a baby." Avoid being pulled into an adversarial relationship. The procedure is reasonable because it is has been discussed with students. If you negotiate with students or respond to objections, the student ends up taking control of the situation and it becomes a "big deal."

Step 6: If you have to take a chair away from a student, treat the student normally and interact positively in regard to academic work.

Make it a point to interact positively with the student. If students are doing independent work, walk around the room. Check to see how several students are doing, and include the student who has lost his chair.

For the next several days, make it a point to interact with the student when he is working. This will demonstrate that the past incident is forgotten and that you are aware of the student's efforts to follow the rules.

Problem 13
HYPOCHONDRIA

DESCRIPTION

Vonn raised her hand. When Mr. Mousseu called on her, she complained of stomach pain and nausea and asked to go to the health room to see the school nurse. This is the second time during the week and the fifth time in three weeks that Vonn has gone to the health room.

Mr. Mousseu is concerned about the amount of class time Vonn misses. He has also found himself avoiding Vonn. Any time anyone talks to her, she complains about how she is feeling. You don't dare ask her how she's doing. Vonn doesn't have many friends.

CONTRIBUTING FACTORS

One cause for complaints is that the student is in fact ill. Without medical training, one cannot assume that a health complaint is not valid.

However, this problem is more likely the result of the attention the student receives when she complains about her health. She is given one-to-one attention from the teacher. She may momentarily be the center of attention in class, and then she receives attention from the school nurse or office staff. This student gets attention by complaining because she has not learned appropriate ways of interacting with people. The student's symptoms may be very real to her, as she has gotten reinforced for feeling sick. This student may no longer know the difference between feeling ill and just feeling tired or emotionally down. Unfortunately, the more she complains, the more people ignore her, and the more she will feel the need to get attention.

Another factor in this problem may be that the student has also learned to avoid unpleasant or difficult class activities by using health excuses. Regardless of the motivation, the student may or may not be aware that her health complaints are not real.

Note: If the student is suffering from health problems, medical intervention will certainly be necessary. If the student is well enough to attend school, as with allergies, the student will also need to learn behaviors that do not interfere with her social interactions and classroom success. If the student does not learn to function on a daily basis without complaining and going to the health room, the student will have a difficult time in later life holding a job.

Step 1: Recommend that the student receive a physical examination.

You may wish to contact the school nurse to document the student's health-room visits and frequent complaints. Next, parents should be contacted and a physical exam should be recommended. If the parents are unwilling or unable to arrange a physical exam, the school administration should be involved to make sure the student is examined by a physician.

Step 2: Once a physical has been completed, establish consistent procedures for dealing with any health complaints.

Work with the school nurse and health aide to determine how you will respond to complaints. Once a procedure has been established, enlist the cooperation of other staff members who are likely to deal with the student.

Step 3: Any time the student complains about health, immediately send her to the health room.

As soon as the student begins to complain about her health, she should automatically go to the health room. This should be nonnegotiable. Teachers should plan to give the student as little attention as possible in response to health complaints. When the student begins complaining about her health, the teacher should immediately say, "That's too bad. You need to go to the health room." This comment should be made in a matter of fact way. The tone should not be overly sympathetic and should not be at all sarcastic.

Step 4: In the health room, the student should be required to lie down and do nothing for a set period of time.

Standard health-screening procedures should be completed as usual, but the health attendant should give the student as little attention as possible. Sympathy should not be apparent. This may seem harsh, particularly if the student has a diagnosed health problem. However, if the student gets a lot of attention when sick, it could lead to the student having more and more symptoms. The student should always receive any necessary health monitoring or treatment, but should not get a lot of attention.

Once the student has reported to the health room, she should automatically be required to spend a minimum of fifteen minutes. This will help eliminate the possibility of the student finding that she can go to the health room, get some attention, and still miss only five minutes of class time.

Step 5: Establish a consequence for class time the student misses.

Whenever the student misses class, she should be required to make up the time that was missed by doing an extra-credit assignment. Each make-up assignment should take approximately fifteen minutes and should demonstrate to the student that she has missed something important. For example, if the student has missed a class discussion, you might give her an essay question concerning the topic that was discussed.

If you are using a grading system that incorporates a percentage of the grade for participation and effort, the student can be told that she will not be earning class performance points while she is out of class. These points will need to be made up by doing extra-credit work. (See Chapter 2.) This particular procedure teaches students that how they use class time will affect their grade.

Assigning extra-credit work for class time missed is designed to teach the student that she should make every effort to stay in class. If she isn't feeling terrific, it will be easier to ignore her health problems than it will be to do the extra work. If the student does suffer from hayfever, headaches, or other health problems, she will need to learn to live with the symptoms if she hopes to eventually maintain a job. Thinking about something other than health problems is the best way to learn to live with them.

Step 6: Discuss the problem and plan with the student.

At a neutral time, explain to the student that you are all concerned about her and want to help her learn to cope with any health problems. Explain that complaining about health all the time will only make her feel worse and that it is difficult for others to enjoy interacting with her if she never feels well. Tell the student that everyone will take her complaints seriously if she decides she doesn't feel well. This means that any time she complains, she will automatically need to go to the health room. Explain that since class time is valuable, she will also need to make up the time she has missed by doing extra credit work. Give examples of the kinds of assignments she will be given for missing class.

Step 7: Increase the number of positive interactions you have with the student.

It will be very important to teach the student that she can get a lot of attention and support without having to be ill. Enlist the help of other staff members. Greet the student as she enters the classroom. Stop to talk with the student in the halls. Ask the student how her special interests are going. If possible, encourage the student to become involved in activities that will take her mind off her own health. She might enjoy working with a community service group or a 4-H group where she needs to take responsibility for something other than herself. Take an active interest in the student's academic efforts. (See Chapter 7.)

Step 8: Provide the student with feedback on improved classroom performance and a decline in health complaints.

As the student learns to cope with real or imagined health problems, let the student know you are proud of the way she has managed to work hard in class. Let her know privately that you are pleased to have her in class every day.

Problem 14
BEING OFF TASK DURING INDEPENDENT SEATWORK

DESCRIPTION

Each day, Mr. Gillette's ninth-grade English class has fifteen minutes of independent study time to work on assignments and write in a required journal. During this time, students are frequently off task. Some quietly talk or read the school newspaper. Others sit and do nothing. When Mr. Gillette reminds the class that they need to work on writing, most of the students start to work again. However, within a few minutes, more and more students begin to do other things. During the fifteen-minute study period, Mr. Gillette has to remind students over and over again to get back to work.

CONTRIBUTING FACTORS

Many students find it is more enjoyable to socialize or do nothing than it is to work. When the only consequence for off-task behavior is a reminder, there is no compelling reason for students to become self-motivated. In the preceding example, students have found that Mr. Gillette has taken it upon himself to keep students working. Whenever a number of students are off task, Mr. Gillette tells them to get back to work. Why should students be responsible for working independently when Mr. Gillette will take the responsibility for them?

Off-task behavior during independent work may also be the result of a teacher falling into the criticism trap. Students may have found that an effective way to get the teacher's attention is to be off task. If you find yourself reminding students to get back to work more than once in forty-five minutes of independent work time, the criticism trap is probably part of the problem.

Finally, many students do not understand that participation and effort in the classroom will make a difference in their overall grade. Many students are poor managers of time. They do not know how to use class time efficiently.

PROBLEM SOLVING

Step 1: Avoid falling into the criticism trap.

There will be occasions when students need to be verbally reminded to get back to work. However, to reduce the amount of attention individuals receive for off-task behavior, remind the whole class to get back to work. If this class reminder does not result in everyone returning to task, look directly at the student or students who are off task. Maintain eye contact until everyone is back at work.

To avoid giving students attention primarily for off-task behavior, give students who are on task feedback about their efficient behavior. Avoid phony praise. Quietly give attention to on-task behavior with adultlike interactions. "Nice job, Joe. I see you won't have much homework tonight." The feedback can be brief and matter-of-fact. Other students will notice that you are paying attention to appropriate behavior. Be sure that you give this feedback periodically to all students who are working hard. Make a point to include students who have a past history of poor work habits.

In addition, give individual students *more* attention for appropriate behavior than you do for inappropriate behavior. Every time you must remind a student to get back to work, try to catch that same student working hard at least three times. Your goal will be to give the student attention three times more often for appropriate behavior than for inappropriate behavior. This three-to-one ratio will demonstrate to students that it is easier to get feedback for working hard than it is to get feedback for goofing off.

Step 2: Make it a habit to visually scan the room during independent work times.

When first implementing this plan, it will be important to visually scan the room fairly frequently during independent work times. Students need to know that the teacher is observing their behavior. If you become engrossed in grading papers or in working with individual students for the entire work period, students will fall back into their off-task behavior.

Take a few seconds in between papers, or between student questions to survey the room. Try to avoid being predictable about when and how you will scan the room. Initially, you will want to survey students at least once a minute. Students should not know when you will scan the room again so it will be important to vary your routine slightly. Eventually, you should be able to reduce the frequency of the scanning to about once every five minutes.

When visually scanning the room, begin with one corner and quickly gaze across the entire room. You should observe every student. Avoid starting in the same place and always looking across the room in the same direction. If you are predictable, some students become very sophisticated at determining when the teacher has begun observing. By the time the teacher has reached these students, they are always back on task and never accountable for their off-task behavior.

Try to avoid scanning only when you hear a problem. Scan frequently enough to let students know they are being observed when they are on task. This indicates that you are observing frequently enough to observe the class before problems occur.

Step 3: Establish a procedure for students to get assistance from you while continuing their work.

In some classes, students may need assistance with independent work. If students must wait for long periods with their hands up, they will tire and find other things to do while they are waiting for help. This encourages off-task behavior.

Establish a procedure for students to signal for help while they continue to work on other parts of the assignment. There are several methods for getting teacher assistance other than hand raising. Perhaps the easiest method is to have students stand a partially opened book on their desk in a vertical position. This type of signal leaves the student's hands free to work on an alternative portion of the assignment. Let students know that you will answer their questions only if they signal with the book and are busy working on the task. They need to realize you will not help them if they are just staring off into space. This type of procedure will eliminate any excuses students might have for being off task.

Once you have established a method for students to get your attention during independent work times, be consistent in responding only to students who follow the established procedure.

Step 4: Establish an efficient system for recording off-task behavior during independent work time.

When you visually scan the room, record any off-task behavior you see. This information will be used to implement consequences for inappropriate behavior.

Recording off-task behavior can be done efficiently by keeping a class list handy. Any time you notice someone off task, mark an *O* for "off task" next to the student's name. The Weekly Record Sheet discussed in Chapter 2 was designed for this purpose.

This simple system will teach students that their inappropriate behavior has been noticed and that they will be accountable for failing to make use of class time. A mild consequence will then be implemented, and most students will learn to use their independent work time. This system will work only if you systematically scan the room. Students must see that you are monitoring everyone in the class and that anyone who is off task will be accountable. If you see the procedure but are not systematically scanning, you will end up responding only to inappropriate behavior and some students may end up feeling they are picked on.

Step 5: Establish a consequence for off-task behavior.

Establish a percentage of the students' grades for participation and effort. (See Chapter 2.) The percentage of the grade for participation and effort in class can vary from 5 percent to 50 percent of the final grade depending on the type of class you teach and the type of students in your class.

Once you have determined the percentage of the grade to be based on participation and effort, determine how many points students can earn each week for their classroom performance. Next determine a set number of points students might fail to earn for being off task. For example, if students can earn 20 points per week for classroom performance, each incidence of off-task behavior could mean the student has failed to earn one point.

If you are not including participation and effort in your grade, follow all of the preceding procedures but in addition establish a set of formal consequences for off-task behavior. Possible consequences include owing time, after-school detention, parental contacts, or work assigned. For example, you might establish that three off-task notations in a week will result in ten minutes of owed time or in an after-school detention. You will need a mild consequence that demonstrates to students that class time is as valuable as their free time.

Step 6: Discuss the problem and plan with students.

Explain to students that too much time is being wasted during independent work times. Let them know that you expect work times to be used efficiently. This means that students will work quietly by themselves. Explain your system for getting help, and emphasize that students should continue on with the remainder of the assignment until you are able to help them.

Let students know that you will be periodically observing the entire class and that you will record any students who are off task during those times. Next explain the consequences. If you are going to use participation and effort points as a part of student grades, fully explain the number of points students may earn during the week and the number of points they will fail to earn for off-task behavior. If you have selected one of the other consequences, explain carefully how the system will be implemented.

Step 7: Periodically reinforce students for working during independent work periods.

As students learn to work successfully, praise their efforts. At the end of a ten-minute period with everyone on task, let the entire class know that you are pleased with their efforts. Make a matter-of-fact statement. "Everyone has really worked hard during the last ten minutes. I'm impressed with your concentration." When students are able to go for several days without any off-task notations, give the students five minutes of free time. "You have used your work time so efficiently this week that you deserve to have five minutes of free time."

Problem 15
TALKING DURING CLASS—ONE OR TWO STUDENTS

DESCRIPTION

Mrs. Radziski has a sixth-grade student in her reading class who talks incessantly. During class discussions, Kent always wants to dominate the discussion. Once he is called on, it's almost impossible to get him to stop talking. During independent work times, Kent is always talking to someone, whether they're listening or not. Kent even talks while Mrs. Radziski is trying to talk. Mrs. Radziski has tried discussing the problem with Kent. She has scolded him, she has reminded him, and she has even tried isolating him. In spite of all this, Kent continues to talk and bother students around him. Mrs. Radziski is considering isolating Kent from other students for the remainder of the term.

CONTRIBUTING FACTORS

The truly chronic talker talks out of habit. He doesn't seem to care whom he's talking to or if anyone is listening. This may be a student who wasn't listened to when he was younger. He learned to keep talking until he was finally noticed. Now talking is reinforcing in itself. It will be difficult to teach this student to change his behavior because he is reinforced for talking regardless of the reactions of people around him.

Some chronic talkers are also reinforced by the attention they get for talking. These students have learned that they can control the classroom by engaging in a behavior that obviously upsets others.

PROBLEM SOLVING

Step 1: Assign a desk to the student that is close to where you spend the majority of the class period.

By doing this, you can monitor the student's behavior as closely as possible without isolating him from other students. Select a desk that is a part of your regular student seating, but as close to you as possible.

Step 2: Provide positive feedback to the student when he is being quiet.

Recognize that being quiet is very difficult for this student and that it requires an ongoing effort on his part. Acknowledge that effort by providing positive feedback. "Kent, you have been working very hard in class today."

Avoid praising the student for not talking. Your goal is to increase appropriate participation and effort in class. If the student has tried to dominate class discussions in the past, you might say something like, "Kent, I really appreciated your comments in class today and your ability to give everyone else a chance to participate too."

Step 3: Establish a sequence of consequences for inappropriate talking.

A sequence of consequences is discussed here. You may choose to use this sequence or design your own.

a. First incident—one verbal reprimand and warning: Tell the student that he is talking at an inappropriate time. Also remind the student that the next incident of inappropriate talking will lead to isolation for the remainder of the period and the next class period. Give only one verbal reprimand per period.

b. Second incident—isolation area for the remainder of the period and during the same class period the next day: Calmly tell the student that the remainder of the period and the same class period the next day will be spent in the isolation area. Do not negotiate, and ignore any comments from the student. In order to leave the isolation area, the student will need to complete a full period without talking.

c. Talking in isolation—fifteen minutes owed for each incident of talking in isolation: If the student talks while in isolation, he will owe fifteen minutes after school, before school, or during lunch for each additional incident of talking. During owed time the student should sit quietly and do nothing. In addition, the student will need to stay in isolation until he has completed one full class period without talking. When the student talks, calmly inform him that he owes fifteen minutes.

d. One full period without talking in isolation—normal seating the next day: When the student has demonstrated that he can work a whole class period without talking, quietly inform him that he may return to his normal seat the next day. Tell him you are pleased that he was able to show such restraint.

Step 4: Set up an isolation area in the classroom.

The isolation area should be as far away from other students as possible, but the student doesn't need to be completely isolated. If the distance from other students will be minimal, make sure that your most mature students are the closest to the isolation area. Train these students to ignore anyone who is in isolation.

Step 5: Discuss the problem and procedure with the student.

At a neutral time, privately discuss the problem with the student. Explain that people have a hard time knowing when it is important to listen to him because he is always talking. Tell the student that his incessant talking also interrupts class. Explain to the student that you realize that talking all of the time is a habit and that you are going to be following a plan that should help him learn to control his talking. Explain the sequence of consequences you will be using.

Step 6: When the student has shown a significant improvement, reinforce the student for his improvement.

Any number of reinforcers can be used to demonstrate to the student that you are impressed with his increasing sense of responsibility and maturity. If the student's parents are interested, write a note home. Have the principal congratulate the student on his growth. Allow the student to choose where he would like to sit for the next week. Ask the student to assist you in a class activity or to take on a responsibility.

Problem 16
TALKING DURING CLASS—SEVERAL STUDENTS

DESCRIPTION

Mrs. Skyles teaches a senior journalism class. This is a class that she typically enjoys because students are very able and rarely need disciplining. During independent work times, students are free to move about the room to work on paste-ups, to use the typewriter and recording equipment, and to do whatever is needed to complete individual assignments. Mrs. Skyles also allows students to talk during these times as she encourages them to work out their ideas with each other. Most years, students take full advantage of the time. Although there is a fair amount of movement and quiet talking, students are on task.

This year Mrs. Skyles has three students who seem to talk nonstop. Marta, Bonnie, and Sue are all close friends. Unfortunately, their talk is rarely related to journalism. Mrs. Skyles has spoken to the students. They quiet down for a short time, but within minutes always seem to be talking and laughing again. Mrs. Skyles is disturbed because the girls are not completing work up to their abilities, and because she is beginning to feel like a nag.

CONTRIBUTING FACTORS

The most obvious factor in this problem is that the students enjoy talking to each other, and the pleasure of talking together outweighs the consequences. In this instance, teacher reprimands are punishing only to the teacher.

PROBLEM SOLVING

Step 1: Try using a gentle verbal reprimand first.

Calmly ask the students who are talking to stop talking. Give a one-sentence explanation why you would prefer that they didn't talk. For example, the teacher might say, "I would prefer that you didn't talk about your date last night because that will not help you complete your article on the food drive."

The gentle verbal reprimand can be used between three and ten times. If this procedure is needed more than ten times over the course of a term, plan to change your strategy by implementing the following steps. If you have already been nagging your students, eliminate this step and proceed directly to Step 2.

Step 2: Identify the borderline between appropriate and inappropriate talking during class time.

List the different types of activities that students will engage in during class time. Next determine whether students should be allowed to talk during these activities.

Example: Talking between students

Not allowed	Allowed
Class lectures	Writing articles
Student reports	Working on paste-ups
Typing	Setting up interview questions

Next, identify the parameters of allowable talking. How loudly may students talk? Will they be restricted to particular topics? With whom may they talk? How far away may the other person be?

1. While you are writing your article, talking must be restricted to topics that are pertinent to your article or the project of another person.

2. While working on paste-ups, you may talk quietly with whoever is at the paste-up table. As long as you can stay on task, you may discuss anything quietly. This means that people at the next table should not be able to overhear what you are talking about.

3. While setting up interview questions, you may talk with others to get additional ideas and to practice; however, your talk must be restricted to working on the interview.

Step 3: Set up a consequence for inappropriate talking.

If the problem is primarily between two or three students, it might be reasonable to separate the students if they fail to stay within the boundaries of acceptable talking. For example, you might establish that inappropriate talking will lead to assigned seats for one week, with students sitting apart. If you have a grading system that includes participation and effort, inappropriate talking should also affect the student's grades. If students are moved apart for inappropriate talking, they should fail to earn participation points for that day.

Step 4: At a neutral time discuss the problem with the students.

Avoid having this discussion when students have just been reprimanded. The discussion will need to be calm and nonaccusatory. Therefore, it is best to have the discussion during a neutral time. Tell the students that you would like to help them learn to keep their conversation related to class assignments. Explain that their talking has interfered with their ability to use class time well. It has affected the quality of their work, and it has disturbed others in class. Because reminders have not worked, inform the students that you will require them to sit apart for a week whenever they fail to keep their discussion within the prescribed limits. Go through your list of activities, and describe exactly what will be acceptable and what will not be acceptable.

If a student complains that the consequence is babyish, explain that you will impose it only if she fails to act maturely.

Step 5: If students talk inappropriately, calmly explain how they have violated the limits of acceptable talking, and implement the consequence.

If the students make a wisecrack or complain, ignore them. Give the students as little attention as possible. Their misbehavior does not deserve your attention.

If a student should refuse to move, calmly inform the student that you will keep track of the time it takes the student to get to her assigned seat. She will owe you that time after school or during a lunch period. (See Chapter 8.)

Step 6: If students continue talking after they have taken their new seats, inform them that they will owe five minutes of time for each additional incident of inappropriate talking.

Record the amount of additional time the students owes. When you inform the student of the total time that is owed, be as brief as possible. Do not argue, and do not discuss the consequence.

Step 7: Increase the amount of positive interactions and feedback these students receive in class.

When students are working appropriately, give them your attention. Let them know that you are pleased with their mature behavior and their ability to determine when socializing is appropriate. Feedback can be given verbally, via notes, or private confer-

Figure IV-1   Daily Report Card

DAILY REPORT CARD

Student Marta Coffel
Week of April 12

Each day that Marta restricts talking to appropriate topics during appropriate tasks, Mrs. Skyles will sign this report card. Marta will earn the right to watch TV if she chooses any evening that the card is signed. If Marta forgets the daily report card, she will also not be allowed to watch TV.

Monday _____   Thursday _____
Tuesday _____   Friday _____
Wednesday _____

---

ences. You can also express your confidence in these students by giving them responsibilities and by working on increasing your positive interaction with them.

Step 8: If the problem continues for two weeks after implementing the above steps, set up an individualized reinforcement system.

If the problem persists, contact the student's parents and inform them of the problem. See if the parents would be willing to assist you. If they seem supportive, ask them if they would be willing to withhold TV, use of the family car, or free time on weekends if the student fails to behave appropriately in class. If the parents agree, you can set up a system that requires a certain number of good reports to earn whatever privilege is selected. Set up a daily report card similar to that in Figure IV-1.

If it seems unlikely that parents will follow through with a daily report card system, set up your own contract. Instead of working for a privilege at home, students can work for a privilege in your classroom.

Problem 17
MISBEHAVING DURING INDEPENDENT SEATWORK TIME

DESCRIPTION

In Ms. Hausman's eighth-grade science class, students work on lab exercises two or three times each week. While working on the lab assignments, students frequently have questions. There are often five or six students with their hands up. Students sometimes wait as long as five minutes before Ms. Hausman is able to help them. In the meantime, some of the students become impatient and end up trying to get Ms. Hausman's attention by calling out to her. Other students simply quit working and begin visiting with those around them. Ms. Hausman feels that her classroom is sometimes chaotic. Her students seem to be very immature and unable to function independently.

CONTRIBUTING FACTORS

When several students are unable to complete assignments independently, this is often an indication that more instruction is needed prior to beginning independent work. Students may not have the skills or concepts needed to complete work independently.

A second factor may be that several students do not listen to preliminary instruction, or they may be unable to remember instruction sufficiently to complete independent work.

A final contributing factor is the length of time students are expected to wait with their hands up if they need help. If students must wait more than fifteen seconds for assistance, their arms tire and they become bored. If students must wait several minutes for help, they are likely to tire, rest their arms, and possibly lose their turn. This situation can lead to students waiting for help the majority of the period. Some students will undoubtedly stop trying and will find other things to occupy their time.

PROBLEM SOLVING

Step 1: Identify the types of questions students typically ask during independent work times.

a. Do students ask basic questions about the assignment—which pages they are supposed to read or which questions they are supposed to answer?

b. Do students ask questions about procedures or use of equipment?

c. Do students ask questions that show they do not comprehend vocabulary or important concepts?

d. Do students ask questions because they fail to understand written or verbal instructions?

Step 2: If students frequently ask questions related to what they should do, require students to write the assignment at the top of their papers before beginning work.

If students frequently ask questions related to what they are supposed to do for their assignment, write the assignment on the board and require students to copy the information on their papers. Tell students that you will not accept papers if the assignment has not been written at the top of their paper. After students become used to copying the assignment, begin giving the assignment orally. Continue requiring students to write the assignment at the top of their papers.

In addition, when giving assignments try to anticipate student questions. If students typically ask whether they need to answer in complete sentences, include this information on your assignment. Discuss the expectations for the assignment. Ask for questions. Then inform students that you will ignore any questions regarding information that you have already covered.

Sample Student Heading with Assignment Copied:

Jonathan Smith
5th Period Psychology
Due: January 13
Assignment: Read pages 15–30
                    Answer questions 1–5 in complete sentences

Step 3: If students frequently ask about procedures or use of equipment, work on notetaking skills.

a. While you are teaching students new procedures or how to use equipment, be explicit. Identify exactly what should be done first, second, third, and so on. The less sophisticated your students, the more tightly you will need to break down the steps.

b. At each step, paraphrase your directions and write them on the board for students to copy as you are going through them.

c. After a few days of modeling these procedures, have student volunteers help you paraphrase the information that they will copy from the board.

d. As students learn this technique, begin calling on lower-performing students to paraphrase. Initially, ask the less able students to paraphrase the easiest steps. Continue writing the notes on the board for students to copy as you are going through the instructions.

e. Continue having students paraphrase, but eliminate writing the notes on the board for students to copy. Inform students that members of the class will take turns paraphrasing, but it will be up to individual students to write their own notes. They may use the paraphrase suggested in class or they may use their own words. Check to make sure that students are writing notes at each step of your instructions.

Throughout these exercises let students know that they will be accountable for their notes. You can assign a small percentage of the grade to notetaking or you can make notetaking a part of participation-and-effort points. You will periodically need to check student notes to determine whether anyone is having difficulty.

Students should also be told that they will be accountable for having their notes available when they are working on related assignments or projects. You may wish to require that students keep a notebook. Prior to beginning independent work on a related assignment, have students practice using their notes. Set up hypothetical questions. Ask students to identify where they would find the information. Have students locate the information in their notes and read the step that would answer the question.

Step 4: If students seem to be having difficulty because they do not understand important concepts or vocabulary, work on potential problems prior to assigning independent work.

One of the easiest ways to try to determine what students will have difficulty with is to go over assignments and try to anticipate where problems will lie prior to assigning work. During instruction, drill students on basic information and collectively work through application exercises. If only a small percentage of the class has difficulty, you might want to structure additional instruction for a small group of students.

Step 5: Establish a procedure for students to get help.

Select an alternative to hand raising that would allow students to continue on with other work while waiting for help. A very common and effective technique is to have students stand a book on their desk, slightly open, in a vertical position.

Inform students that you will help only students who have a book up and who are continuing to work quietly. Let students know that you will not help anyone who calls out for help during independent work times.

This procedure will require that you frequently scan the room to determine whether anyone needs help. If you let long periods go by while you are correcting work, students will quickly find out that the signal does not work. Their only alternative will be to go back to calling for your attention.

If your class structure requires students to work on independent tasks that may be difficult for many students, it may be necessary to have higher-performing students serve as student assistants. Ask three or four higher-performing students if they will help you answer questions if there are a lot of students waiting. When you see many students waiting for help, ask one of the "assistants" to help answer questions. Do not always use the same student as the assistant. By using a different student, you reduce the chance that the assistants will fall behind because they spend too much time helping to answer questions.

Problem 18
MAKING "WISECRACKS" OR BEING A "SMART ALECK"

DESCRIPTION

Chris is bright, talented, witty, and a pain in the neck. He is always ready with a wisecrack or a joke. He sometimes pulls minor pranks and practical jokes. Most of the time he is really funny, but he often comes very close to getting his laughs at the expense of the teacher and other students. He sometimes comes very close to putting others down, and occasionally he crosses the line.

In Mrs. Sorenson's fifth-period advanced math class, Mrs. Sorenson has decided to spend a few minutes explaining how advanced math skills may help students meet the requirements of challenging and rewarding careers. Before Mrs. Sorensen has a chance to proceed, Chris chimes in by saying, "Yeah, like you—getting a highly paid job as math teacher, making about two bucks an hour." Mrs. Sorensen ignores this comment.

The next day, Mrs. Sorenson begins class by admonishing the class for getting behind on their independent assignments. As she is talking, Chris says nothing but sits with a big grin on his face. Finally, Mrs. Sorenson says, "Chris, wipe that grin off your face. I do not mean this to be funny." At that, Chris takes his hand, raises it above his head and slowly lowers it in front of his face, changing his expression from a grin to a frown as his hand passes in front of his face. This pantomime receives the attention and laughter of the entire class.

CONTRIBUTING FACTORS

There may be many factors affecting this complex behavior. A smart aleck is a bright and capable person. Part of his behavior is the result of being really "funny." People enjoy his cleverness and fast wit. The smart aleck is reinforced by others because he is entertaining. This may result in the student continually experimenting to find out what will get a laugh and what will not. Making wisecracks can become a nonthinking habit for a student, his way of interacting.

Another factor to consider is that the student may be bored. If work is too easy, the student may occupy himself by thinking of comebacks and smart comments instead of focusing on academic tasks. When school is too easy, a bright student may have too much time on his hands. The humor and smart comments may be his way of filling time and entertaining himself.

Wisecracks may also be the student's way of engaging in intellectual competition with the teacher. The student may not know that some of his jokes and comments are actually cruel and destructive; his intellectual abilities may outstrip his social sensitivities.

Finally, some students may use humor as a subtle way to manipulate the classroom and teacher. This may be a bright student's way of challenging authority. If the student has had primarily negative interactions with adults, he may actually enjoy being able to put teachers down in subtle ways that are unlikely to result in punishment. Bright students recognize that it is often difficult for teachers to respond to derogatory comments that are made humorously. But where is the line between insult and humor?

Note: This plan will not attempt to squelch the student. The wise guy is often a very dynamic quick-witted individual. If you want to "contain" the student, you may create an adversarial relationship. If the student feels you are against him, he may use his many talents to continually put you down. Your goal will be to channel this student's talent and humor into appropriate classroom behaviors.

If you are able to handle this problem by using your own quick wit and sense of humor, you may be able to help channel the student's comments. You may be able to use his sense of humor as a way of making class more fun and material more interesting. As the student finds you also have a quick comeback, he will be less likely to put you down. Your interactions will be lively, but fun. You may want to study the following plan, but you may find that some or all of the steps are unnecessary.

This plan is for most of us who are not so fast on our feet. If you tend to think of the perfect comeback an hour too late, implement the plan below.

PROBLEM SOLVING

Step 1: Examine the level and amount of work the student is expected to do in class.

If work is too easy or the student has too little to do, adjust the amount of work. Every student needs to be challenged by school. Provide the student with extra-credit assignments that stretch his abilities. Make adjustments in regular assignments or have the student work on more sophisticated assignments in place of regular assignments. If the student has obviously mastered the material you are covering in class or can master it rapidly on his own, you may want to consider having the student work on a course of independent study.

Step 2: Establish a mild consequence for unacceptable wisecracks.

If the student needs to learn how to be sensitive to the feelings of others, you may need to establish a mild consequence for comments that have demonstrated a disregard for someone else. One consequence is having the student owe you two minutes from his lunch time for each unacceptable comment. Another possible consequence is to deduct points from the student's grade. This will be effective only if you have a grading system that bases a percentage of the grade on participation and effort. (See Chapter 2.) Inform the student that each infraction will mean that he has failed to earn a certain percentage of his participation grade.

Step 3: Arrange a private conference with the student at a neutral time.

Prior to this discussion, write a list of several comments and jokes the student has made. Choose some examples where the student's behavior was funny and an appropriate contribution to class. Choose other examples where the student's behavior was insensitive, hurtful, or where it disrupted instruction.

The goal of this discussion is not to make the student feel punished for what he has done. Instead, you are trying to get the student to step outside himself and look at his behavior from someone else's perspective. Help the student see that humor is fine, but that he sometimes places you and other students in an untenable position. Show him how some of his actions and comments are humiliating rather than funny.

Go through the list of comments, examining the difference between acceptable types of humor and unacceptable. Try to explain why one type of comment is all right and others are disruptive or destructive. Differences will serve as guidelines to the student for evaluating whether a future comment will be acceptable or unacceptable. Explain that ultimately you will make subjective evaluations, but also express confidence in the student's abilities to make these judgments.

Inform the student of the consequence you are going to use. Make sure the student understands that the consequence will be implemented when you feel a comment is inappropriate. If the student isn't sure whether a comment is appropriate, it might be best not to say it.

Step 4: When the student participates appropriately in class, interact with the student in a supportive way.

If the student makes an appropriately funny comment, laugh. If the student makes a serious comment, expand on the student's contribution. Encourage the student to continue taking part in class in appropriate ways. This will demonstrate that you are not asking the student to sit and do nothing.

Step 5: When the student makes an unacceptable comment or engages in an unacceptable behavior, calmly inform him of the consequence.

Do not lecture the student. Simply tell the student, "That was an unnecessary comment, and as we discussed, you owe me time after class." If the student disagrees with the consequence, tell him that he can talk to you about it after class.

If the student does talk to you privately, explain why you thought his behavior was unacceptable. Listen to the student's concerns. If they are reasonable, adjust your procedures. If you still think the student's behavior was unacceptable, tell the student that you are going to follow through on the consequence and that he should refrain from that behavior in the future.

Step 6: If the student makes a significant improvement, reinforce him for his self-control.

When the student has had a week or two of successful classroom behavior, do something to let the student know that you are aware of his improvement. Some possibilities might include writing the student a note, sending a note to his parents, or discussing his improvements in private after class.

You can also reinforce the student in indirect ways. For example, when you see the student in the hall, tell him a joke. Ask the student to tell you a joke. Relate an amusing anecdote. Any of these things will let the student know that you have a sense of humor and appreciate his sense of humor, especially now that he is channeling that humor into acceptable directions.

Problem 19
MISBEHAVING AFTER BEING REINFORCED

DESCRIPTION

Robert is a disruptive student. Though he has remained in regular classrooms, Robert has a long history of arguing with teachers, shouting out, throwing books to the floor, and tearing up papers angrily. In between times, Robert rarely does much more than stare sullenly at the floor.

As Robert's science teacher, Mrs. Henry has just recently attended a staff meeting on Robert. Robert has been put on an individualized motivational plan to try to improve his behavior. One of the things that teachers have agreed to help with is increasing positive feedback to Robert when he has small successes. Mrs. Henry has tried very conscientiously to follow through with the plan, but she is very close to giving up. Every time Mrs. Henry gives Robert recognition for appropriate behavior, he begins misbehaving. In fact, his behavior is worse after being praised than it normally is. Mrs. Henry is to the point that she is afraid of giving Robert positive feedback for fear of sending him into another episode of severe misbehavior.

CONTRIBUTING FACTORS

It is not uncommon for a student with a long history of behavior problems to react negatively to positive feedback. The student has had so little success and praise that positive comments are unnerving—especially if praise is contingent. It will make the student uncomfortable. His reaction will be to resort to behaviors that he is more familiar with. He will begin misbehaving to reassure himself that he is still capable of generating negative interactions. If the student can force the teacher back into a negative interaction pattern, his self-image as a loser is left intact.

These students will also be hypersensitive to praise. If the student has cultivated a "tough guy" image, an open acknowledgment of praise will be embarrassing. The student may misbehave to show others that he is not a "goody-two-shoes."

PROBLEM SOLVING

Step 1: Resist the natural impulse to quit giving the student positive feedback for appropriate behavior.

Though the student will usually be unaware of his motives, his misbehavior is aimed at ensuring that you will acknowledge only his failures. If the student wins, there is no hope of changing his behavior.

Step 2: Plan to reinforce the student more frequently for smaller successes and smaller increments of appropriate behavior.

By increasing the amount of positive feedback you give, the student will soon learn that you are not going to give in. You will acknowledge his successes whether he likes it or not. Eventually, the student will learn to be comfortable with praise. Though misbehavior prompted by praise may initially occur more frequently, it will diminish quickly in intensity and duration.

Step 3: Establish procedures for giving the student positive feedback that will not be embarrassing.

When you give positive feedback, do not act as if it is a big deal or a surprise. If you overreact, you will imply that you are "amazed" that the student could do something appropriately.

When you praise the student, move quickly on to something else. Change the subject. Address another student. Try to avoid giving the student an opportunity to respond with misbehavior.

Avoid evaluative statements and flowery praise. Simply describe what the student did that was appropriate.

"Your penmanship was very easy to read. Thanks."

"Nice to see that you were able to complete your homework in class."

Be somewhat discreet about your praise. Talk to the student quietly at his desk. Write a note. Give him a thumbs-up signal. Overall, remember that simply interacting with the student can also give the student positive feedback. If the student is paying attention during a class lecture, ask him a question that he will be able to answer. If the student quietly accepts a paper from you when he would normally rip it up, ask him to pass out the remaining papers.

Step 4: When the student does misbehave after you have praised him, implement the consequences that had been set up initially for misbehavior.

Calmly implement any consequence that has been set up. If the misbehavior has not been discussed previously, issue a gentle verbal reprimand. While you implement consequences, avoid looking frustrated, exasperated, or disappointed. These emotions imply that you believe he is a failure. Treat misbehavior as though it is a momentary interruption in success.

Step 5: Discuss the problem with the student.

At a neutral time, meet privately with the student. Describe the pattern of behavior you have noticed. Avoid trying to "psychoanalyze" the student. Simply let him know that you are interested in helping him learn to be as successful as possible in your class. Tell the student that you want him to be aware of behaviors that will help increase his success. Ask the student if he can suggest ways for you to let him know that he's doing well without embarrassing him. Make suggestions. Overall, let the student know that you intend to continue encouraging his successes.

Step 6: Be persistent.

A secondary student will have had years and years of seeing himself as a loser. It will not be easy for him to give this up. Your positive expectations will be threatening, but wanted all the same.

However, if things do not appear to improve over time, be sure to continue evaluating the individualized reinforcement system. There may be problems in the reinforcement system rather than in your efforts to give the student positive feedback.

Problem 20
DOING NOTHING—PASSIVE RESISTANCE AND FAILURE TO BE MOTIVATED BY ANYTHING

DESCRIPTION

Ella does not seem to care about anything. She never does any work in class and never completes any homework. She has never turned in any assignments or participated in class discussions. When asked a direct question in class, she may answer or she may just shrug her shoulders. Ella never acts out or is disruptive; she just never does anything. She does not seem at all interested in grades, and is totally unresponsive to the attempts of teachers to give her encouragement and positive feedback.

CONTRIBUTING FACTORS

There are probably many causes for this problem. However, no matter what the underlying causes, the true problem lies in the fact that the student has become so discouraged she has given up. If she were still acting out or being disruptive, it would indicate that she still cared enough to rebel against school. The student described above is convinced that she cannot be successful and is not even willing to try.

Another factor in this problem may be that the student does not have the academic skills to complete the tasks. Sometimes students who know they cannot do the expected work will become passively resistant as a way of covering up the fact they cannot be successful. If she never shows what she can do, nobody will know what she can't do.

Note: This is one of the most difficult types of behavior problems on which to have an impact. There are no easy techniques that are likely to work. Most of the steps here described refer to other parts of this book. Passive resistance and poor motivation are a combination of many different problems.

Recognize at the outset that this may be a student in desperate need of help, and she may need more help than the classroom teacher can provide. It may be necessary to involve other resource people such as a school counselor, school psychologist, or social worker.

PROBLEM SOLVING

Step 1: Determine if the student's withdrawn behavior is a recent change or something that has been going on for a long time.

If this passive resistance and withdrawn behavior is a recent change, the student may be going through a very difficult time. Becoming withdrawn and having difficulties with school work are behaviors often exhibited by adolescents prior to suicide attempts. Read Problem 9, "Threatening to Commit Suicide," to see if any of the other common signs are present in the student's behavior. If so, follow those suggestions for getting help for the student.

Step 2: Determine if the student is capable of doing the academic work in your class.

Do not simply ask the student if the work is too difficult, because the student may not give you reliable information. Make arrangements to work with the student individually. Follow the suggestions in Problem 42, "The Student Who Has Poor Academic Skills," to determine the extent of the student's academic problems. If the student is not capable of doing the work, follow the steps suggested for Problem 42 for helping to remediate some of the academic problems.

If the student could successfully perform the majority of the tasks you presented, you know that the student has the academic abilities to do the work. Implement the remaining steps outlined here to try to get the student motivated.

Step 3: Identify all the behaviors that have led you to the conclusion that this student has a problem.

What are the specific things that have happened in the last two or three weeks that have resulted in your being concerned about her? The more detailed and specific you can be, the easier it will be to know what to do about the problem. If in doing this, you notice that your true concern is that the student is not doing assignments and homework, see Problem 34 "Failing to Complete Homework Assignments—An Individual Problem." Other things on your list may relate to poor peer interactions, bored or apathetic behavior in class, and depressed or despondent behaviors.

Step 4: Use the information from the previous step to set goals for the student.

In order to help this student, it will be necessary to clarify exactly what you expect her to do differently. Use the list of behaviors and problems as a starting place. From this list, what is the major problem? Use Goal-Setting Form 1 from Chapter 4 to establish

Figure IV–2   Sample Goal Setting Form for Ella Barnes

GOAL-SETTING FORM 1

STUDENT Ella Barnes

CLASS 3rd Period English

GOAL To show a more positive attitude in class and to answer at least one question in

class each day

STUDENT RESPONSIBILITIES FOR ACHIEVING THE GOAL

Ella will say good morning to Mr. Lopez as she enters the classroom. When asked a question before or during class, she will think about the question before saying, "I don't know." Ella will attempt to answer the question.

TEACHER SUPPORT RESPONSIBILITIES

Mr. Lopez will say hello to Ella as she enters the classroom. He will ask her at least one question per day and will allow her enough time to think about her answer.

EVALUATION PROCEDURE Ella and Mr. Lopez will meet every Friday immediately

after class to evaluate the week.

DATE OF GOAL EVALUATION October 15

STUDENT'S SIGNATURE _Ella Barnes_

TEACHER'S SIGNATURE _M. Lopez_

---

your expectations for her behavior. Figure IV-2 is an example of a Goal-Setting Form that has been filled out for Ella.

Step 5: Meet with the student to discuss the goal and to go over the goal-setting form.

Meet with the student privately to discuss your concerns. Let her know that you want to help and hope that you can work with her to get her to participate more in your class.

Go over the Goal-Setting Form and see if she is interested in trying to meet the goal. Do not be surprised if she acts very ambivalent about the whole thing. Ask if she can suggest any modifications or revisions in the goals. End the meeting by discussing how you and she will evaluate if she is meeting the goal.

Step 6: Provide feedback to the student about how well she is meeting the goal.

If she is being successful, provide positive feedback. If she is making no effort to do the things specified on the Goal-Setting Form, meet with her at the end of the week to reiterate your expectations for her participation in class. Avoid sounding disappointed or exasperated. Try to communicate that you still expect her to begin exhibiting the effort to reach the goals.

Step 7: If, after two or three weeks, the student has still not tried to meet your expectations, consider setting up a highly structured reinforcement system.

See Chapter 6 for information on setting up an individualized reinforcement plan to try to reach this student. If the student has truly given up, even this may not be successful. However, if the student still has some spark of motivation, an individualized reinforcement plan set up by a caring teacher may be what it takes to get her motivated.

Problem 21
BEING EMBARRASSED BY PRAISE OR NOT LIKING PRAISE

DESCRIPTION

Mr. Monero teaches a special reading class at Madison High School. His students have had long-standing reading problems and very little success in school. These students also have difficulty accepting responsibility, and Mr. Monero has found himself frequently nagging students about getting assignments in, about remembering pencils, about staying on task, and on and on. Mr. Monero realizes that he has fallen into the criticism trap.

Mr. Monero decides that he must shift his attention from negative to positive behaviors. Nagging was getting him nowhere quickly. As Mr. Monero begins emphasizing appropriate behaviors, he is disappointed to find that his students seem to be really embarrassed by any kind of positive feedback. In fact, it has gotten to the point that if Mr. Monero says, "Excellent paper, Will," some of the other students will respond with comments like, "Hey, Willie boy. Excellent work." Mr. Monero is beginning to feel as if the situation is hopeless.

CONTRIBUTING FACTORS

Students who are used to getting attention for inappropriate behavior will often be embarrassed by any attention for appropriate behavior. The change makes them uncomfortable, and they may have a difficult time knowing how to respond. If an entire group of students is used to primarily negative interactions, the problem may be compounded by the fact that negative attention is status quo with the group. Group dynamics may make it unacceptable to be recognized for appropriate behavior. Very few secondary students want to be teacher's pet!

Students may also be uncomfortable with praise if they feel it is phony. If students are given recognition for behaviors they are not pleased with, they will have a difficult time accepting praise.

PROBLEM SOLVING

Step 1: Determine whether your feedback is contingent.

Contingency implies that praise must be earned. If the teacher praises behaviors that have required no effort, the student is likely to be embarrassed because he won't feel that he deserves to be praised. He may feel that he is being praised for babyish behavior, or he may feel that the teacher is trying to con him into working hard.

Contingent positive feedback is relevant to students because the teacher is recognizing and acknowledging a behavior that the student himself perceives to be an improvement. Since the student himself feels good about the behavior he engaged in, the feedback from the teacher is appreciated because the student is proud of himself.

Be sure to give positive feedback only when the student or students have exhibited behavior that is more mature or academically advanced than their typical performance. This does not mean that only the highest-performing students get positive feedback. It means that every student who tries to surpass his or her typical performance should get some recognition from the teacher.

Step 2: Praise individual students privately.

If students have demonstrated that they are embarrassed by public praise, establish techniques to provide positive feedback to individuals without making other students aware. One way to do this is to speak quietly to an individual at his desk. Another way is to call a student to your desk for a private conference, or talk to a student after class. Notes on student papers can be very effective, and even sending a letter to a student or to the student's parents can be powerful.

For the student who is extremely embarrassed, you might even need to work out techniques that would be mutually acceptable to you and the student. For example, you might work out with the student that whenever you establish sustained eye contact with him it means he is doing excellent work.

As the students begin to get more comfortable with private praise, gradually introduce praise that is more public. By the end of a term, the teacher should be able to tell a student he has done well, without that student or any other student reacting in a negative way. Positive feedback and encouragement should be a part of any classroom environment.

Step 3: Describe the positive behavior in a nonemotional and nonpersonal manner.

The teacher who says, "Oh Jamie, I am so excited about the excellent work you have been doing" is very likely to embarrass the student. A comment like, "Jamie, you have been consistently getting more than 80 percent on your papers. You are heading for a *B*" is less likely to make the student uncomfortable.

Some teachers try to use positive feedback as a way to get close to their students.

This is a big mistake. The goal of the positive feedback is to get the student to take pride in his own performance. The praise should not imply that the teacher is trying to be a "buddy" to the student. The student will probably be better able to accept praise that is businesslike rather than praise that gives the impression that the teacher is trying to be a friend.

Step 4: Avoid pauses after praising an individual student.

There is a common tendency to give a student positive feedback and then to wait for a response. This pattern puts a tremendous amount of pressure on the student who is uncomfortable with praise. The pause forces the student to give a response, and some students will respond in a hostile or "smart aleck" way simply because they do not know what else to say.

Get in the habit of giving the positive feedback and then changing the subject. This eliminates the pressure that is on the student to respond. If the student wants to respond to you, he can at a later time, but he does not have to.

Step 5: Evaluate the effectiveness of your positive feedback by what students do, not by what they say.

If a student continues to work hard and improve, the positive feedback and encouragement has been effective, even if the student says things like, "Don't tell me I did good work, I hate this stupid class." The student may say things like this to look tough in front of friends, but if he is working and trying, your feedback is getting the desired results—a motivated student.

Problem 22
ACTING VIOLENTLY OR BEING OUT OF CONTROL

DESCRIPTION

Mrs. Scharpfs has just learned that a new student is going to be placed in her seventh-period basic skills math class. She has also been informed that the student has had a history of violent and destructive behavior. Though Daniel has been identified as an emotionally disturbed youngster, his Individualized Educational Plan (I.E.P.) specifies that Daniel should be mainstreamed into basic skills classes in math and reading.

Mrs. Scharpfs has volunteered to work with the lowest math sections, knowing that she is often able to get through to students who hate math. She has always been willing to work with students who have problems. She says they are "her kind of kids." In this instance, however, Mrs. Scharpfs is feeling very frustrated, primarily because no one has given her any functional information on how to deal with Daniel's difficulties.

CONTRIBUTING FACTORS

A pattern of violent behavior will never be the result of a single factor, but the result of many interwoven factors. Violence may erupt from children who have been the object of abuse and neglect in the home. It may be the result of frustration and failure and the failure to learn how to deal with life's difficulties. It may be a student's way of crying for help or it may be the result of childhood tantrums that have accelerated into outright violence. For students with severe problems, violent behavior may be almost addictive. Once the spiral begins, the student seems to lose control and get lost in an emotional pitch that can only do damage to himself and others.

PROBLEM SOLVING

Problem solving will include two basic approaches for the classroom teacher. First, you must plan your strategy for dealing with violent behavior. Planning does not mean that the student won't be given a chance to succeed in your classroom. You will never imply to the student that you do not have positive expectations. Planning is necessary because you must act immediately if a violent incident occurs in your classroom. If the student has already had a violent incident in your classroom, it is not too late to plan in case another occurs.

Your second strategy will be to follow steps to help the student learn to control his violent behavior. Both of these approaches are vital factors in dealing with a student who has had a past history of violent behavior. Because this is a very severe problem, it is also suggested that you carefully study the procedures suggested in Chapter 6.

HANDLING VIOLENT BEHAVIOR

Step 1: Establish a procedure for getting help immediately.

Never attempt to subdue a violent student on your own. Your only chance of stopping a violent episode is if you outweigh the student by at least one third and are extremely strong. Tell your class to move into the hall immediately and then call for help.

The procedure for getting help should be similar to an emergency situation in a hospital. In a code blue situation, preidentified medical personnel immediately drop whatever they are doing and go to the room where help is needed. In this situation, a code should be established that indicates to the office that a dangerous situation is taking place. As students are clearing the room, call the office on the intercom and give the code or send a student to the office. As soon as the office receives the message, they will act immediately to get help.

Step 2: Identify personnel to help in a violent situation.

At least three strong male teachers or administrators need to be identified to help in a violent situation. As soon as the office is contacted for help, two of these men should be alerted. Their instructions will be to immediately leave whatever they are doing and go to the designated classroom as quickly as possible. At least three teachers will need to be identified in case the office has difficulty reaching one of the teachers immediately. Once the office has alerted these men, office personnel should follow procedures for getting people to cover their classes.

Step 3: Train teachers to subdue the violent student.

If possible, the student should be restrained and immediately removed from the room. If this is not possible, the male teacher should lower the student to the floor and hold him there until the student becomes calm enough to be released.

Step 4: The teacher who has subdued the student should escort him to the office and place the student in isolation until he is calm.

This teacher should also remain to supervise until an administrator takes over. See Chapter 9 for information on how to establish an isolation consequence. If the school has no isolation area, the student will need to be escorted to an administrator's office.

Step 5: Set up consequences for violent behavior.

Regardless of the causes for violent behavior, students must learn that it cannot be tolerated in a school setting. If school property is damaged, set up consequences similar to those outlined in Problem 23, "Destroying Property or Vandalism." If someone has been injured, parents of the injured student must take part in determining how the situation will be handled. Certainly, the severity of the injury must be considered. It will need to be the decision of the injured student's parents whether local authorities will be contacted. Formal assault charges may need to be filed.

If no one is injured, the student will need to face a series of consequences. You may choose to follow a schedule similar to the one following. Whatever the consequences, parents and the student should be informed that violent behavior is not acceptable and that any further incidence can result in the school or an injured party pressing legal charges against the student. The administrator handling the parent conference should also stress that corporal punishment at home will not improve the situation, but will only provide an additional model of violence. Parents should be referred for additional help to a counselor, school psychologist, or other professionals who are trained to deal with students in trouble.

First offense:	Parent conference One day of in-school suspension with work
Second offense:	Parent conference Three days of in-school suspension with work
Third offense:	Parent conference Three days of out-of-school suspension Three days of in-school suspension with work
Fourth offense:	Expulsion

Step 6: The administration needs to assign a counselor or school psychologist to work with this student.

It is essential that someone follow through on the needs of this student and the needs of teachers who must work with the student. The remainder of this plan outlines steps that can be taken by an individual teacher to help the student avoid volatile situations and learn to control his behavior. If possible, someone should adapt the plan and the suggested contract to encompass an entire day.

TEACHING THE STUDENT TO CONTROL VIOLENT EPISODES

The next steps are designed for use by an individual teacher. It may be necessary for an individual teacher to deal with a potentially violent student until a cohesive plan can be established for the student's entire day. If you are working alone on this problem, make sure that you seek help.

Step 1: Identify warning signals.

If you have worked with the student for some time, try to identify behaviors that indicate the student is beginning to spiral into an incidence of violence. Most students will demonstrate that they are beginning to tense up in some way. If you haven't worked with the student and are planning for a new school year, get in touch with a former teacher or call the parents in for a conference. Explain that you are really interested in helping the student learn to control his temper. Ask them to help you identify specific behaviors that the student exhibits prior to exploding. Explosive students typically demonstrate some of the types of behaviors listed here prior to losing control:

Breathing heavily
Gritting their teeth

Clenching their fists

Changing the tone, pitch, or loudness of the voice

Step 2: Set up a time-out area where the student can go to cool down.

This area should be set up strictly for the student's use. It should be as quiet and private a place as possible.

Step 3: Meet with the student privately.

Tell the student that you really hope he can be successful in your classroom. Explain that you are aware of some of his past history, but stress that you are certain that he can succeed in your room. Explain that everyone has some things that are difficult to learn. His priority will be learning to control his temper.

Tell the student that you would like to help him learn to recognize his own warning signals. Tell the student about the things he tends to do *before* he loses control. Explain that you would like to let him leave the room as soon as these warning signals appear, that you have set up a time-out area where he will be free to go. Explain that this will give him a cooling-off period. If he chooses to leave, he will need to remain in the time-out area for a minimum of ten minutes, but that he can stay as long as he needs to cool off. The only stipulation will be that he will need to complete a short assignment to make up the time he has lost in class.

Next, tell the student that you know you are asking him to do something that is very difficult. Tell the student that you would like to help make it a little easier by setting up something for which to work. Explain that each class period completed without an incidence of violence will earn credit toward something he would like to have or toward earning a privilege. Help the student brainstorm ideas of things for which he would like to work. Once you have a fairly lengthy list, help the student evaluate the ideas and jointly select two or three things the student would like to have.

Tell the student that you will be contacting his parents, checking into the things he would like to work for, and writing a contract. Set up a time for a second meeting and tell the student that he will be earning credits in the meantime.

Step 4: Contact the student's parents.

Explain to the student's parents that you are really interested in helping their child be successful in your class. Tell the parents that you will be working to help their son recognize when he needs to remove himself from a potentially volatile situation. Try to determine whether the parents will be supportive of your efforts. If they appear to be supportive, try to determine whether they can help out by supplying the reinforcer.

Step 5: Secure the reinforcer.

If the parents cannot provide the reinforcer, check with the administration or counselor to see if special funds can be used. If this is not possible, check to see whether a local merchant would be willing to donate the item. You may wish to see whether the administration would be willing to ask a local service group to support the school's efforts to help high-risk students by providing special funds.

Step 6: Draw up a contract.

You may wish to do something similar to that shown in Figure IV–3.

Figure IV–3   Sample Contract re: Control of Behavior

SAMPLE CONTRACT RE: CONTROL OF BEHAVIOR

GOAL: Daniel Brown will demonstrate growth and maturity by learning to control his own behavior when he must deal with frustrating situations.

STUDENT RESPONSIBILITIES:

1. When the teacher raises one finger, Daniel will immediately go to Room 12. He will wait quietly for at least ten minutes. If his breathing has returned to normal and he feels that he is able to read and study quietly, Daniel will return to class. If Daniel still feels agitated, he may remain in Room 12 until he decides that he is calm enough to read and study quietly.
2. When Daniel realizes that he is breathing very quickly, that his voice has become high pitched, or that he is feeling disturbed in any way, he will immediately go to Room 12 and follow the other procedures identified in item 1.
3. When Daniel has made use of Room 12, he will willingly complete a brief assignment to make up the time that was lost in class.

MONITORING: Daniel will write the date of each class period that is completed without an emotional outburst on his monitoring card.

INCENTIVE: When Daniel has completed four periods without an emotional outburst, he will have earned a dinner with his father.

TEACHER RESPONSIBILITIES:

1. Mrs. Scharpfs will signal Daniel with a raised index finger, whenever she notices that his breathing has become rapid, that his voice has become high pitched, or that he is becoming disturbed in any way.
2. Mrs. Scharpfs will clear this procedure with the staff so that Danny is allowed to go to Room 12 without being stopped for a hall pass.
3. Mrs. Scharpfs will make sure that Daniel has a desk in Room 12 that he may use without being disturbed or questioned.
4. Mrs. Scharpfs has prearranged the dinner with Daniel's father. Daniel's mother has agreed to allow this incentive.
5. Mrs. Scharpfs will make it a point to make sure that Daniel has understood the assignments. When a study period begins, Mrs. Scharpfs will check to see that Daniel is on the right track and provide any assistance that is needed.
6. Mrs. Scharpfs will let Daniel know when he is handling situations in the classroom maturely.
7. Mrs. Scharpfs will contact Daniel's parents as soon as the incentive has been earned and make sure that the contractual agreement is completed.

_____
Teacher's Signature

_____
Student's Signature

Step 7: Set up a monitoring system.

You will want to keep a record of the number of times the student uses time-out each period and a record of each period that the student completes successfully. You can make quick notations on a Weekly Record Sheet or in your lesson plan book.

The student will also need to keep a record. You can set up an index card like the one in Figure IV–4. Suggest that the student keep his record in his notebook or textbook. Each day that he completes without having a violent incidence will earn the student one point. If this plan works for this class period, consider extending the plan and the record sheet to include the entire school day.

Step 8: Meet with the student.

Go through the contract, and at this time also outline consequences for any problems that might occur. Stress that you are sure the student can make it with this plan, but in fairness to him you also need to make sure that he understands the consequences for failing to control his behavior. You may also want to set up a nonverbal signal that will tell the student that he should go immediately to time-out. Let the student know that at first he might need your assistance but that he will learn to recognize the signs on his own.

Give the student his self-monitoring card. Tell him that he will be responsible for filling in the date of each successful period. A successful period will be defined as one in which the student has demonstrated self-control by going to the time-out area anytime he has felt himself getting upset or by not needing to use the time-out area at all.

Step 9: Work on keeping up a high degree of positive student-teacher interactions.

Make it a point to greet the student at the door. Carefully monitor academic progress and make certain that the student receives any special help that is needed. During independent work times, casually stop and see how several students are doing. Be sure to include the student who is on this plan. When the student is participating in class, give him the hard-earned attention he deserves. As the student leaves your class, give him a thumbs up signal to let him know you are proud of him.

Step 10: Set up periodic private conferences.

Make sure the student has access to you. As you first begin the contract, meet with the student one or two days later to see how things are going. Then meet with the student once a week. If everything is going fine, you can just meet briefly to let the student know that you do not take his improvement for granted. These times can also be used to adjust the contract when needed.

Figure IV–4   Self-Monitoring Card

Student: Daniel

Record the date for each successful period. When each blank is filled, you will have completed your first contract.

_____   _____   _____   _____

Step 11: Keep a record of the number of times the student must use the time-out area and adjust the contract as the student becomes more and more successful.

When the student has successfully avoided violent behavior for *several weeks,* adjust the contract. Be sure to congratulate the student. Emphasize that he has learned to control himself.

Next, have the student work on using the time-out area less and less. This should be a gradual process as the student needs to know that it is acceptable to remove himself when a situation becomes difficult. If the student currently uses the time-out area an average of once a week, have the student work to stay within this range.

Have the student count every half period that he is able to remain in the classroom. His new goal will be to earn six half-period credits. Remind the student that his willingness to use time-out will continue to demonstrate self-control and maturity. The change in the contract demonstrates the tremendous amount of growth he has made. Remind the student that his points are cumulative. Whenever he earns six half-period credits, he will have earned whatever he is working for. Explain that this may happen in the first three days, or it may take a week or more. When the student has successfully reached this goal two or three times, adjust the contract again. This time the student will begin working for full-day credits. His contract should stipulate that he needs five full-day credits to earn whatever he is working for. When the student is completing a contract in five to seven days, he has made remarkable progress. He is no longer having violent episodes, and he is only using the time-out area once each week.

Step 12: Keep in touch with the parents.

Even if the parents did not initially seem supportive of your efforts, keep in touch. As you begin the contract, let them know when their son has had one or two successful days. Parents of children with severe problems rarely have any positive contacts with the school.

Problem 23
DESTROYING PROPERTY—VANDALISM

DESCRIPTION

Mr. Zoref has just noticed two of his students gouging their initials into the top of a desk. He has asked the students to quit, and they have stopped. Mr. Zoref isn't sure whether he should follow through with additional consequences. The students have purposefully damaged public property. On the other hand, the desk was already badly scarred from the abuse of other students.

Jefferson High School is frequently the target of vandalism. It is not uncommon to find a broken window in the old facility. Once-beautiful hardwood banisters have been marred by pencil marks and carvings. Bulletin boards crumble where students have picked at them. Bathrooms are filled with graffitti, and there are even holes in the walls where students have kicked them in. Building maintenance funds are available, but it doesn't take long for students to destroy all traces of improvement.

CONTRIBUTING FACTORS

Vandalism will occur when some students find that there is no accountability for their actions. As vandalism becomes more apparent, students begin to feel that it really doesn't matter if they absentmindedly write on their desks or pick the paint off a wall. It becomes a joke if someone "accidentally" knocks another hole into a wall. As destruction becomes more visible, even responsible students begin forgetting that they are destroying public property.

PROBLEM SOLVING

Step 1: Establish consequences for minor vandalism in the classroom.

Require students to repair or clean up the damage they have done—and more. For example, if a student writes on a desk, he should be required to wash off all the desks in the room. If a student sticks gum under her desk, she should be required to scrape off all the gum found in the room. If a student is caught loosening a screw in a desk, he should be required to tighten screws in all of the desks.

Parents should also be contacted. Many students would never write on furniture at home, but do not think twice about writing on school property. Parent contact can be made by sending home a letter similar to the one in Figure IV–5.

Step 2: Work with the administration to establish consequences for vandalism causing permanent or serious damage to school property.

When serious damage has been done, students should be referred to the office. The custodial staff should be requested to assess the extent of the damage as soon as possible.

Figure IV–5   Sample Letter to Parents re: Vandalism

SAMPLE LETTER TO PARENTS RE: VANDALISM

Dear Parent,

Kimberly spent part of my first-period class writing on her desk. Though this may have not have been purposeful destruction of public property, I did feel that you, as a taxpayer, should know.

Kimberly will be required to stay after school on April 7 to clean all the desks in my room. This consequence is designed to teach Kimberly to respect public property. This project should take roughly one hour. Please help Kimberly arrange transportation home at 4:00 if necessary.

Please sign and return the bottom portion of this form to school.

Sincerely,

Mr. Zoref

I have been notified that Kimberly will need to stay after school on Thursday, April 7, to make reparations for her misuse of public property. We will make arrangements for transportation home at 4:00.

Signed: _____

If repairs can be made, an estimate of labor and material costs will be needed. If damage is permanent, you will need an estimate of replacement costs.

Once an estimate of damages has been made, a building administrator will need to meet with the student and her parents. Parents should help determine how the student can pay for the damage that was done; however, the parents should not pay for the damage themselves. If the student has no outside job, nor any possibility of getting an outside job, the student will need to work with the custodial staff at a rate slightly lower than the minimum wage. If the minimum wage is $3.50 per hour, the student should work for an equivalent of $3.00 an hour until damages have been paid for. For example, at $3.00 an hour, a student would need to work a total of 30 hours to pay for a $90.00 repair estimate.

A contract should be drawn up indicating specifically how and when the student will pay for damages. The administrator should make it clear that failure to uphold the agreement may result in the school's pressing formal charges with the police. The student and parents should also understand that a second incidence will be dealt with by legal authorities. A sample contract is shown in Figure IV-6.

Step 3: Discuss the problem and consequences with your class.

At a neutral time, discuss the problem of vandalism. Tell your students that you cannot allow students to abuse public property in your classroom. Explain that taxpayers have made it possible for young people to have a building and equipment to assist them in getting an education, and it will be everyone's responsibility to keep things in as good a condition as possible.

Figure IV-6   Sample Contract re: Vandalism

SAMPLE CONTRACT RE: VANDALISM

On May 4 Julia Braches was involved in breaking windows at Jackson High School. The school is holding Julia responsible for damage estimated at $90.00.

Julia has agreed to make reparations by working with the custodial staff for a total of 30 hours. She will work from 3:00–5:00 Monday through Friday, beginning May 7 and ending May 25. Any excused absences will be made up.

Julia will be responsible for reporting to Room 12 promptly at 3:00 each afternoon. She will work cooperatively with the custodial staff, completing every job conscientiously and without complaining.

If Julia fails to meet her work commitment, or if a similar incident of property destruction occurs, the school will work with legal authorities to press formal charges.

_____   _____
School Administrator   Date

_____   _____
Parent   Date

_____   _____
Student   Date

Explain that you will be helping students learn to treat the classroom and equipment with respect by expecting everyone to use the building and furniture as it was designed to be used.

Next identify various forms of vandalism and the types of consequences that will be required. Explain that parents will also be notified of any destruction as they have helped provide the materials that are gradually being ruined.

Step 4: If vandalism is a school-wide problem, the staff will need to work together to establish a consistent policy for vandalism.

Steps 1 and 2 can be used as models for designing consequences for school-wide consequences. Staff members will need to agree to implement consequences for any incidence of vandalism, no matter how small. Once the policy has been established, it will be important to inform students of the procedures.

Encourage the custodial staff to remove any evidence of vandalism as soon as possible. The less damage visible, the easier it will be to get students to take care of the school.

You may also want to begin building student concern and awareness by encouraging any of the following groups to become involved:

Student Council

Lettermen's Club and Rally

Journalism Classes

PTA or community groups

If students can be encouraged to tackle this problem, tremendous improvements can be made in a short time. Student groups might be encouraged to sponsor a school clean-up week. Journalism students could feature before-and-after articles. If things improve dramatically, an article in the local newspaper can help to fire student spirit. The more people involved, the greater your chance of improving student pride and concern in the maintenance of their school.

Problem 24
NAME-CALLING

DESCRIPTION

In Mr. Contrerras's seventh-grade homeroom class, students frequently get into arguments and minor scuffles. Most of the altercations begin when one student calls another student a derogatory name. These incidents occur five to ten times during the four periods that Mr. Contrerras works with the students. Mr. Contrerras is tired of running interference. When he tries to get to the bottom of these scuffles, he usually hears, "I was only teasing. Jessie here is my friend." Regardless of the intent, this "teasing" disrupts class time, and sets up adversarial relationships between students.

CONTRIBUTING FACTORS

Chronic name-calling is usually a habitual interaction pattern between students. Because the pattern is habitual, it is also difficult to change. Students are used to initiating stimulating interactions by provoking each other.

PROBLEM SOLVING

Step 1: Work with the class to define the difference between name calling and nicknames.

Begin resolving this problem by explaining to the class that name-calling and the ensuing arguments interfere with class time. Explain that everyone's tolerance to name-calling seems to vary; therefore, the class needs to clarify what is friendly teasing, and what is intolerable name-calling.

Label one column on the board "name-calling" and a second column "nicknames." Ask students to help you categorize names they have been called or heard. You might begin by listing some of the names you have heard. Ask students to come up with other names. Tell them that any name that is bothersome to anyone will be put in the name-calling category.

Step 2: Determine a mild consequence for any student who is involved in name-calling.

Tell students that the class needs to decide on a consequence for any student who becomes involved in a name-calling incident. Explain that some students may not feel that some of the names are derogatory, but that people who are intelligent and mature will respect the wishes of others. Because the use of nicknames is entirely unnecessary, they will not be tolerated unless the group has determined that they can be accepted in fun and good humor.

Explore possible consequences with students. These include time owed during a break or after school, loss of a privilege, and classroom isolation.

Explain to students that you will implement the consequence any time you see or hear any name-calling. If two students are calling each other names, both students will pay the consequence regardless of who started the sequence.

Step 3: Discuss how students should behave if someone calls them a name when you are not around.

Students must understand that you can only implement consequences when you have witnessed the name-calling. This will be your responsibility.

When you are not around, students will be responsible for turning and walking away from students who call them names. Explain that this takes a great deal of maturity but by taking such an action they tell name-callers they refuse to be manipulated.

Step 4 (optional): If you know of a few students who will have a very difficult time ignoring name-calling, hold individual role-playing sessions.

Step 5: Implement consequences consistently and calmly.

Step 6: Periodically give the class a free period or a special privilege when they have significantly reduced the amount of name-calling.

Let students know that you have seen increased maturity and that you are impressed with their ability to maintain that demonstration of maturity over time.

Step 7: If the problem is still prevalent after two weeks, set up a group reinforcement system.

Design a system where each day that students can function without any name-calling, they earn a point. When they have accumulated 5 points, everyone in the group has earned five minutes of free time. For more information on setting up group reinforcement systems and for ideas on group reinforcers, see Chapter 5.

Problem 25
FIGHTING

DESCRIPTION

The faculty of Rosemont High School is becoming more and more concerned about the number of fist fights that break out on the school grounds—outside, in the halls, and in the cafeteria. Teachers are not only concerned about the safety of students involved, but they are also concerned that fighting is becoming a way of life at Rosemont High. Whenever a fight breaks out, students gather around and cheer students on.

CONTRIBUTING FACTORS

Sometimes fighting occurs because students have learned that violence is a way of life. "Being tough," "standing up for yourself," and "showing them who's boss" are values that have been taught at home or on the streets. These values may not be changed by the school; however, the school can teach students that fighting will not be tolerated.

PROBLEM SOLVING

Step 1: Establish a school-wide consequence for any student involved in a fight.

Because fighting will not be tolerated, any student involved in a fight will need to pay the same consequence without differentiating between who started the fight. The only exception to this will be the rare case of an unprovoked assault.

The faculty will need to agree upon a schedule of consequences. The consequence for the first incident of fighting should be relatively mild, but the severity of the consequence should accelerate sharply after the first and second incident of fighting. The staff might decide upon a schedule similar to the following series of consequences:

First Incidence: Parent conference
                      One day of in-school suspension with work

Second Incidence: Parent conference
                      Three days of in-school suspension with work or
                      Saturday School

Third Incidence: Parent conference
                      Three days of out-of-school suspension and three days of in-school
                      suspension

Fourth Incidence: Expulsion

Step 2: Make a staff commitment to immediately report any fights.

If a fight occurs, staff members should intervene immediately. If the teacher is alone, she should make no physical attempt to break up the fight. Students should be told firmly to stop the fight. If they continue, inform them that the consequences will be more severe if they do not stop immediately. If the students break up the fight themselves, escort them to the office. If the fight continues, step into the nearest room and call on the intercom or get another teacher's assistance. When help arrives, the fighting students should be escorted immediately to the office.

Step 3: Implement consequences.

If the students have broken the fight up on their own, follow the schedule of consequences already laid out. If staff members have had to break up the fight, the students will also be required to pay additional consequences for defying the orders of the teacher.

Step 4: Design a consequence for onlookers.

Fights are frequently egged on by a cheering crowd. The student body needs to know that fighting will not be tolerated. Therefore, a mild consequence should be implemented for any student who is obviously egging on the students in the fight. For example, any identified onlooker may be required to report to after-school detention.

Step 5: Discuss the problem and consequences with students.

This may be done in homerooms, via the intercom, or during an assembly. Students should be told that the school and student body will not tolerate fighting. It presents a physical danger to students and will be regarded as assault. Students should be informed of the consequences for fighting. Make it very clear that there will be no equivocation when implementing consequences.

Inform students that anyone involved in a fight will be required to pay the consequences, regardless of who provoked the fight. Tell students that everyone has the choice of walking away from a fight. Let them know that an unprovoked assault on a student who refuses to become involved will result in immediately pressing charges with the local law enforcement agencies.

Also inform students that getting faculty assistance when a fight does break out may keep someone from getting hurt. While you cannot demand that students report fights, you can demand that they do not encourage others to fight. Let students know that they will be expected to walk away from fights. When a fight breaks out they should immediately disperse. Anyone seen egging others on, or being a spectator will also pay a consequence.

Let students know you are confident that students can work on demonstrating to the public that your school is made up of rational, intelligent people.

Step 6: You may wish to call the press in to document improvements.

If a significant reduction in fighting does occur, you might send a press release to a local newspaper. Too often, students hear only of the negative actions of peers. Work to develop a sense of pride at your school.

> The students of Rosemont High have worked hard over the past few weeks to reduce fighting on school grounds. They have demonstrated a sense of responsibility and the ability to control what happens at their school. The students of Rosemont High are to be congratulated. No incidences of fighting have been reported for the last two weeks.

When the item appears in the paper, make sure that students are aware of the article.

Step 7: Give private recognition to students who have demonstrated self-restraint.

Ask teachers to quietly demonstrate their support of student efforts by increasing positive interactions with students who have had a past history of fighting. These students need special attention and guidance if they are to change their values. Faculty members should make a conscious attempt to provide these students with support and positive feedback for handling conflict in mature ways. You may wish to set up individualized plans for the students who have had chronic problems with violent behavior. (See Chapter 6.)

Step 8: If the problem continues, set up classes in conflict resolution for any students who fight.

If the preceding steps are not successful, add to the consequence for fighting. Establish a procedure where any students involved in a fight must attend a class after school. The class could be taught once a week by a counselor or a school psychologist or an administrator. Any student involved in a fight could be assigned to go to the class for four successive weeks. The class should discuss and role play mature methods of conflict resolution.

Problem 26
THREATENING VIOLENCE OR EXTORTION

DESCRIPTION

Rumors have been circulating in the school for a couple of weeks now that someone is involved in extortion. Teachers keep hearing little bits of conversations and allusions to a problem, but no one has been able to find out what is really happening. When directly confronted, students say that they have heard things, but it is nothing they can prove. Finally three students have let teachers know that Jerry Baskins has threatened to beat them up if they don't pay him a dollar a day. These students are afraid of being hurt if it comes out that they "squealed." The students are not certain, but they think that Jerry has threatened other students too.

CONTRIBUTING FACTORS

Extortion obviously involves a student who is seeking power and control. If only one student is involved, it is often a student who lacks social skills and friends. Out of alienation and frustration, the student makes victims of other students. Since he can't "join 'em," he is going to "beat 'em." By engaging in extortion, the student sets up an image that makes him feel important. This individual probably experiences very little success anywhere. Extortion is a way of venting anger at an academic and social system that he perceives does not seem to be able to include him in any positive way.

If students are being threatened by an extortion ring, the problem may be the result of peer pressure. Harassment can easily lead to extortion. If several "tough" kids get involved in pushing students around, it may not take long for someone to say, "Hey, give me your lunch money and we won't bother you." A malicious game becomes a serious racket. If none of the students involved in the original incident are willing to back down for fear of looking "soft," the whole group gets themselves deeper and deeper into serious trouble.

PROBLEM SOLVING

Step 1: Try to identify how serious the problem is and how long it has been going on.

If the problem is pervasive and well organized, it may be necessary to get the civil authorities involved from the start. If someone has been physically hurt, it will be important to meet with the parents of the injured student to see whether they wish to file charges. Once the problem is in the hands of local authorities, the school should support investigations in any way possible.

If the problem does not seem severe enough to warrant calling in the police, make sure that your information is accurate. If you are unsure whether reports are true, do not progress with the recommendations below. Investigate the situation more thoroughly to make sure reports are accurate. Interview a number of students privately. If a student divulges information, protect his identity by continuing to interview more students. Substantiate the claims by asking the student if he knows of others who might have been threatened. If you meet systematically with several students on an individual basis, you are likely to begin tracking down what is happening. No victim enjoys being a victim. While students may not let school officials know what is happening on their own, they are likely to talk if they feel no one will know who talked.

Step 2: Meet with the problem student and confront him about the reports of his behavior.

If more than one student is involved, meet with each of the perpetrators privately. If you meet with students as a group, they will each need to act "tough" to impress the others. During this meeting, inform the student of your knowledge of the problem. There is no need to divulge who gave you the information. The tone of this meeting should reflect the serious nature of the offense.

First, let the student know that any action against a student for reporting the problem will result in the school pressing assault charges. Try to dispel any thoughts of revenge before the meeting goes any further. Be sure to emphasize that the situation will only get worse if anyone tries "to get" anybody.

Next, make sure the student understands that he is not playing a game; he is engaged in a serious crime. It may be useful to ask a police officer to participate in this meeting to get the student to take the situation seriously. However, if a police officer is present, conduct the meeting after school or the whole student body will wonder why the "cop" is in the office.

Inform the student that you are going to arrange a meeting with his parents and that he will be kept in in-school suspension until the conference takes place. Tell the student that you will be considering how to handle the problem and suggest he should also give it some thought.

With the student present, call his parents and briefly describe the problem. Arrange that a meeting take place as soon as possible. If the parents seem unwilling to come in for a meeting, let them know that you will need to consider getting in touch with legal authorities to handle the situation if it can't be handled at school.

Step 3: Before the meeting with the parents, decide on a reasonable consequence and think about preventative measures.

Until the meeting, the student should be kept away from the other students in an isolation environment. This reduces the likelihood that he will start acting like a tough guy or try "to get" the students who reported him.

Determine a relatively severe consequence for the problem. A reasonable consequence would be three days of in-school suspension and paying back any money gained from illegal activities. Obviously the amount of money would have to be a fair estimate based on the damages reported by the victims.

Determine what your actions would be if the student engages in the extortion or in physical violence in the future. In all probability, you should report the problem to authorities for prosecution. If this would be your reaction to a future incident, prepare a letter for the student and his parents to sign that states he understands the severity of the problem. A sample letter is shown in Figure IV–7.

Step 4: Meet with the student and his parents.

Do not allow this meeting to become a session of accusations and denials. Simply inform the parents of the problem. Ask the student whether he has any suggestions for a fair consequence to the problem. If he has a reasonable suggestion, modify your consequence to incorporate some of the student's ideas. If the student has no ideas, outline the consequences you have prepared.

Make sure the parents and the student understand the severity of the problem. Have the student and parents sign the letter stating that they understand the criminal nature of extortion and assault and battery. If the parents deny their child's involvement, let them know that the letter is not a confession. It merely states the student understands that there are laws against extortion and assault. The goal of this procedure is to make the student and the parents realize that if a problem occurs in the future, this letter would be given to the police or the courts as evidence that the student had prior knowledge of the law.

End the meeting by discussing what happens when the consequences have been paid. Everyone involved should understand that once the money is paid back and the in-school-suspension time has been served, everything is back to normal. The end of the meeting should have a tone of positive expectations for the future.

Step 5: When the consequences have been paid, interact positively with the student.

Greet the student in the halls. Ask him how things are going. Comment positively on his appearance. This will demonstrate that you do not hold a grudge, and that you do not view him as a "criminal."

Figure IV–7   Sample Letter re: Extortion and Threats of Violence

SAMPLE LETTER RE: EXTORTION
AND THREATS OF VIOLENCE

To Whom It May Concern:

I, _____, fully understand that making someone pay to avoid being beaten up is a criminal act called extortion. I also understand that carrying out threatened violence is a criminal act called assault and battery. I fully recognize that if anyone engages in these criminal acts, the police will be notified and charges will be pressed against any of the people involved.

_____   _____
Student's signature   Date

_____   _____
Parent's signature   Date

Step 6: Examine the student's ability to be successful in his classes.

If the student is an academically low achiever, he may be experiencing a lot of frustration. Unless something is done to alleviate this problem, extortion and violence may recur as the student again feels a need to seek power or revenge. See Problem 42, "Poor Academic Skills," for more information on diagnosing and remediating academic deficits.

It may also be useful to set up a highly structured reinforcement system with this student. See Chapter 6 for information on procedures that may help a student having severe problems. It may be worthwhile to set up an individualized motivational system to teach the student how to engage in appropriate social interactions with peers and adults.

Problem 27
POOR TEST-TAKING SKILLS OR TEST ANXIETY

DESCRIPTION

While posting grades for a history exam, Miss Hernandez notes that Charlotte Smith has failed another test. This is surprising because Charlotte typically does well on her weekly assignments. A quiet student, Charlotte seems to be very conscientious. The test scores do not seem to be an accurate reflection of her knowledge.

CONTRIBUTING FACTORS

Test anxiety is probably the result of a number of interrelated factors. There may be too much parental pressure to excel. The student may put undue pressures on herself to excel and then clutch under the strain. The student may initially have had real difficulty on a few tests and developed a self-defeating attitude toward tests. "I don't know what happens. I just can't take tests." Once the student has decided she cannot take tests, her self-defeating prophecy becomes very real. Finally, this may be a student who has never learned test-taking strategies. As she fails more and more tests, the feeling of panic impedes her ability to develop the kinds of test-taking approaches that would help her to demonstrate her knowledge.

PROBLEM SOLVING

Step 1: During the next scheduled test or during a special mini test observe the student's test-taking strategies.

Be unobtrusive, but position yourself so you have a clear view of the student. The best way to observe her unnoticed is to stand somewhere toward the back of the room, out of her sight. Note how she approaches the test. Which items does she complete first? What are her general mannerisms during the test period?

Step 2: Call the student's parents in for a conference.

Describe their daughter's test-taking behavior. Explain that you have grown concerned because her exams do not seem to reflect her knowledge. Let the parents know that you would like to help the student with this problem. Encourage the parents to be supportive but not pushy. Explain that you will need their help in getting the student to relax a little about her grades because her sense of needing to do well is actually working against her. If the parents seem to be responsive, see whether they would be interested in having the student work with the school counselor or school psychologist. If the parents are interested, find someone in the school who can work with the student on relaxation training. There are many books, tapes, and filmstrips that deal with how to teach students deep muscle relaxation skills. These resources may be useful if no one in the school currently has expertise on teaching relaxation.

Step 3: Consider giving your class a few minutes of training on test-taking skills each week.

Though you may have only one student with severe test-taking anxiety, you may have many students who have poor strategies for taking tests. Have students practice some of the following strategies:

a. Complete all of the easy items first.

b. Mark difficult items so you don't forget to come back to them.

c. If the test is lengthy, take a brief relaxation break in the middle to collect your thoughts.

d. Once easy items are completed, see if some of the answers to the harder questions are provided in another question.

e. Use a process of elimination on difficult multiple-choice questions.

f. Monitor your time.

g. Use the last several minutes of available time to fill in guesses on blank items.

Step 4: Make short quizzes a frequent part of your daily routine.

Routine quizzes can be graded by the students or they can simply be opportunities for students to rehearse information they will be tested on. Students are less likely to be anxious about midterm and final exams if short tests have become a regular part of the classroom routine.

Step 5: Conduct help sessions prior to tests.

Some fear of testing may be alleviated if the student feels she is adequately prepared for the test. Help sessions can give many students additional practice on mastery of course objectives and skill application.

Problem 28
POOR LISTENING SKILLS AND NOT FOLLOWING VERBAL DIRECTIONS

DESCRIPTION

Mr. Goldstein has noticed that several students in his ninth-grade geography class do not seem to listen. They appear to spend a large part of class time daydreaming. Whenever Mr. Goldstein gives instructions, he has to repeat himself three or four times before all the students know what they are to do. This problem has gotten worse as the year has progressed. Mr. Goldstein frequently tells students they need to listen. Things are generally better for a short time, but within minutes the class is again inattentive.

CONTRIBUTING FACTORS

Students generally fail to listen because they don't have to. If they happen to miss something the first time, the teacher will repeat it. In fact, some students get into the habit of tuning out until an adult shouts or demands their attention in one way or another.

PROBLEM SOLVING

Step 1: Establish a rule of listening.

An example would be, "Listen and pay attention when other people are speaking." Your rule has to tell students that you need their attention; however, it should not demand that students always "look" attentive. Attentiveness means that students should be able to carry out instructions and repeat back information you have given. "Looking attentive" is sometimes deceptive. Some students learn to appear very attentive while completely tuning out.

Step 2: Select a statement that you will use to get students' attention.

Decide on a phrase with which you are comfortable because you will use it frequently. Some examples are:

"I need your attention."

"Everyone please listen."

"This is important."

"I am about to give some important information."

"Listen carefully."

Make it a habit to use this phrase prior to giving any information, directions, or instructions that you are not willing to repeat.

Step 3: Establish a consequence for dealing with questions about information that you are not willing to repeat.

The most logical way to handle these questions is not to answer them. Calmly explain that you can't answer and tell students when you give the information. "I'm sorry I can't answer that. I gave that information at the beginning of class."

If students complain, tell them they can discuss the problem with you after class. Students will need to get the information from another student.

In using this consequence, you must be consistent. If you answer some students and not others, students are bound to feel that they are picked on when you will not answer their questions. Consistency is the only way to keep this procedure from turning into a big game. During the first week, try to train yourself to pause before answering any questions. This pause will give you a moment to evaluate whether the question should be answered. If you answer questions spontaneously, you are bound to give information to students that they should already know.

Step 4: Provide students with positive interactions as they demonstrate they are listening to your instructions.

When you see that students are listening, interact positively. Give them attention for listening. If this has been a group problem, give students an occasional reinforcer. "I really appreciate the way you have learned to listen to instructions. It is really saving me a lot of time. You may have five minutes of free time at the end of the period today."

Problem 29

HANDING IN LATE OR INCOMPLETE ASSIGNMENTS

DESCRIPTION

In Mrs. Nozaki's tenth-grade social studies classes, about one third of the students turn in late assignments. Some of these assignments are only a day late, but others are as much as four weeks late. Mrs. Nozaki has told students that she will subtract 10 percent of the total possible points for late papers and that she will not accept any papers during the last week of the term. This usually results in Mrs. Nozaki's being deluged by late papers right before her cut-off date. Mrs. Nozaki has asked students to work harder at getting their assignments in on time. These discussions help for a short time, but students continually fall back into their old habits. When some students finally get around to completing their work, they have so much to do that they end up turning in work that is not up to their abilities.

CONTRIBUTING FACTORS

Late papers are the result of a number of factors. Many students do not learn to manage their independent time well. They may make good use of structured class time, but fail to pace themselves at home. If the consequences for late papers are too mild, or delayed, students may intend to get papers in but put off doing the work because the consequences are so far removed.

Other students have problems getting assignments in on time because they have periodically been reinforced for doing their assignments at the last minute. They have managed to avoid working at home by doing their math assignments in Spanish and their English in math. Unfortunately, leaving assignments until the last minute means that there is no room for underestimating the time an assignment will take, or for not having time to actually complete the assignments. In the foregoing example, students have also learned that once a paper is late, it doesn't matter how late it is. Procrastination goes on until the next final due date.

Students will also frequently fall into the habit of turning in late papers if they are not always accountable for their assignments on the due date. If the teacher sometimes forgets to collect assignments, or the class or the teacher doesn't get around to correcting an assignment until the day after it is due, students will sometimes run the risk of not having assignments ready 100 percent of the time.

PROBLEM SOLVING

Note: The following plan is for a class that has difficulty getting work in on time. It assumes that students are capable of completing work; they simply turn it in late. Also see Problem 33, "Failing to Complete Homework Assignments—a Class Problem," which includes suggestions for individual students who have chronic problems completing homework due to academic and time management problems.

Step 1: Establish a procedure for checking off student work at the beginning of the period on the assigned due date.

Use a class list to check off student work at the beginning of the period. Students can turn in work as you call roll, or you can collect work as students enter the classroom. This will teach students that they are immediately and directly accountable to you for their homework assignments.

Step 2: Establish consequences and final deadlines for late assignments.

Students should learn that late papers will adversely affect their grade. Regardless of the quality of work, evaluation on a job will always be affected by work that is not completed on time. Therefore, it is not unreasonable to teach students that they will be accountable when they fail to meet deadlines.

Establish a schedule of consequences and deadlines for late papers. Papers should lose value each day they are late. You may wish to give students a little more leeway on longer assignments, but all assignments should have a preestablished set of consequences for being late and should have a final deadline. You will need to determine a schedule that fits your particular class structure.

The fine for late assignments will work best with grading systems that use points. In the following example, students will lose a total of 10 percent of the assignment's value each day it is late. If your subtract a letter grade for each day a paper is late, students will learn that C papers have no value if they are more than one day late. On the other hand, if your grading system uses points, students will still earn points, even though the grade might equal an F. For example, if a student earned 75 out of 100 points on an assignment and lost 20 points because the paper was two days late, the student will still get 55 points. While this equals an F, the points will help the student's final grade. If you are using only letter grades rather than points, some students may fail to turn in papers at all. "If I already have an F, why bother?"

SAMPLE SCHEDULE OF FINES FOR LATE PAPERS

Regular Assignment
(Completed in one evening)

1 day late	−10%
2 days late	−20%
3 days late	−30%
4 days late	−40%
5 days +	Not accepted

Long-Term Assignments

1 day late	−10%
2–3 days late	−20%
4–5 days late	−30%
6–7 days late	−40%
8 days +	Not accepted

Step 3. Establish additional consequences for students who habitually turn in late assignments.

If students are not sufficiently motivated by grades, you may also need to include additional consequences. A schedule of suggested consequences is listed here:

Third late assignment: Parents contacted

Fifth late assignment: Required after-school sessions until work is caught up.

Step 4. Keep clear and easy-to-read records of work handed in.

It will be important for students to recognize that you are keeping careful records of student work. Immediately checking student work off as it is handed in, recording late fines, and tracking habitually late students will demonstrate to students that they are always accountable for their work. (See the Weekly Record Sheet discussed in Chapter 2.)

Step 5: Discuss the problem of late papers and all future consequences with students.

Prior to implementing any set of consequences, it is important to discuss them with students. Explain that being late will affect how one is evaluated on a job and will therefore affect how students will be evaluated in their school work. Go over your plan. Discuss your homework routine. Explain that papers will always be collected at the beginning of the period when they are due. Explain the schedule of consequences you have determined. Show students your record-keeping system.

Step 6: Consistently implement all consequences.

The only acceptable excuse for late work is illness. When a student has been absent for a period of time, work out a reasonable schedule with the student for getting make-up work in.

Step 7: Consider providing a group reinforcer if the problem has been chronic and improvements are noted.

You may wish to provide a group reinforcement when the entire class has been successful at getting work in on time. For example, you may wish to tell students that they can earn one point every time everyone in the class gets work in on time. When the group has earned seven points, the class will earn ten minutes of free time, or you may want to eliminate one homework assignment.

Problem 30
FAILING TO FOLLOW WRITTEN DIRECTIONS

DESCRIPTION

In Mr. Washington's English classes, students seem to be very careless about following written directions. Mr. Washington has surveyed students while they are working on in-class assignments and has noticed that several students don't even bother reading directions. They immediately begin working on assignments without reading to find out what they should do. This carelessness is obvious in complete work. If an instruction tells students to write in complete sentences, there are always several students who write one-word answers. If instructions tell students to circle the verbs, there will always be a number of students who underline. When students work with written rules, some students fail to apply the rule at all. Mr. Washington has just had students complete a worksheet with the following instructions.

Read the rule.

When a suffix beginning with a vowel is added to a word ending in a silent "e," the "e" is usually dropped.

Add the suffixes as shown and write the new word.
   Example: amaze + ing = amazing

1. relate + ion = _____
2. fame + ous = _____
3. create + ive = _____

Mr. Washington is discouraged to find that several of his students have failed to do this simple task correctly. They have combined all the words without dropping a single "e."

CONTRIBUTING FACTORS

In some cases, students fail to read and follow written directions because they are unable to read and understand the directions. Unfortunately, this aspect of the problem is very common.

Other students fail to follow written instructions because they have learned that worksheets are frequently laid out so that they do not have to read the instructions to complete them. They simply look at an example and complete the assignment. In addition, many worksheet directions are written so poorly that it is much easier to ignore the instructions and simply follow the format of the worksheet, or the examples given.

Finally, students quickly learn which teachers will accept assignments even if they have not bothered to follow the instructions. In many instances, teachers will give students the benefit of the doubt if they have not read questions or instructions carefully.

PROBLEM SOLVING

Step 1: Determine whether students can read and understand the exercises.

Students who have difficulty with written instructions because they cannot read and understand the directions will also be students who have difficulty with all assignments. They will typically spell and write poorly. Errors and difficulties will be apparent in most exercises, not only those that require students to follow written directions. Identify several of these students.

Find an assignment with which students have had difficulty. Privately, have individual students read aloud approximately 100 words from the assignment. When listening to students read, count the errors as you would in an informal reading inventory. Count omissions, insertions, self-corrections, mispronunciations, and being unable to read a word within three seconds. If the student makes three to five errors, he is functioning at a reading level where he may need to be taught any new or difficult vocabulary before being assigned to read material independently. If the student makes six or more errors, it may be impossible for the student to function independently. This error rate places a student at a frustration level. He does not read well enough to understand the written instructions and exercises independently. If the student reads with zero to five errors, reading at an instructional or independent level, you will also want to test informally to determine whether the student understands what he reads. In the English exercise just described, the teacher might have the student give the following information:

1. Tell me the vowels.
2. Show me the suffix in items 1 and 2.
3. What should you do if a word ends in "e" and you add a suffix that begins with a vowel?

If the student has difficulty with these types of questions, she is missing the prerequisite skills necessary to follow the directions.

Step 2: Work to help students resolve and compensate for reading difficulties.

If a student has an apparent reading deficit, refer him to the building learning specialist for further evaluation and testing. In the meantime, consider providing students who have reading problems with student helpers. You might use student assistants or provide peer tutors. Recruit students who are currently earning *B*s to read and go over assignments with students who are having difficulties. Let the tutors know that they will earn extra credit points for helping another student. This experience will help the *B* student move one step closer to an *A,* and it may also result in better mastery of skills for the *B* student. In order to tutor, a student must focus on the related skills more intensely than if she were simply going through the motions of completing the assignment on her own.

Step 3: For students who are having difficulty reading and for students who seem to lack prerequisite skills provide small group-study sessions.

While other students are working on assignments independently, work with a small group of students who have been having difficulty on assignments. Have students read the instructions. Provide group practice on any prerequisite skills that students are weak on. Work through some of the exercises, but do not allow the students to write the answers. Students can complete the work at home, but they will have had practice following the directions and working some of the items while at school.

Note: The remaining steps are designed for classes where a number of students carelessly fail to follow written instructions.

Step 1: Discuss the problem with students.

Explain to the class that several students are having difficulty learning to follow written instructions. Tell them that this is probably the result of habit and explain that you would like them to make a concerted effort in the future to read and follow instructions.

Step 2: If students continue to make careless errors due to a failure to follow written instructions, set up a classroom consequence.

A logical consequence for students who carelessly fail to follow directions is to have the student do the assignment over again. Because the assignment will be late, 10 percent of the possible grade should be subtracted.

Step 3: Design assignments to include written instructions that require students to read carefully.

When writing instructions, avoid being predictable. Write low probability instructions that will force students to read and follow directions carefully. Some examples are shown here.

- Write your name on the back of this paper.

- Answer only the odd-numbered questions. Any even-numbered questions that are answered will be subtracted from your score.

- Read Chapter 12 and answer questions 1, 3, 4, and 6. Read Chapter 16 and answer questions 2 and 4. When you turn in your assignment, include your lecture notes from Chapter 12.

- In the paragraph below, circle all the verbs, underline all the nouns, and write a list of the adjectives below the paragraph. Next, rewrite the list of adjectives in alphabetical order on another sheet of paper.

Step 4: Discuss the consequence with students.

Tell students that papers have not improved since your original discussion. Explain to them that following written instructions is a skill they will need to succeed in many jobs.

Inform students you will no longer accept papers that show a student has not bothered to follow instructions. If any section or exercise is done without following instructions, you will require the student to do the assignment over. Explain that the paper will be late and that 10 percent of the possible grade will be subtracted.

Tell students you will also be writing instructions that they *must* read before beginning the exercise. Show students examples of unpredictable written instructions.

Step 5: Periodically have students work on tasks that require them to follow directions.

To demonstrate the importance of being able to follow written instructions, have students practice filling out job applications, applications for a driver's permit, a tax form, or a standardized test form.

Problem 31
TURNING IN SLOPPY WRITTEN WORK

DESCRIPTION

Several students in Mr. McGahay's ninth-grade science classes turn in written work that is messy and difficult to read. Mr. McGahay is aware of the fact that it is difficult for him to grade these papers objectively. Grading papers is time consuming, and these papers require twice as much time as others. The messiness and sloppy handwriting are obviously due to carelessness rather than to a lack of ability. Mr. McGahay has admonished these students several times, but the problem has not changed.

CONTRIBUTING FACTORS

Sloppy papers are frequently the result of unclear guidelines. Students may have no clear idea of the quality of written work that is expected. If expectations are not clear, student work will deteriorate over time as students test to see how careless they can be with their work. It is much faster for students to do sloppy work, even though much of it may be accurate.

Students may also hand in work of poor quality because there is no consequence for carelessness and no perceived benefit in producing work more carefully. Sloppy work is a habit for many students. It develops over the years and becomes ingrained as students realize there may not be any added recognition for taking the effort to hand in work of better quality.

PROBLEM SOLVING

Step 1: Define your expectations.

Establish a clear definition of "neat work." Unless this term is specifically defined in observable terms, it will be difficult for you to evaluate papers fairly, and it will be impossible for students to identify how they might improve their written work. Without a clear criterion for evaluating papers, students will find that work of an equal quality is acceptable one day and not the next. Factors outside of how carefully an assignment was prepared will affect how the paper is perceived. For example, if the teacher is tired or if the student was difficult in class, the paper many appear messier than if the teacher was in a good mood when grading and basically pleased with the student.

To establish clear criteria for "neat work," examine several papers you find offensive. Identify things that the students have done that make the paper difficult to grade. Your list may include some of the following things:

- Rumpled
- Ink smeared
- Answers scribbled out
- Writing in margins
- Printing and cursive writing mixed
- Letters written on top of each other
- Writing of differing slants mixed
- Capitals and small letters mixed inappropriately
- Writing inappropriately above and below the lines
- Failure to punctuate and capitalize appropriately
- Misspellings

Identify positive expectations that would eliminate these types of papers:

- Papers may be folded evenly in half. All other creases and wrinkles will not be acceptable.
- Mistakes in pen should be crossed out with a single line.
- Mistakes in pencil should be cleanly erased.
- One or two ink blots will be acceptable. Beyond that, you will be expected to have obtained a different writing tool.
- Work must be completed in either cursive or printing. Papers with mixed writing types will not be acceptable.
- Handwriting must be on the lines provided.
- Write with a uniform slant.
- Small letters should be small. Capital letters should be capital letters.

Note: Specify your expectations for spelling. If your class is composed predominantly of high-performing students, you may want to say that any misspellings will reduce the grade by 5 percent. If you are working with low-performing students, you may need to say that any misspellings of work where the word missed is spelled correctly on the worksheet will reduce the grade by 5 percent; however, other misspelled words will not reduce the grade. Design your policy for spelling based on the academic abilities of your students. Your criteria should demonstrate to students that they need to be careful, but that you have realistic expectations of their abilities.

Step 2: Decide on a consequence for students who turn in work that does not meet your expectations for neatness.

A logical consequence for papers that do not meet your standards for neatness is that they must be redone. The work should not be graded until it meets your requirements. Give the student a new deadline to resubmit the work.

When work needs to be redone, there should be a fine of approximately 10 percent of the value of the paper. If the assignment was worth 50 points, the student will automatically lose five points. If the work is resubmitted by the student, but still not up to expectations, the student should not receive credit for the assignment.

Step 3: Determine if any students have a handicapping condition that prevents them from meeting the criteria you have established for neatness.

If a student's best work is not "neat" due to some circumstance like a physical handicap, a learning disability, or because he has never learned to write neatly, you may have to determine a special set of criteria that teaches the student to always do his best within realistic expectations.

To determine whether a student is being sloppy or if he is doing his best, ask yourself if the student has ever done neater work. If he has, you know that your expectations can be at least as great as the student's best work. If you expect too much of an improvement, too rapidly, the student may become so discouraged that he will not turn in work at all. Your expectations must always be within reach for each student.

Step 4: Discuss why neatness is important.

Discuss with the class the importance of neatness. Stress the fact that every teacher is likely to grade a paper more leniently if work is neat and easy to read. Students should have a clear understanding that two papers that are identical in content, but one sloppy and one neat, may be graded differently. No teacher in the world would give the sloppy paper a better grade than the neat paper. However, many teachers would consciously or unconsciously give a higher grade to the neat paper. Students should also understand that neatness will affect job applications, bank loans, college assignments, and the perception of their eventual work by a boss.

Step 5: Communicate your expectations for neatness with students, and explain the consequences for failing to turn in "neat" work.

Be specific about what you will look for to determine whether work is of sufficiently high quality to be acceptable. Show examples of the types of papers you would accept and the types of papers you would not accept. Examples should not be from your classes. You may wish to use papers from several years back. You could use examples of papers completed by students in another school. Or you may wish to set up your own models that demonstrate the kinds of problems you have actually seen on student papers. You can also demonstrate to students what is acceptable and what is not acceptable with examples on the chalkboard.

Step 6: Provide positive feedback to students when they make an effort to improve the appearance and neatness of written work.

A student who is used to getting by with sloppy work will have to put forth a lot of effort to change. Acknowledge that extra effort. Periodically let the student know that you have seen the change. Positive feedback will help the student learn to take pride in the work she has turned in. Failure to notice improvements will result in the student falling back into old habits.

A brief note on the student's paper is easy to carry out. On neat papers, write the kinds of comments listed here:

Neat work

Professional appearance

Nice writing

Very legible

Occasionally, give the student verbal feedback about the neatness of her work. Notes on a student's paper are meaningful, but privately telling the student that the quality of her written work has really improved will help the student take additional pride in her accomplishments. Eventually, you hope that the student will learn to turn in high-quality work because she takes pride in her abilities to do neat work.

Problem 32
POOR PLANNING ON LONG-TERM ASSIGNMENTS

DESCRIPTION

Mr. Lehming assigned his World History class a five-page report on the fall of the Roman Empire. The assignment was given three weeks prior to the time it was due and was to be done entirely outside class time. When the reports were due, Mr. Lehming was dismayed to find that only half the students turned in papers. Of the papers that were turned in, it was obvious that several had been thrown together in no more than an hour of time. Mr. Lehming is very discouraged with this problem. Given the number of students who had not completed the assignment, he feels that he must teach his students how to handle long-term assignments. Mr. Lehming recognizes that this is a skill that will be important for his students in all their classes.

CONTRIBUTING FACTORS

The major cause for this problem is that the students have not learned how to manage their time and how to pace themselves through a long task. Both of these are very sophisticated behaviors that are rarely taught. The more immature and the less capable your students, the less likely that they will have learned to do these things on their own. Students who have difficulty handling long-term assignments need to be taught to pace themselves over a long block of time.

PROBLEM SOLVING

Step 1: Initially, assign short-term assignments.

The younger and less mature your students, the shorter the initial homework assignments should be. For the first few weeks of school a sixth-grade teacher should begin building independent work skills by assigning work that is due the next day. A teacher of high school students should initially assign work that takes no more than two days.

Step 2: Gradually lengthen assignments.

As you learn your students' maturity level and their level of self-discipline, gradually build longer and longer assignments.

Step 3: Provide pacing guidelines for students by assigning work that will require more than one night to complete.

Pacing guidelines can quickly be given to a class as an assignment is handed out. For example, if you give a four-page worksheet assignment to students that is due in two days, suggest that students complete two pages the first evening and the remaining pages the next evening.

Step 4: Determine which students need help with pacing.

As you read through the following steps, you may determine that your entire class will benefit from the time management training suggested. Frequently, high-performing students lack the ability to pace their work over a long period of time as much as lower-performing students. However, these academically able students continue to succeed because they are able to assimilate large amounts of material in a relatively short period of time. This may mean that the students are staying up all night to complete a long assignment. If they get a good grade, this can actually be reinforcing poor study habits.

While the following suggestions may be beneficial for high-performing students, they will be critical for the success of lower-performing students. This will generally include students who are earning a *C* or less.

Steps 5 through 11 can be completed with only a portion of the class that is having difficulty, or it can be completed with the entire class. As students demonstrate an ability to manage time, these steps may be continued with only a few students who have a difficult time completing schoolwork.

Step 5: Set up multiple checkpoints on long assignments.

Multiple checkpoints divide a long assignment into smaller increments and demonstrate to students how much should be completed at given times.

For example, Mr. Lehming could have assigned his class the report, given three weeks to complete the report, and then assigned multiple checkpoints to students who might have difficulty reaching their goal. The checkpoints might follow a schedule similar to the one here:

Friday, Nov. 1	Report assigned
Tuesday, Nov. 5	One page of reading notes due
Friday, Nov. 8	Two pages of reading notes due
Tuesday, Nov. 12	Three pages of reading notes due
Friday, Nov. 15	Outline due
Tuesday, Nov. 19	Rough draft due
Friday, Nov. 22	Final report due

Multiple checkpoints teach students how to manage time while simultaneously teaching students how to complete different types of long-term assignments. Many students have never been taught how to design and complete a project or the basic steps in writing a report. Frequently, students will learn skills in isolation, but never learn how to combine the skills needed to complete long-term projects. For example, some students may have learned to take notes, to outline, and how to put writing into final copy, but they may never have learned how to integrate all these skills into writing a report.

Step 6: Adjust your grading system to include meeting checkpoints.

Determine how many points the assignment will be worth. Students should be able to earn a little over half the points possible by turning in completed work at each checkpoint. In Mr. Lehming's example, he might assign 55 points out of 100 for meeting checkpoints. The breakdown might look like the following:

Nov. 1	Report assigned	
Nov. 5	One page of reading notes due	5 points
Nov. 8	Two pages of reading notes due	10 points

Nov. 12	Three pages of reading notes due	10 points
Nov. 15	Outline due	15 points
Nov. 19	Rough draft due	15 points
Nov. 22	Final report due	45 points

If the student turned in work at all the checkpoints, she would have accumulated 55 points. The remaining 45 points are given for grading the content and organization of the paper in the same manner that would be awarded normally. Even if all the checkpoints are met, the teacher is able to award a grade of *F* to *A,* or 55 to 100 points.

The advantage of this system of grading is that lower-performing students are more likely to have reasonable content, and the grade will reflect their efforts. Higher-performing students will have not only content graded, but their efforts as well. If higher-performing students must work on an assignment over a period of time, they are likely to put more thought into their work than if it is a last-minute effort.

If only a portion of your class is working on the formal checkpoint system, the remainder of the class should receive the same number of checkpoint points for turning the paper in on time. In Mr. Lehming's example, students who were not in the formal checkpoint system would automatically earn 55 points for turning in an acceptable paper on time.

Step 7: Assign the work and discuss the checkpoints with students.

When assigning long-term work, discuss the advantages of completing work in small steps. Students frequently procrastinate because they feel the work is difficult. However, the longer students procrastinate, the more difficult the work becomes because too much must be done in too short a time period. Make sure the students understand that avoiding work because of fear of failure inevitably results in failure.

When discussing the advantages of carefully learning to pace oneself, include examples of life situations that require people to work at tasks in small increments. What kinds of things cannot be done at the last minute? What kinds of things will require that a little be done over a long period of time?

Give the students the long-term assignment. Discuss the checkpoints and how you determined how much should be accomplished at each checkpoint. As students become more sophisticated with checkpoints, you can have the class help break down a long task and determine the appropriate checkpoints.

Step 8: Collect work at each checkpoint and record points.

At each checkpoint, collect papers at the beginning of the period from students who are working within this system. Content does not need to be graded. Simply record points for having done the work and return the work to students by the end of the period. This is also a good point to check with the remainder of the class to determine how well they are pacing themselves independently. "Class, at this point you should have about four pages of your reading notes completed. If you have fallen behind, you should plan to complete that work this evening."

Step 9: Provide positive feedback and encouragement to students who typically fall behind but are trying to complete tasks at the established checkpoints.

Students who typically fail are usually convinced they will always fail. As students turn in completed work at different checkpoints, be sure to let them know that the work they have already done will make a difference in the grade they earn.

Step 10: Increase the amount of time and work required between checkpoints.

With each new long-term assignment, increase the amount of time required between checkpoints and the amount of work due. For example, on the next five-page report that Mr. Lehming assigns, instead of having three checkpoints on reading notes, he might have two checkpoints with more due at each checkpoint.

Step 11: As students demonstrate an ability to handle long-term assignments, gradually require that more and more of the students pace themselves independently.

Your eventual goal will be to have formal checkpoints with only a few of the lowest performers in each classroom. Truly low performers may require guidance and support over a long period of time because the actual work is difficult and must be monitored frequently.

Problem 33
FAILING TO COMPLETE HOMEWORK ASSIGNMENTS —A CLASS PROBLEM

DESCRIPTION

Mr. Brannigan has difficulty getting students in his literature classes to turn in their homework assignments. Sometimes as many as half of his students don't have their assignments ready to turn in. Mr. Brannigan is convinced that many of his students simply don't care enough to get work in. The prospect of a bad grade just doesn't seem to matter.

CONTRIBUTING FACTORS

Students will neglect homework for a number of reasons. The first reason may be that work is not always collected or recorded when it is due. If the teacher is inconsistent about making students accountable for work when it is due, students will learn that they can sometimes get away with not doing their work.

If there is a long delay between the time students hand in work and the time they get it back, some students will lose their incentive to get assignments done. Low-performing students will assume that they did not do well anyway. Why try?

Finally, some students will fail to do assignments because they lack the academic skills necessary to complete the assigned tasks.

PROBLEM SOLVING

Step 1: Determine whether students have the ability to complete homework assignments.

This can be accomplished by having students do homework assignments during class time. If students are able to complete the work independently in class, they should be able to complete the assignments on their own at home. If some students have difficulty completing the assignments in class, try to determine more specifically what is causing the problem.

Arrange to meet with a few of the students independently. Work through tasks that are typical of homework assignments. Determine whether the student is able to read the material independently. For more information on diagnosing and remediating academic deficits, see Problem 42, "Poor Academic Skills."

If a student is at a frustration reading level, she cannot be expected to independently complete homework assignments that require reading and writing. For students who are able to read the material, but have difficulty completing assignments, try to determine what is causing the problem. Determine whether the students have a strategy for working the assigned tasks. If the students are missing information, see if they have a strategy for finding the needed information. Problem 42 gives suggestions for remediating academic deficits.

Step 2: Design a grading system that encourages motivation and effort.

Chapter 2 presents information for designing a system that demonstrates to students how to be successful and pass a class. With an effective system, every student will know exactly what is necessary to be academically successful. The more the teacher can increase student motivation with the grading system, the fewer problems there will be with students not completing homework.

Step 3: Establish consistent routines for assigning, monitoring, and recording homework.

A consistent routine means that each week there should be a fairly standard amount of homework, collected and due at relatively routine times. If you have academically unsophisticated students, small amounts of homework should be assigned every night, due at the beginning of the next class period.

If students are working on lengthy assignments, help students learn to pace themselves. If you wish students to read a chapter by the end of the week, spend a few minutes of class time on Monday teaching students how to break the task into manageable units of homework for each night.

> This week your assignment is to read Chapter 8 and complete the study questions. Open your books to page 258. Find out how many pages are in the chapter. Yes, there are sixteen pages. Approximately how many pages should you read each night? Remember, you have four weeknights.
>
> Right, you will probably want to read about four pages each evening. However, you don't want to arbitrarily stop reading in the middle of a topic, so it would make sense to keep reading until you come to the end of a section. Count four pages and determine where it would be most logical to stop reading on Monday evening. Let's go ahead and identify how much work you should do each evening. I will write the assignment breakdown on the board.
>
> Now look at your study questions. Notice, they are numbered according to the correlated sections in your text. Let's determine which questions you should answer each evening. I'll also write the study questions you should complete.
>
> Your daily assignments are now listed on the board. I will do a work check on Wednesday to see how you are keeping up. Everyone who has completed the appropriate amount of work will receive bonus points. Remember, the whole assignment is due at the beginning of class on Friday. If you keep up, you should be able to complete each night's work in fifteen to twenty minutes. If you wait until Thursday night, you may have difficulty completing this assignment and the work you have in other classes.

> Monday: pages 258–263, questions 1–4
> Tuesday: pages 264–266, questions 5–10
> Wednesday: pages 267–272, questions 11–14
> Thursday: pages 273–274, questions 15–20

Step 4: At the beginning of a new term inform parents of the homework routine you have established.

If you have a basic homework routine established, parents can be informed of the approximate amount of work they should expect to see their children doing each evening. Without a routine, it is virtually impossible to enlist the help of parents. If parents do not know when homework will be assigned and how much homework students will have, the most they can do is periodically lecture their children. This is typically ineffectual.

At the beginning of the term, send a letter home to parents explaining your homework routine. If you wish, you can use the sample letter in Figure IV–8 to give parents suggestions for helping their children learn to manage their time. Figure IV–9 shows a sample which has been filled in.

Step 5: When a homework assignment involves new or difficult tasks, try to provide a few minutes of class time for students to get started.

Allowing students some class time to work on homework assignments gives them time to identify whether they have any questions. Sometimes students may think they understand an assignment and may not realize that they have questions until they begin working at home. If the student has not learned to problem solve, his frustration level will be very low. These students will simply give up if help is not available.

Step 6: When assignments are due, collect them at the beginning of the class period.

If papers are collected at the beginning of the period, students will learn that they cannot leave homework for the last minute. A last-ditch effort in class will not be possible. Homework is to be done prior to class time. This will help students learn to manage their assignments better and will also reduce the possibility that students are working on homework instead of attending to lectures or class discussions.

Work can be collected as students enter the door. Use a class list to mark whether students have handed work in on time. This procedure will give you a structure for greeting students as they enter the door, and students will learn that they are immediately accountable when work isn't ready. If a student has failed to complete work, she will have to directly face the teacher. This is much more difficult than simply not turning in a paper. Turning papers in directly to the teacher emphasizes the teacher's expectations.

This procedure is also effective if students exchange or correct their own papers. As students enter the room you can still check off completed assignments, but have students keep their papers for correcting in class.

Step 7: Establish a policy for late work.

The main consideration in dealing with late work is that you have an established policy. Students should lose a predetermined percentage of points for each day the assignment is late. "Late" should be defined as any work turned in after the final bell rings for the beginning of class. Ten percent of the assignment's value is a standard deduction. This tells the student that the overall quality of the assignment has been affected by turning the paper in late.

Step 8: Provide intermittent feedback to the group and to individuals for handing in work on time.

As students turn in their work at the beginning of the period, occasionally let students know that you appreciate their efforts and sense of responsibility.

With some groups, it might also be useful to provide a group reinforcer. For example, if all the students turn in their work for a full week, you might eliminate one homework assignment from the next week or you might give students additional class time for homework.

Step 9: Send progress reports home.

Every two to three weeks, send home progress reports. This can be a very simple note to parents informing them of the number of homework assignments that were complete, incomplete, and late. This simple procedure can help encourage parents to support your efforts.

Problem 34
FAILING TO COMPLETE HOMEWORK ASSIGNMENTS —AN INDIVIDUAL PROBLEM

DESCRIPTION

Nathan has been in special reading classes since second grade. On entering the junior high school, he has been dropped from special classes as there are many students with greater skill deficits.

On his first-quarter report, Nathan is failing in most of his classes. Nathan's parents contact the school and are referred to Miss Stein, a school counselor. In checking with classroom teachers, Miss Stein finds that Nathan has not turned in most of his homework assignments. Teachers report Nathan's test scores and classroom assignments are marginal, but that Nathan has failed courses primarily due to missing homework assignments.

CONTRIBUTING FACTORS

A student like Nathan may fail to complete homework assignments due to a number of interrelated factors. First of all, low-performing students have rarely learned how to manage homework assignments. They do not write down assignments, they do not keep track of completed assignments, and they do not know when assignments are due. If these students are given long-term assignments, they are rarely able to break the task into manageable units. When the assignment is due, they have no chance of completing it at the last minute.

Students who fail to turn in homework assignments are also students who typically do not understand grading systems. If classroom assignments are of passing quality, these students frequently have little understanding of how their missing assignments will affect their grade. If the student has low abilities in math, the concept of averaging will be nonmeaningful.

Low performers also have long lists of excuses. "We went to my grandmother's house over the weekend, and it was too late to do my homework when we got back." The bottom line is generally that the student has not learned to manage time. The end result is a failure to take responsibility for school work.

Finally, low performers will have a difficult time with regular class work. Homework will take longer. Vocabulary and directions may be confusing. Some homework may be impossible for a student with low academic skills. If the student has no chance of succeeding, he will soon give up. When a student gives up, he will rarely try even the easier

Figure IV–8   Sample Letter to Parents re: Time Management

SAMPLE LETTER TO PARENTS RE: TIME MANAGEMENT

Dear Parents,

In addition to teaching World Geography, we will be working on helping students learn to manage their homework responsibilities. Most weekday nights, Monday through Thursday, students will have fifteen to twenty minutes of homework from this class.

Every two to three weeks, I will send home a progress sheet indicating how well your son or daughter is keeping up with homework. If study habits need improvement, it may be useful for you and your child to do some advance planning. An exercise for helping your child establish homework routines is enclosed.

Please sign the bottom of this letter and return it to school. We appreciate your support of our efforts to improve student responsibility and increase learning.

Sincerely,

Mr. Brannigan

_____

Parent   Date

ESTABLISHING HOMEWORK ROUTINES

The weekly calendar shown below demonstrates how you can assist your son or daughter in establishing a study time. A blank copy of the weekly calendar is attached if you decide that this would be a worthwhile exercise to complete with your child. Begin by filling in other time commitments. This would include chores, dinner time, and any extracurricular commitments. With the remaining time, help your child identify times that could best be used for studying versus relaxation time.

	Mon.	Tues.	Wed.	Thurs.	Fri.
4:00					
4:15					
4:30					
4:45					
5:00					
5:15					
5:30					
5:45					
6:00					
6:15					
6:30					
6:45					
7:00					
7:15					
7:30					
7:45					
8:00					
8:15					
8:30					
8:45					
9:00					
9:15					
9:30					
9:45					
10:00					

Students who are fairly responsible and self-disciplined should be able to select which times will be used for studying. For example, a student might decide to watch a particular TV show on Tuesday evening. On this day, homework needs to be done after school. On other days, the student may decide to do homework later in the evening.

If your child has difficulty carrying out responsibilities and needs to learn better self-discipline, I would suggest that you help your child select a set time for studying each day. This time should be as early as possible so that completing homework assignments is a prerequisite for watching TV, talking on the phone, and so on.

Figure IV–9   Establishing Homework Routines (Sample)

ESTABLISHING HOMEWORK ROUTINES
(Sample)

The weekly calendar shown below demonstrates how you can assist your son or daughter in establishing a study time. A blank copy of the weekly calendar is attached if you decide that this would be a worthwhile exercise to complete with your child. Begin by filling in other time commitments. This would include chores, dinner time, and any extracurricular commitments. With the remaining time, help your child identify times that could best be used for studying versus relaxation time.

	Mon.	Tues.	Wed.	Thurs.	Fri.
4:00	Arrive home				
4:15					
4:30	Free choice, time with friends,				
4:45	or relax at home				
5:00					
5:15					
5:30	Help with dinner preparation				
5:45					
6:00	Dinner				
6:15					
6:30	Clean up				
6:45					
7:00					
7:15					Friday's homework
7:30	Homework				can be done on
7:45					Friday or Saturday
8:00					
8:15					
8:30					
8:45					
9:00	Free choice				
9:15					
9:30					
9:45					
10:00	Go to bed				

In this planning chart, the free choice indicates times that could be used for studying or for relaxation.

assignments. If success is unattainable, there is no reason to keep struggling through frustrating assignments.

Individual students will fail to complete homework assignments for many of the same reasons that several students in a classroom may fail to complete homework assignments. However, if the problem is with only one individual, the problem-solving plan will vary slightly. Check the plan for Problem 33 to determine which plan is more relevant to the problem with which you are dealing. You may want to use a combination of the two plans.

PROBLEM SOLVING

Step 1: Determine whether the student has the ability to complete homework assignments.

Give the student a timed informal reading inventory on a passage from a homework assignment. (See Problem 42, "Poor Academic Skills.") If the student is at an instructional or independent reading level, have the student try to complete the homework assignment without assistance from you. If the student is able to complete the assignment satisfactorily, proceed with Steps 3 to 5 here. If the student is unable or seems unwilling to complete the assignment, try to determine what the problems are. Does the student understand the directions? Does the student understand the vocabulary? Does the student have strategies for looking up needed information?

Step 2: Make arrangements to get the student academic help.

If the student cannot complete the assignment independently, check with the learning specialist in your building to determine whether the student is eligible for special classes. If the student has reasonable reading skills, he may still be eligible for classes that focus on study skills. It is not uncommon to find secondary students who have had reading skills remediated, but who have no idea how to complete written assignments, how to take notes, how to read maps, and how to study for a test.

You may also want to check into the possibility of pairing the student with a peer tutor.

Step 3: Set up an assignment sheet and grade record for the student.

The Assignment Record (see Figure IV–10) will teach the student how to keep track of assignments and grades. Initially, each teacher will need to check the Assignment Record on a daily basis to make sure the student understands what he needs to record. This will help the student learn to keep consistent records of work. Low performers will typically work in spurts. This results in inaccurate records. The student will learn to complete assignments and understand grades only if he can learn to be consistent.

Step 4: Ask the student's other teachers for assistance in teaching the student how to complete work consistently.

This can be accomplished best through a staff meeting. However, it may be more expedient in some schools to do it by a letter similar to the one in Figure IV–11.

Step 5: Set up a homework routine.

It may be necessary to help the student and his parents design a schedule for when he will work on homework each evening. (See Problem 33, "Failing to Complete Homework Assignments—A Class Problem.")

Figure IV–10   Assignment Record

ASSIGNMENT RECORD

Student _____   Subject _____
Week of _____   Period ____ Teacher _____

Dear Teacher,

Please initial the box under each day that the student has accurately recorded all of the following information:

In-class assignments, tests, and homework
Possible points on assignments or tests
Grades or points on returned assignments and tests
Dates of returned assignments and tests

If there is nothing to record for the day, please initial the space next to the appropriate date anyway.

Your help is invaluable. Thank you for your cooperation.

Sincerely.

_____

DATE	ASSIGNMENTS	Date due	Date Completed	Date Returned	Points Possible	Points Earned
Monday						
Tuesday						
Wednesday						
Thursday						
Friday						

Figure IV–11   Sample Letter to Teachers re: Homework Assignments

SAMPLE LETTER TO TEACHER RE: HOMEWORK ASSIGNMENTS

Dear Teachers,

We are currently working on an assistance plan to help Nathan _____ learn to complete assignments. We will need your help in this plan. At the end of each period, Nathan will ask you to skim his Assignment Record to determine whether he has accurately recorded all of the following information:

In-class assignments
Tests
Homework assignments and due dates
Any grades or points on returned papers

If Nathan has met his responsibilities, please initial this daily report.

Once Nathan has demonstrated his ability to keep accurate records, we will ask you to check his Assignment Record only once a week.

If you will be able to assist us in this effort, please sign the attached contract. Your cooperation and time is invaluable and will be appreciated.

Sincerely,

_____

Problem 35
SKIPPING CLASS OR ABSENTEEISM WITH NO EXCUSE

DESCRIPTION

Barker is a high school junior. He maintains a *C* average in most classes without a lot of effort. Eric is also a high school junior; however, he is a very poor student who often fails courses.

Eric and Barker are close friends. Neither boy has ever had much supervision at home. Most of their time is spent on the street, just hanging around. Not surprisingly, both boys have an attendance problem. They are frequently absent. When one is gone, the other student is also gone.

"So we skipped. Big deal! Sometimes we get hauled into the office and they give us a big talk. Once we got suspended so we hitched to the beach. Some days we just don't feel like going . . ."

CONTRIBUTING FACTORS

Students with severe truancy problems typically have many interrelated problems that are outside the school's influence. These problems—lack of parental supervision, abusive and nonsupportive home environments, and parents with overwhelming problems of their own—are frustrating because they cannot be resolved by the school. However, the school must deal with students who are the products of these homes. In part, these students don't care to be in school because no one at home cares. On the other hand, most truant students do care enough about school to show up more often than not.

Truancy is also a function of students' perceiving that attendance does not make any difference. For a student like Eric, what does absenteeism matter? He is failing anyway. Since being in school doesn't increase his chances of passing, why bother? Barker has the same attitude, only he doesn't mind missing school because he can still pass his courses. He is bright enough to attend school whenever assignments are due or when a test is given. This situation reflects a need to work on establishing a more effective grading system and a need for reorganizing class structure for both the able and the failing student.

Finally truancy can be a problem when the school has failed to implement a consistent policy on unexcused absences. If the established consequence is too severe, administrators may find themselves working to avoid imposing the penalty. If students find there are no clear guidelines, some will test to find out how much they can get away with.

PROBLEM SOLVING

Step 1: Work with the staff and school administration to establish a series of fair and consistent consequences for unexcused absences.

This can be accomplished by developing a graduated series of consequences for truancy. On the first offense the student will pay a relatively minor consequence. This teaches students that truancy is not acceptable, but it is not so severe that staff members would try to avoid implementing the consequence. Each successive infraction results in a more and more severe consequence. The graduated series of consequences should demonstrate to students that it is more trouble than it is worth to miss class. For more detailed information on setting up school-wide discipline policies, see Chapter 9. An example of a graduated series of consequences for misbehavior is shown here:

First Offense:	Parents notified Loss of class points (Step 3)
Second Offense:	Parents notified Loss of class points Three days of after-school detention
Third Offense:	Parents notified Loss of class points One day of in-school suspension with nothing to do
Fourth Offense:	Parents required to come for conference Loss of class points Three days of in-school suspension with work
Fifth Offense:	Parents required to come for conference Loss of class points Three days in-school suspension with work Saturday school
Sixth Offense:	Parents required to come in for conference Out-of-school suspension

Step 2: Make sure that assigned work is within the student's range of ability.

This may require arranging for special help from the school's learning specialists and arranging for peer tutors or special-assistance groups. If the student knows that he cannot do the work, he will see no valid reason for going to class. For more information on diagnosing and remediating academic problems, see Problem 42, "Poor Academic Skills."

Step 3: Design a grading system that bases a percentage of every student's grade on participation and effort.

Chapter 2 outlines a grading system that provides students with daily points for class participation and effort. These points represent a percentage of the student's final grade If the student has an unexcused absence, the teacher automatically deducts the unearned participation points from the student's weekly total. Since the absence is unexcused, the student cannot make up the points.

Step 4: Establish consistent routines that demonstrate the importance of activities conducted in class.

It is human nature to see no value in attending class if it doesn't affect how well you do. Class time must make it easier for students to succeed. Class time should provide students with instruction that will help them master course objectives, pass tests, complete assignments, and make homework easier. If students feel that class time has no direct bearing on their ability to work successfully, the course must be restructured.

When a student is failing, she often thinks that failing is inevitable, "There is nothing I can do about it." If this is the student's perception, coming to class appears completely worthless—a waste of time. The student must understand that if she comes to class and tries, she will probably be able to pass. Until the student realizes that participation in class activities can result in passing grades, her attendance will continue to be a problem.

Step 5: With students who are still truant in spite of the previous steps, set up a highly structured reinforcement system.

Any chronically truant student may need more structured interventions than described in the preceding steps. He may need to have someone in the school whom he perceives as a support person, someone who is taking personal interest in his attendance, with whom to relate. See Chapter 6 for information on setting up teacher volunteers to work with individual students in need of individualized help.

Problem 36
EXCESSIVE NUMBERS OF EXCUSED ABSENCES

DESCRIPTION

Ms. Rosenman has a problem with absenteeism in her classes. Initially the problem was unexcused absences but since the school has worked to establish an effective policy for unexcused absences, these have decreased but excused absences have increased. Some of the excuses Ms. Rosenman gets from the parents of students in her first period class include:

Rita needed to get new track shoes.

Jan had hayfever.

Mary Jane needed to babysit with her sister.

Charles didn't get back from his father's house in time to go to school yesterday.

Jimmy had a headache.

CONTRIBUTING FACTORS

Parents allow students to stay home from school for invalid reasons when they do not recognize that school time is valuable. Students stay home for the same reason. They do not recognize the value of class time and in some cases they are not accountable for class time.

PROBLEM SOLVING

Note: While this problem seems to be a school-wide problem, it must be dealt with by restructuring classroom programs. A school-wide policy to reduce lame excuses for absenteeism is typically ineffective. The school cannot get caught in the middle of negotiating with parents over whether the student should be excused from school or not.

School-wide policies that require illnesses to be verified by physicians are also not effective for reducing the types of excuses already noted. This type of verification can be required only if the student is out of school for a long period of time. Students who miss large blocks of time are usually legitimately ill. Students who miss school for marginal reasons are generally not gone for more than a day or two at one time.

Reducing absenteeism does need to be a school-wide effort. However, it will be important for teachers to individually implement the kinds of steps suggested here.

Step 1. Demonstrate to students that they are accountable for class time even when they are absent.

Structure class time so that activities are clearly related to instructional objectives and student accountability. Students should recognize that they are less likely to pass tests and accurately complete assignments if they are out of class. In other words, class time should make a difference in the amount that a student learns. If the student can miss school and not have it matter, then the assumption that class time is not valuable is true.

Step 2. Require extra-credit work to make up for class time that was missed.

In addition to requiring completion of regular assignments, extra-credit work should be required to make up for class time that was missed. This procedure should hold true for all valid excuses, questionable excused absences, and for any loss of class time due to musical events, athletics, or student leadership activities. While the procedure may seem harsh, you will demonstrate to students that class time is valuable. When class is missed, they will need to do extra work to make up for the instruction that was missed.

The one exception to this procedure would be legitimate extended illnesses. Your goal is not to make it impossible for a legitimately ill student to get caught up after a long absence. An example of an exception to requiring extra-credit work would be an illness due to something like chicken pox, a broken leg, or pneumonia. Most of these problems would result in several days of absence, but would be easily documented. In most cases the student will have been treated by a physician. The one time that students are generally absent for long periods of time without seeing a physician is during a flu epidemic. During these times large numbers of students are out of school for several days at a time, frequently returning with coldlike symptoms. This would also be a reasonable time to waive the extra-credit requirements for absenteeism.

If a percentage of your grade is based on classroom participation and effort, the extra-credit assignment would make up class performance points that were missed for being absent. If students have an unexcused absence, however, they would not have the opportunity of making up the points.

If a percentage of your grade is not based upon participation and effort, you can still require the extra-credit work. If the extra-credit work has not been turned in within three days of the student's return to school, extra-credit work should be completed after school.

Step 3: Structure extra-credit work to make up for instruction that was missed.

Extra-credit work should take the student fifteen to thirty minutes to complete. If at all possible avoid busy work. Students should see that extra work is given in an effort to make up for the instruction that was missed. You might have a student summarize an article upon which a lecture was based or write an essay on a topic that was discussed in class.

Step 4: Obtain administrative support for your plan.

Before you implement this plan, explain your policy to the administration. Some parents may complain that this procedure is unfair. If so, you may need the administration to back your efforts.

Step 5: Discuss the procedure with students.

Explain to students that you are concerned with the number of absences in class. Explain that school is much like a job where absences will affect the quality of one's work. Tell students that extra-credit work will be required when they miss school to make up for time lost. Give examples of the types of assignments students will be required to complete.

If you are using class performance points, explain that students will earn missed performance points by completing the assignments. If you are not using class performance points, inform students that they will have three days to turn in the first day's extra-credit work. If they are gone more than one day, a new extra-credit assignment will be due each day until all work is made up. If extra-credit work is not made up on schedule, students will need to report after school to make up the work.

Also explain to students that this requirement will be waived for legitimate extended illnesses. In these cases, parents should contact you.

Problem 37
ARRIVING LATE, OR BEING TARDY

DESCRIPTION

Mr. Berman teaches in a middle school. He has two sections of an elective sixth-grade audio-visual class, two sections of seventh-grade English, and two sections of an elective eighth-grade computer science course. Mr. Berman's classes are well liked by students, both for their content and for Mr. Berman's personable teaching style. At the beginning of each class, Mr. Berman chats with students, answers questions about assignments, and gathers materials to get class started. By the time he takes roll, he is about five minutes into the period. In first-period computer science, Joe saunters into class about ten minutes late. Since students have already begun working on an assignment, Joe has to ask his neighbor what to do. Mr. Berman marks Joe tardy for the fifth time in two weeks. What Mr. Berman doesn't realize is that Joe has actually been tardy several other times, but he has been able to slip into class unnoticed.

In third-period English, three students come running into class. They quickly slide into their chairs but totally disrupt a class discussion. Mr. Berman marks the three students tardy.

When Mr. Berman is filling out grades, he notices that over the course of the term there have been a tremendous number of students tardy. Even some of his best students have poor records of tardiness. Surprisingly, Mr. Berman's sixth graders actually do a better job of getting to class on time than his older students.

CONTRIBUTING FACTORS

There are several factors involved in chronic student tardiness. The first problem is that in some schools there is no significant consequence for being tardy. At the end of the term, students simply take home a record of tardiness as part of their overall report card.

A second factor may be that students don't feel that they have lost important class time if they are a few minutes late. They enjoy socializing in the halls and linger a little too long. Because the consequences are negligible, the benefits of socializing outweigh the consequences for getting to class late.

Other students may realize that they can sometimes get away with being tardy. "Some days I can get away with it, so why hurry?" Getting away with being late may become a little game.

Being on time requires a little initiative. If students are frequently tardy, the benefits of being tardy are obviously outweighing the negative effects of being tardy. Sometimes it just feels good to lie in bed a little longer.

PROBLEM SOLVING

Step 1: Work with the entire school staff to set up procedures for tardiness.

Students need to know that tardiness is a relatively severe problem. Tardiness is not tolerated in most jobs and therefore is not acceptable at school. The staff will need to work collectively to resolve this problem.

Step 2: Establish a definition of tardiness that is acceptable to all staff members.

Work with the staff to determine a clear, consistent definition of tardiness. Some teachers do not mark students tardy if they are a few minutes late but the teacher hasn't begun class yet. Other teachers do not consider students tardy if they have stepped into the room by the time the final bell rings. Still other teachers consider students tardy if they aren't in their seats with all materials ready when the final bell rings. A sample definition is provided below. Your staff goal will be to write a definition by which everyone will abide.

Students must be in the classroom *before* the final bell rings with all needed materials. If a student must return to his or her locker for materials, he or she will be considered tardy.

Step 3: As a staff, work to consistently report and record each incident of tardiness.

Every teacher must agree to make an effort to immediately report and record each tardy. This should be reported to the office on attendance slips picked up each period. Students must see that being late to any class will result in the office being notified. If some teachers fail to follow through with the procedure, some students will continue to test the procedures to determine if they can get away with being tardy.

Step 4: Determine a consistent set of consequences.

The school will need to determine the consequences to be administered over a set period of time—over the year, for a term, or for a semester. A set of consequences will be most effective if planned over the course of a year, as chronically truant students will quickly realize they have exhausted the milder consequences and will realize that their problem with tardiness is a severe problem warranting strong consequences. The following sample demonstrates the kind of schedule your staff may want to design:

First offense:	Warning
Second offense:	Written warning Student is informed that parents will be notified on the next offense.
Third offense:	Parents notified
Fourth offense:	Parents notified, after-school detention Conference with counselor to help identify ways that the student can get to class on time
Fifth offense:	Parents notified 30 minutes of in-school suspension with student doing nothing
Sixth offense:	Parents notified 60 minutes of in-school suspension with student doing nothing
Seventh offense:	Parents brought in for conference Three days of in-school suspension with school work
Eighth offense:	Out-of-school suspension

Step 5: Implement consequences through the main office.

The office will need to keep cumulative records on individual students. This can be easily accomplished by keeping a clipboard or notebook of tardy forms similar to the one shown in Figure IV–12. Each time a student is tardy for the first time, the office should start a tardy form on the student. Each new incident of tardiness should be logged on the student's tardy form.

Forms for all students tardy in a given period of time (one quarter or semester) should be marked and turned over to a person in charge of implementing the consequences. Consequences should be imposed as soon as possible. As soon as the consequences have been implemented, the student's tardy form should be returned to the office notebook. If forms are kept in alphabetical order, office personnel should have no difficulty logging incidences of tardiness.

Step 6: Determine who will be responsible for implementing consequences.

Consequences may be dealt with on a rotating basis by counselors or building administrators. Warnings and letters of notification to parents can be easily implemented by using form letters. The effectiveness of this plan lies in a consistent application of all consequences. Students must see that they are accountable for all tardy incidents at any time of the day.

Note: The remaining steps are procedures that can be used by the individual teacher to reduce tardiness in their own classes.

Step 1: Establish a grading system that allows you to award points for participation and effort.

For details on how to set up a grading system that teaches students behaviors that will increase academic success, see Chapter 2. If you have a percentage of your grade based upon participation and effort, being late to class can result in a loss of points. This system teaches students that a behavior such as tardiness will affect their overall perfor-

Figure IV–12   Student Tardy Form

STUDENT TARDY FORM

Name _____

Consequence	Date	Period
First offense: Warning	_____	_____
Second offense: Written warning informing student that parents will be notified on the next offense	_____	_____
Third offense: Parents notified	_____	_____
Fourth offense: Parents notified, after-school detention, training with counselor on ways to get to class on time	_____	_____
Fifth offense: Parents notified, 30 minutes of in-school suspension with student not allowed to do anything	_____	_____
Sixth offense: Parents notified, 60 minutes of in-school suspension with student not allowed to do anything	_____	_____
Seventh offense: Parents brought in for conference, three days of in-school suspension with school work	_____	_____
Eighth offense: Out-of-school suspension	_____	_____

mance. The consequence is relatively mild, but it is very similar to how students would be evaluated on a job. Students will learn that there is a consequence for being late.

Step 2: Organize class time in such a way that students learn that the first several minutes of class are important.

Give students a short quiz or board exercise at the beginning of every period. This short exercise should take no longer than four or five minutes, but it will keep students actively engaged while you are taking attendance. This procedure will demonstrate to students that they need to be in class and ready to work when the bell rings.

Step 3: Stand at the door to greet students the last minute or two before the bell rings.

If you can stand at the door a minute or two before the bell rings on a fairly regular basis, students will learn that you are also ready to begin class. This will eliminate the possibility of students testing the borderline of the tardiness definition by trying to sneak into class later and later.

Problem 38
STEALING

DESCRIPTION

Phil is a low-performing sophomore who has developed the reputation of being a thief. Although he has only been caught stealing twice, everyone assumes that Phil is the culprit when something is missing. Most of the time, no one really knows whether Phil is involved or not. Though everyone is obviously suspicious, Phil is usually not confronted openly because no one wants to accuse Phil unfairly of taking something.

CONTRIBUTING FACTORS

Occasionally a student will steal because he actually needs or wants the items that he takes. Though this is generally not the cause for stealing, it is a factor that must be considered.

A few students steal because they want to get caught. These students may have serious psychological problems. In this case, stealing should be viewed as a cry for help.

Unfortunately, the most common cause of stealing is that the student has a very poor self-image. The student steals out of a need to develop a niche for himself. Since the student has no other image to hang onto, he may try out the role of "thief" to see if he can be successful at something. This student doesn't necessarily need the items he steals, and he is not necessarily trying to get caught. This student steals because he is coming to think of himself as a thief.

PROBLEM SOLVING

Step 1: Try to determine why the student steals.

Discuss the problem with other staff members. This is a problem that needs a team approach. It would be wise to involve the school counselor or psychologist and several staff members who have daily contact with the student.

Make a list of items that the student has been suspected of taking. It should be fairly obvious if the student is stealing out of a specific need or desire for the items. In that case, the student will have very little compared to his peers. The items taken will include things that are needed for school or personal care and items that are currently in high demand by students of his age.

If the student has gotten caught stealing several times, he is probably stealing to get attention. Blatant stealing is probably an unconscious cry for help.

If it is difficult to prove that the student is stealing the student is probably stealing because he has come to think of himself as a thief.

Step 2: Regardless of the cause, establish a consequence for stealing.

Regardless of the cause for stealing, any proven case of stealing must result in a consequence. The consequence might involve in-school suspension, Saturday school, working with the custodial staff, or working in the kitchen. The actual consequence is relatively unimportant because no consequence is likely to result in a long-term change in the behavior. The primary reason for providing the consequence is to demonstrate that stealing is not acceptable.

Step 3: If the student is frequently "suspected" of stealing, establish a procedure for dealing with unproven suspicions.

The only way to deal with suspicion is to discuss the problem openly with the student. At a neutral time, tell the student that you would like to trust him. Explain how his past has made this difficult. Tell the student that you will need his help. This means that you would like to talk with him any time he is suspected of taking something. Tell him that this will help keep things in the open and give him a chance to demonstrate his innocence. Explain that you will not be "out to get him," but that you would like to keep lines of communication open. Assure the student that you would like any discussion to be calm and that you will always talk to him in private.

Step 4: Work to improve interactions with the student.

Throughout the day, it will be important for the staff to take an active interest in the student. Greeting the student in a friendly, nonchalant way as he enters the classroom, occasionally taking the time to ask the student how things are going, stopping to chat with the student in the halls, and taking an active interest in the student's academic efforts can help him begin to recognize his self-worth.

Step 5: Work to help the student become more academically successful.

If the student is a poor student, self-concept will improve only if he can become more successful in school. Check out the student's reading abilities. For information on diagnosing and remediating academic problems, see Problem 42, "Poor Academic Skills."

If the student does seem to have difficulty reading, a referral should be made to the school reading specialist. In the meantime, provide the student with a tutor when he must deal with written materials. You might also consider providing this student with additional small-group instruction and study sessions with other students wanting help prior to a test.

Take a personal interest in the student's grades. This can be accomplished by helping the student track his grades and assignments. (See Chapter 2.) Take the time to make sure the student knows his current grades and what he can do to improve them.

If the student is unmotivated, you may also want to set up an individualized reinforcement system. (See Chapter 6.) This would involve getting the student motivated to complete assignments, pay attention in class, and stay on task.

Step 6: Try to get the student involved in extracurricular activities, a volunteer group, or a hobby.

Frequently, students develop a better self-image when they become involved in something other than themselves. Check with the counselor to see if there is a school or community organization that the student could become involved with. Visiting senior citizens in a rest home can help a student develop self-worth by interacting with someone who needs and enjoys his company.

Step 7: If the student seems to be stealing because he needs the items he is taking, implement steps 1 to 5 and also explore the possibility of helping the student get a part-time job.

Paper routes, yard work, stacking wood, and helping with odd jobs are all work possibilities for young people. Setting up a work program for students might be something the student council, counselors, or the PTA might like to sponsor. Students could advertise their skills with a neighborhood flier, in the local newpaper, and through the school newspaper. Small businesses might be able to use secondary students to stuff envelopes or provide other services that would otherwise require overtime for their employees. Work with your school counselors and school psychologists to teach students job skills, to supervise, and to match students with jobs.

Step 8: If the student seems to be trying to get caught, implement steps 1 to 5 and also explore the possibility of getting the student involved in some kind of therapy.

Work with your school counselor and school psychologist to see what resources might be available to the student.

Problem 39
USING AND ABUSING DRUGS

DESCRIPTION

Paul is a high school sophomore. He is a bright, verbal student who usually takes an active part in class. During a twenty-minute study period in history class, Mr. Lessing notices that Paul seems to be very distractible. This normally productive student doesn't get a thing done. During the class lecture, Paul is equally inattentive. When asked a question, Paul simply looks at the floor and says that he doesn't know the answer. This is the third time in two weeks that Paul has acted strangely in class.

Carla is an average-performing eighth-grade student. Carla's home economics teacher has begun suspecting that she is having problems. During the last three weeks, Carla has seemed different, though not in a way that Mrs. Maxim can really put her finger on. Carla just doesn't seem to be herself.

CONTRIBUTING FACTORS

There may be several causes for the types of behaviors described above—only one of which is a use of drugs. A student who appears to be unusually distractible or unfocused may be going through a period of psychological stress. The problem may be a simple lack of sleep or the student may be having difficulties with an allergy. It is not safe to assume that any behavior change is the result of a use of drugs.

PROBLEM SOLVING

Step 1: Talk to the student privately.

When a student begins acting strangely or demonstrates atypical behavior, talk to the student privately. Avoid making accusations or insinuations. Let the student know that you are concerned. Describe the behaviors you have observed and discuss how they are different from the student's normal behavior. Ask the student if she has any problems that she would like to talk about or whether she has any physical problems that she would like to see the nurse about.

If the student does not wish to see the nurse and indicates there are no problems, tell the student how you expect her to behave for the remainder of the class. Let the student know that if you observe the same kinds of behaviors again, you will need to refer her to the nurse or principal so that steps can be taken to ensure she is well.

The objective of this step is not to threaten the student, but simply to let her know that you are aware of a change in her behavior. If the student is using drugs, this discussion will let her know that the effect of the drug is not acceptable in your classroom. If the student is not using drugs, you will avoid falsely accusing the student. If a health problem is present, something does need to be done.

Step 2: If the student does poor academic work, establish procedures for helping the student work more successfully in your class.

If a student feels that academic work is hopeless and she is already using drugs recreationally, it is likely that she may increase her use of drugs before class. She may feel that she might as well have fun in class if she can't pass it. For more information on diagnosing and remediating academic problems, see Problem 42.

Step 3: Check your grading system and make sure that students clearly see how class participation and effort will affect their grade.

A daily class participation-and-effort grade will demonstrate to all students that they need to be attentive in your class if they hope to earn this percentage of their final grade. If you do not have a daily participation-and-effort grade, see Chapter 2.

Step 4: At a neutral time, discuss appropriate behaviors with the student.

Meet privately with the student when she is obviously her "normal" self. Discuss the kinds of behaviors that will help the student be successful in class and the kinds of behaviors that have recently interfered with academic progress. You do not have to address the problem of drugs. Simply focus on your expectations for classroom behavior.

Step 5: If the student comes to class exhibiting the same types of abnormal behaviors that were discussed, send the student to the health room to be examined by the school nurse.

The student needs to see that you are aware of and concerned by the continuing problem. It is unnecessary for you to make any judgments about the student's possible use of drugs. A referral to the school nurse sets up a situation where someone with medical training can try to determine whether the student needs additional medical evaluation. At this point, the school's medically trained staff member should contact the parents, and measures should be taken to resolve the problem.

Step 6: If the problem continues and no health problem has been diagnosed, discuss the problem with school administrators and counselors. Determine how future incidents will be handled.

Jointly make decisions about how to involve parents and how to react to behavior that would indicate drug use. You may wish to set up a series of consequences similar to the ones here:

First incident: Parental contact simply describing the student's actual behavior—(We are still concerned about John's behavior in class. Today, he giggled at inappropriate times and was not able to control his laughter when the teacher asked to talk with him.)

Second incident:	Parental contact with description of student behavior
	One hour in-school suspension with nothing to do
Third incident:	Parental contact with description of student behavior
	3 days in-school suspension with work
Fourth incident:	Parent conference together with a local mental-health worker, school psychologist, or someone trained in working with drug problems
	3 days out-of-school suspension

Step 7: Discuss the problem with the student and outline the consequences.

Avoid moralizing. Simply explain to the student that the behaviors she has been exhibiting are not compatible with the objectives of your class. Describe the behaviors that are needed for a student to remain in your classroom. Explain the consequences that have been set up for behaviors that are not consistent with the expectations.

Step 8 (optional): Set up an individualized reinforcement system for the student.

See Chapter 6 for more detailed information. Basically, you will need to define behaviors that will be acceptable in class, set up a Daily Report Card system for monitoring student success, establish an incentive, and discuss the plan with the parents and the student. The Sample Contract and Daily Report Card in Figures IV–13 and IV–14 will give you an idea of the type of individualized system that may help the student decide that drug use at school is not to her benefit.

Step 9: Recognize that a severe abuse of drugs and alcohol will not be resolved by the efforts of school personnel.

If improvements are not noted, it will be important to meet again with the parents and take steps to ensure that the student receives the help of professionals trained to deal with drug abuse and addiction. If you are unsure of community resources, check with a local mental health clinic or community referral agency.

Note: The preceding plan does not discuss how to educate students on the use and misuse of drugs. This does not imply that an ongoing educational program is not of value. Students need to have information regarding the realities of any substances to which they might be exposed and the risks they take if they choose to use these substances. For additional information on drug education, you might begin with a pamphlet published by the federal government called "This Side Up—Making Decisions About Drugs." It is available by writing:

National Institute on Drug Abuse 560 Fishers Lane
Office of Communications and Public Affairs Rockville, Maryland 20857

Figure IV–13   Sample Daily Report Card

SAMPLE DAILY REPORT CARD

Dear Teachers: Please initial the space next to your class period if Melissa Dressel has behaved appropriately in class, watched the teacher or taken class notes, and/or worked consistently to complete assignments.

| 1st period _____ | 3rd period _____ | 6th period _____ |
| 2nd period _____ | 5th period _____ | 7th period _____ |

Figure IV–14   Sample Contract re: Drug Use and Abuse

SAMPLE CONTRACT RE: DRUG USE AND ABUSE

GOAL: The following contract is designed to help Melissa Dressel learn to pay attention and follow directions in class.

STUDENT RESPONSIBILITIES
1. Melissa will sit at her desk comfortably, but without slouching or lying across the desk.
2. Melissa will show that she is paying attention by watching the teacher, writing class lecture notes, and answering questions to the best of her ability.
3. During independent work times, Melissa will work on the assigned material until she has completed the work. If she has problems, she will raise her hand to get help.
4. Melissa will ask each teacher to sign the Daily Report Card at the end of the period.

TEACHER RESPONSIBILITIES
1. Each of Melissa's teachers will make a conscious effort to notice Melissa's attentive behavior. When Melissa is demonstrating her attempt to work hard in class by sitting up and watching what is happening in class, her teachers will give Melissa direct eye contact.
2. Each teacher will make it a point to include Melissa in class discussions and lectures by asking questions that she can answer because of paying attention.
3. When class notes are taken, Melissa will be given bonus points in classes where classroom performance points are included in the grading system.
4. During independent work times, teachers will frequently check to see that Melissa is working hard on her assignments and has no questions.
5. Teachers will initial Melissa's Daily Report Card when she has carried out her responsibilities.

INCENTIVE
When Melissa has earned 30 initials for attentive behavior during a class, she will be allowed an extra hour on her Saturday evening curfew.

TEACHER ADVOCATE RESPONSIBILITIES
1. Mrs. Gawthorne will meet with Melissa at 7:55 each morning to give her a new daily report card and to collect the previous day's card. She will keep Melissa informed of her progress.
2. When Melissa has collected thirty initials, Mrs. Gawthorne will get in touch with Melissa's parents and make sure that she is given an additional hour on her curfew for the coming Saturday.
3. When a contract has been filled, Mrs. Gawthorne will help Melissa set up a new contract. As Melissa demonstrates her maturity and growth, Mrs. Gawthorne and Melissa will begin establishing new goals that demonstrate her increased sophistication.

Student Signature	Date	Classroom Teacher	Date
Teacher Advocate Signature	Date	Classroom Teacher	Date
Classroom Teacher	Date	Classroom Teacher	Date
Classroom Teacher	Date		

Problem 40
SMOKING

DESCRIPTION

Claremont High School has a "no smoking" policy. As in many buildings the policy is obviously not effective. Cigarette butts are often found between buildings and in the school courtyard. In an effort to reduce smoking in the restrooms, doors have been removed from the stalls. Students complain bitterly that this is an invasion of their privacy. Why should the entire student body lose privileges due to the smoking of a few?

CONTRIBUTING FACTORS

Students smoke because they enjoy smoking. Some find that it is a demonstration of their independence. Others feel it is their way of rebelling against authority. Once the habit has been established some students may smoke at school because they, like many adults, feel they cannot get through the day without smoking.

PROBLEM SOLVING

Smoking can be handled in two ways. The first is to set a "no smoking" policy and the second is to allow smoking in designated areas. Schools, counties, and states differ widely in their laws and regulations regarding smoking on school property. Therefore, this plan will outline steps that need to be taken for either approach.

A "NO SMOKING" POLICY

Step 1: Set up a sequence of consequences that gradually progresses from mild to severe.

If a "no smoking" policy is to work, students must know that there will always be a consequence. The gradual series of consequences tells students that smoking will not be tolerated, but the early consequences are not so severe that staff members would avoid implementing them due to their severity. One possible sequence is shown here:

First offense:	Warning from office Parental contact
Second offense:	After-school detention Parental contact
Third offense:	One half hour of in-school detention, doing nothing Parental contact
Fourth offense:	One hour of in-school detention, doing nothing Parental contact
Fifth offense:	Three days of in-school suspension with work Parent conference
Sixth offense:	Three days of in-school suspension with work and Saturday school Parent conference
Seventh offense:	Out-of-school suspension

Step 2: Once the policy is established, the staff must make a commitment to report any student who is caught smoking, regardless of the circumstances.

If students find that some teachers sanction smoking by their lack of action, they will smoke. Some students will smoke to see how often they can get away with it, while others will smoke because they can get away with it.

Step 3: Design procedures for intermittent monitoring of places where students congregate to smoke.

A "no smoking" rule is ineffective without monitoring. This situation is analogous to setting a fifty-mile-per-hour speed limit with no patrols. Without monitoring, the consequences for misbehavior will not be taken seriously.

Have the staff identify all the areas in the school and on school grounds where students typically smoke. A team of staff members should be assigned to each area. Initially, these areas will need to be monitored frequently. As students learn that they cannot smoke in these areas, the amount of monitoring can gradually be decreased, but never stopped.

Step 4: Discuss the smoking policy with students.

In homerooms, or during a regularly scheduled assembly, outline the "no smoking" policy and consequences. Let students know that no one will get upset if they choose to smoke at school; however, students will consistently be required to pay the consequences.

SMOKING ALLOWED IN DESIGNATED AREAS

Step 1: Establish specific times when smoking will be allowed in the designated areas.

A major problem with programs that allow students to smoke in designated areas is tardiness. As students linger to finish a cigarette, they may be late for class. This can be alleviated by opening the smoking area only during the morning break, lunch, before and after school, and closing the area five minutes prior to the first bell. A consistent school-wide policy on tardiness should also be paired with this plan.

Step 2: Designate an area for smoking.

Select an area that is not within open view of the public. You will inform the community of the policy and your reasons for allowing smoking. However, an open display of students smoking on the school grounds will make it appear as if the school condones smoking.

Step 3 (optional): Require students to have written permission from home to use the smoking area.

You may want to require students to have written permission for using the smoking area. Students can register with the office when permission has been obtained. Students can be given special cards or may have their student body cards stamped.

Step 4 (optional): Require smokers to attend three after-school sessions on the effects of smoking.

You may wish to stipulate that anyone using the smoking area attend a set of after-school seminars on the health effects of smoking. Check with your local American Cancer Society. They may be willing to sponsor these sessions. This type of activity will demonstrate that the school is not willing to make decisions for the students, but that they do accept responsibility for giving students the information needed to explore their options.

Step 5: Set up a series of consequences for students who smoke in nondesignated areas or during nondesignated times.

You may wish to set up a schedule similar to the one shown here:

First offense:	After-school detention
	Parental contact
Second offense:	One half hour in-school detention, doing nothing
	Parental contact
Third offense:	One hour of in-school detention, doing nothing
	Parental contact
Fourth offense:	Three days of in-school suspension with work
	Parent conference
Fifth offense:	Three days of in-school suspension with work and Saturday school
	Parent conference
Sixth offense:	Out-of-school suspension

If you are going to require parental permission for smoking, you may also wish to use these consequences for students who smoke without parental permission.

Step 6: Set up a monitoring system to make sure that students smoke only in designated areas and during specified times.

Assign a team of staff members to periodically patrol areas that students have typically used for smoking. Another team should be responsible for making sure that students have cleared the smoking area at appropriate times. When students fail to follow the smoking policy, consequences should be imposed consistently.

Step 7: Inform students of the smoking policy.

In homerooms or during an assembly inform students of the smoking policy. Clearly outline the times the smoking area may be used, by whom, and the consequences for smoking in any other places or during undesignated times. Make it clear that a misuse of the smoking area will result in its being closed.

Problem 41

MISBEHAVING IN HALLWAYS AND OTHER SCHOOL AREAS

DESCRIPTION

Northrup Junior High has a student body of 620 students. Nine times every school day all 620 students move from one place to another. Before school, after school, during lunch, and between classes the halls are crowded, noisy, and chaotic. Some students run, many slam lockers, couples are often making out, most verbal exchanges are shouted. Things have gotten so bad that when the bell rings for the start of a class, many of the students carry the boisterous behavior into the classrooms. Many of the teachers feel they have to spend the first three to five minutes of class just getting the students to settle down.

Note: While the plan here is for hallway problems, most of the suggestions can be modified for problems in bus waiting areas, the cafeteria, and even during assemblies.

CONTRIBUTING FACTORS

Most misbehavior in hallways is a result of students behaving in a natural way. They are interested in interacting with friends, they are in a hurry, they are glad to see their girl friend after the intolerable forty-five-minute separation, and they talk loudly to be heard above the other noise. The more this type of behavior goes on, the more students feel free to become faster, louder, and more boisterous. The misbehavior is no different than adults exceeding the speed limit on highways not frequently patrolled. If there were more supervision and accountability, students would be less inclined to follow their natural impulses.

PROBLEM SOLVING

Note: All the following suggestions assume that the staff is working together to solve this problem. Steps 1 to 4 require the faculty to meet as a group and come to a consensus on the expectations and procedures. Unless the majority of a staff agrees on the problem and on the steps toward solving that problem, it is unlikely that a significant improvement can be made in the student's behavior.

Step 1: List any behaviors that will be considered unacceptable in the halls.

It is important to come to agreement as a staff on what behaviors are unacceptable because students must see that the staff is consistent about implementing consequences for inappropriate behavior. Some of the decisions will be easy. Running, shouting, slamming lockers, talking back to an adult, and swearing are clearly unacceptable.

However, some problems will be harder to define. The staff must decide what are acceptable ways for students to show affection in public and what represents interactions too intimate for public places. Other behaviors that may need to be defined are name calling, racial slurs, and disagreements between students. In making these decisions, think about what types of things have been going on in the halls for the last couple of weeks. For each example decide if that behavior is considered acceptable or unacceptable.

Step 2: Establish consequences for misbehavior.

For each of the unacceptable behaviors, establish what an adult should do when a student is observed engaging in one of the behaviors. For the minor misbehaviors, the consequence should be mild and simple to implement. An example of a mild consequence is that students who run should be sent to the end of the hall and told they need to walk. This may sound silly, but it is effective if students know they are likely to be caught running and if they know that any adult will make them go back and walk. This same consequence can be used for students who slam lockers, shout or swear, or are overly intimate. Having to go clear to the end of a hall and walk back is boring. When students find out they will have to do something boring when they misbehave, they become less likely to misbehave. The advantage of the consequence is that it is simple, mild, and requires no paper work.

For more severe behaviors, students should be referred to the office. Talking back to a teacher, refusal to comply with a teacher's instruction, and any other serious misbehaviors should result in the student being taken immediately to the office. For ideas on what happens to the student as a result of the referral, see Chapter 9.

Step 3: Establish procedures for significantly increasing the amount of adult supervision in the halls.

Increased supervision accomplishes three things. First, seeing adults prompts appropriate behavior in the same way seeing a police car prompts driving at the speed limit. Second, increased supervision increases the likelihood that students who break the rules will be caught and will have to pay the consequence for the infraction. This will result in the halls becoming more quiet and orderly, and this results in everyone being more calm and orderly. When halls are quiet, there is no need to shout when talking to a friend.

The third result of increased supervision is that it prompts interactions between staff and students. While in the halls, adults should not be acting like police officers. They should be interacting positively with students. Talking, greeting, even joking with students demonstrates that teachers are interested in students as people, not just as students. This also gives students an increased opportunity to see teachers in an environment other than the classroom. Increased positive interactions between teachers and student will have many benefits beyond improved hallway behavior. The tone of a school should be relaxed and friendly, and positive interactions in halls can go a long way toward accomplishing this type of atmosphere.

For the first week of implementing this plan, it would be a good idea to have every teacher in the halls during every passing time. This massive amount of supervision will help get the behaviors changed rapidly. If things improve significantly within that first week, go to a schedule that suggests that each teacher plan on being in the halls during at least two passing periods every day. Unless this is structured in some way, such as each teacher being assigned specific times, the amount of supervision usually decreases. Soon, there is little supervision and the misbehaviors begin all over again.

Step 4: From the list of unacceptable behaviors, design a positively stated rule for hallway behavior.

One example of such a rule might be, "In all public areas of the school—halls, courtyards, cafeteria, and so on—students will be orderly, polite, and reasonably quiet." This rule will be used to introduce to students the new expectations for hallway behavior.

Step 5: Teach students the new expectations and consequences.

After the staff has made decisions on the foregoing steps, plan to communicate all the information to students. This might best be accomplished by having each teacher during first period discuss the problem and the new plan with students. It will be important for students to know and understand why the changes are being made in the hall. They should know that if they run or shout, they will be told to go to the end of the hall and walk. If they do not comply with a teacher's instruction, they will immediately be taken to the office. Students should understand that this is being done in an effort to improve the learning atmosphere of the school.

Step 6: If improvement is noted, provide students with positive feedback.

Within two weeks, the halls should be much more orderly. Let students know that their efforts have been noticed. This can be done in several ways: an announcement over the intercom, an announcement at a pep assembly, an article in the school paper, an article in a community paper, and announcements in a parent newsletter. One other very effective strategy to let students know that they have done well is to have the faculty invite the mayor or a city commissioner or another dignitary to come and see the quality of the student behavior at Northrup Junior High.

One of the goals of this type of feedback is to try to get the student body to take pride in the fact that they are functioning in a very adult manner.

Problem 42
POOR ACADEMIC SKILLS

Note: Behavioral problems are frequently related to academic problems. If a student cannot do work, he will often misbehave out of boredom, or in an attempt to cover up the fact that he is too "dumb" to do the work. Every secondary class will have at least one or two students who lack the academic skills to succeed, and some classes may have as many as half of the students in serious academic difficulty. Any attempt to get these students to behave better—without doing something to remediate academic deficits—is at best only a short-term remedy.

The information presented here provides introductory information on how to remediate academic problems. Its objective is to give you a place to start when dealing with students who have academic deficits.

These basic steps should help you identify students who are having academic difficulties and provide a few suggestions for giving these students additional support within the regular classroom setting.

PROBLEM SOLVING

Step 1: Conduct an informal diagnosis of the reading abilities of any students you suspect of having academic problems.

Find an assignment that the student has had difficulty with. Privately, have the student read aloud approximately 100 words from the assignment. Time how long it takes him to read the passage. When listening to the student read, count the errors as you would in an informal reading inventory. Count omissions, insertions, misidentifications, and the inability to read a word within three seconds. Make note of any times the student corrects himself, but do not count these as errors. If the student makes three to five errors, he is functioning at a reading level where he may need to be taught any new or difficult vocabulary before being assigned to read the material independently. If the student makes six or more errors, it will probably be impossible for the student to function independently. This error rate places a student at a frustration level. He does not read well enough to independently understand the material or any written instructions and exercises.

If the student takes longer than forty seconds to read the 100 words, he is reading below 150 words per minute. A student in sixth grade or above should be able to read books and assignments at 150 words or more per minute. Slower rates make comprehension and retention very difficult.

If the student reads with zero to five errors in less than forty seconds, you will also want to determine whether the student understands what he reads. Ask the student some basic questions about the material he has just read. First see if the student can answer basic factual questions. If he can, ask some questions that require the student to make an inference or a judgment about the material. If the student has difficulty with these types of questions, he is missing the prerequisite skills necessary to answer written questions, make judgments, follow directions, or retain information.

Step 2: Work to help students resolve and compensate for reading difficulties.

If a student has an apparent reading deficit, refer him to the learning specialist for further evaluation and testing. In the meantime, consider providing students who have reading problems with student helpers. You might use student assistants or provide peer tutors. Recruit students who are currently earning *B*s to read and go over assignments with students who are having difficulties. Let the tutors know that they will earn extra credit points for helping another student. This experience will help the *B* student move one step closer to an *A,* and it may also result in better mastery of skills for both students. In order to tutor, a student must focus on the related skills more intensely than if he were simply going through the motions of completing an assignment on his own.

Step 3: For students who are having difficulty reading and for students who seem to lack prerequisite skills, provide small-group study sessions.

While other students are working on assignments independently, work with a small group of students who have been having difficulty on assignments. Provide group practice on any prerequisite skills on which students are weak.

In some classes, you may have only one or two students who need this extra instruction. In other classes, you may have ten or twelve students involved. The goal is to have from five to fifteen minutes on at least three days each week where you can work directly with the lowest-performing students in the class. During these sessions, directly teach the information and concepts students will need to be successful in your class. Spend the majority of the teaching time on the most important concepts, operations, skills, and information. Students will soon see that participation in these exercises helps them complete assignments and pass tests.

INDEX